MW01010643

THEATRE IN BRITAIN

HAROLD HOBSON

THEATRE IN BRITAIN

A PERSONAL VIEW

PHAIDON · OXFORD

Phaidon Press Limited, Littlegate House, St Ebbe's Street, Oxford
First published 1984

British Library Cataloguing in Publication Data

Hobson, *Sir* Harold
Theatre in Britain.
1. Theatre—Great Britain
I. Title
792'.092'4 PN2595

ISBN 0-7148-2339-2

Printed in Great Britain at The Pitman Press, Bath

Frontispiece: *John Gielgud as Romeo in the 1935 production of Shakespeare's* Romeo and Juliet *at the New (Albery) Theatre, London.*
Cecil Beaton photograph courtesy of Sotheby's Belgravia.

CONTENTS

To Nancy, with love

PREFACE

This book is not a history, nor is it an academic analysis. It is an entirely personal record and interpretation of what I have seen on the stage from Martin-Harvey to Edward Fox; or, to say the same thing in another way, from John Gielgud to John Gielgud. Since it is personal many doubtless important things have been missed out, and many trivial things put in which I consider to be more important than the important omissions. I may, of course, on occasion be wrong. I may even be wrong all the time.

Nevertheless, in this personal survey of British theatre since 1920 I have tried to do two things: first, to show that all theatre is politically and socially relevant; and, second, to put into perspective the theatrical revolution usually associated with the name of the Royal Court Theatre, but which really began in the Queen's Hall in Barnstaple, Devon, with the first British professional production of a play by Brecht. I have tried to show both the sort of drama this revolution brought us out of, and the sort of drama it has led us in to. The theatre has certainly gone the way I wished it to. The results surprise me.

Theatre in Britain is in some ways a summary of my career as a theatre critic, and I should like to thank all the proprietors and Editors of *The Sunday Times* under whom I have worked since 1947. They have given me unfailing help and opportunities. I should also like to thank *The Times Literary Supplement* and *The Christian Science Monitor*. They are not, of course, responsible for any mistakes the text may contain. Those are my own.

Harold Hobson

CHAPTER ONE
The Gentlemen Fail
1920–1930

In the early days of peace after the war of 1914–18 the theatre seemed to be in a very prosperous condition. London playhouses were crowded, and every Sunday touring companies sped throughout the length and breadth of Britain from one 'date' to another, carrying with them a provincial version of the latest metropolitan successes. Even in the middle of the war the number of touring companies had been prodigious. Five separate companies were needed to satisfy the nation's demand for a single play, *Peg o' My Heart*, and in the fifth and least important of these a small part was played by the future film actor, Leslie Howard. Sheffield, where I passed the first twenty years of my life, was reckoned to be amongst the least theatrical of cities. Yet even in Sheffield there were two theatres, two music halls, and a repertory theatre, whose company was led by a young actor of great emotional power called Donald Wolfit.

Wolfit, then aged not much more than twenty, was not the first actor who struck me as destined for a distinguished future. The first player under thirty who, I thought, had the stamp of greatness on him was Henry Baynton. Baynton, though of comparatively tender years, had his own company, and presented memorable performances of the plays of Shakespeare – a dramatist at that time considered a guarantee of empty houses. Baynton, however, a tall, elegant figure and a master of the languorously graceful gesture, with a carefully cultivated voice of cloying lyrical beauty and a deep sense of his own importance in the world of art, regularly filled the Lyceum Theatre on his annual visits to Sheffield. Thus, before I had seen any play in London, I came upon two actors convinced of their own genius; I agreed with both: one of them went on to noisy critical battles, a knighthood and fame; the other became gradually forgotten, and in 1934 was playing Capulet in *Romeo and Juliet* at the Open Air Theatre in Regent's Park.

Wolfit and Baynton were young men with eyes fixed on London and the future. For them the provinces were merely an approach to the magic of Shaftesbury Avenue. But the big stars of Sheffield and similar places were actors

---

Donald Wolfit as Touchstone in Shakespeare's As You Like It *(1929/30) at the Old Vic, London.*

like Sir John Martin-Harvey, Fred Terry, and Matheson Lang. Each of these players appeared in London from time to time between the last decade of the nineteenth century and the outbreak of the Second World War. But it was in the provinces that their fame and their fortunes were made. They supported companies of thirty or forty actors and actresses, most of them of little merit; it was the star who counted. The great figures of the London stage, like Sir Gerald du Maurier and Marie Tempest, were mere shadowy names in the provinces, which they rarely visited; and when they occasionally came they were not much encouraged to repeat their visits. In Sheffield, for example, Marie Tempest played to empty houses. Her reception was such that the critic St John Ervine declared that the motto of the people of Sheffield was 'Back to protoplasm'. Ervine's well-justified indignation left us unmoved, and unrepentant.

Marie Tempest's Dresden china delicacy, her subtly malicious wit, her predilection for small contemporary plays like A. A. Milne's *Mr Pim Passes By* were considered by us Sheffielders to be trivial and frivolous. We wanted something robust, resounding, and romantic, plays that dealt with people of rank and flamboyance, rich in costume and high in language, flaunting the bigger passions (but in quite a nice way), and making our spines tingle with deeds of courage and self-sacrifice. Preferably they were historic, like Matheson Lang's *The Wandering Jew*. It pleased us that the sombre and stately Lang, the hero of this tremendous denunciation of adultery, was the cousin of the Archbishop of Canterbury, though it came as a bit of a shock when the author of the play, Temple Thurston, was the principal figure in a particularly unsavoury divorce case. We were snobs and Puritans, as well as theatregoers.

That Martin-Harvey and his wife, Nina de Silva, or Fred Terry and his wife, Julia Neilson, should get mixed up with divorce was inconceivable: this was part of the charm they exerted over us. Martin-Harvey had an additional recommendation. Whenever he came to Sheffield, he always read one of the Lessons in the local St Paul's church, whose vicar was the Reverend Spencer Elliott, a keen supporter of the drama and reputed to be a great rhetorical preacher. Whenever I heard him, however, he always seemed to be off form, and I never thought he was really justified in taking round with him, as he invariably did, a reporter in order that his words should appear in the *Sheffield Daily Telegraph*. The close connection between performances in church and performances on the stage lasted, at least among the older actors, until our own day. Jack Hulbert regularly read the Lessons; and Richard Goolden used to take up the collection at Chelsea Old Church.

Fred Terry and Julia Neilson played very fairly by each other. They each had one outstanding part: Fred Terry that of the hero in *The Scarlet Pimpernel* and Julia Neilson Nell Gwyn in *Sweet Nell of Old Drury*. They played these parts more or less an equal number of times, and thus escaped the jealousy which

---

Miss Marie Tempest (1864–1942).

often ruins stage marriages when one partner is more successful than the other. Martin-Harvey and his wife were held together by a different bond. He was a handsome man, with a beautiful, soft, romantic voice; she was very plain, and when she had to express emotion (he would never appear on the stage without her, and he told me that she was the only woman he had ever kissed, either on the stage or off it) she screamed harshly. Very late in his long life (he died in 1940 at the age of eighty) he movingly told me that without her he would have achieved nothing. She had cared for him, and guided him for more than fifty years; it was she who persuaded him to play Sydney Carton in *The Only Way* by F. Wills. This was his greatest triumph, and he played the part for more than forty years. He never tired of it, nor showed any sign of staleness. I saw him in it six or seven times. The last occasion was at the King's Theatre, Hammersmith, in the 1930s. I congratulated him at the end of the performance. 'Yes,' he said, with complete simplicity, 'I never played Carton better than I did tonight.' After that he went on a tour of farewell performances, in which he was of course accompanied by Miss N. de Silva, as he always used to call her. They had played together in *The Only Way* more than five thousand times, and to the end Miss de Silva was playing in her seventies the teenage girl Mimi she had played at the piece's first performance on 16 February 1899.

He held her hand as he, unshaken, and she, timidly, mounted the steps of the guillotine, and disappeared into the wings as a terrifying voice thundered out the order of their execution, 'Fifty-four, fifty-five', against a background roar of bloodthirsty hatred from the crowd who had gathered to see the heads of the aristocrats fall. A moment later the scene was transformed, and Carton stood alone, high in the centre of the stage, the knife of the guillotine suspended over his head, and, in an exactly modulated tremulous voice (he touched the same notes at every performance) spoke those famous words 'It is a far, far better thing that I do than I have ever done. It is a far, far better rest that I go to than I have ever known', causing thousands of people ever since to believe that these were the last words Carton ever spoke. Anyone who reads Dickens's *A Tale of Two Cities* (from which the play is adapted) will be aware that Carton never spoke these words; he made no speech from the scaffold. But if he *had* spoken, these are the words he might have uttered.

They are the most famous thing in the play, but not to me the most moving. I was more deeply affected by a scene that immediately preceded the execution. Prisoners of all classes, working girls like Mimi as well as noblemen and ladies, were waiting for their dreadful call. Some were frightened; others cool and untroubled. It was one of the latter who, in looking at Carton, suddenly realized that he was not the Charles Darnay, the *ci-devant* Marquis de St Evremonde, he was supposed to be. Quizzing him with his elegant lorgnette, he said in a low voice, incredulously, 'You are *dying* for him?' And Carton replied quietly, but

---

John Martin-Harvey and Nina de Silva in F. Wills's The Only Way *(1899) at the Lyceum, London.*

with ever so slight and significant a modification, 'Yes, and for his wife and child.' Whereupon the man, dressed as for a ball in powdered wig and silk knee breeches, turned away with a slight bow, and said, 'In the words of your great poet

Hereafter in a better world than this
I shall desire more love and knowledge of you.'

It was very melodramatic and theatrical; but it was also undeniably grand. Anyway, the words were better placed than they had been by Shakespeare, who had given them to the fop, Le Beau, in *As You Like It*. I wish I could remember that actor's name. He had nothing else to do in the play, but he indeed had his moment. For it was the suppressed astonished doubt in his question that enabled Martin-Harvey to show us the full extent of Carton's courage, and of his love for Lucy Manette.

I went to the theatre purely for enjoyment. It never occurred to me that in plays like *The Only Way* and *The Scarlet Pimpernel* there was any question of political commitment. Yet unconsciously there was as much political commitment in them as there was in the work of Brenton and Hare later in the century. An argument might be put up in defence of the impartiality of *The Only Way* in that it opened with a scene showing the total indifference of the French aristocracy to the sufferings of the poor. The carriage of the Marquis de St Evremonde ran over and killed a child in the street. The Marquis tossed a coin to pay for a doctor, but viewed the death of the child as a casual incident of no interest. Indirectly Charles Darnay, and in his place Sydney Carton, was called on to pay the penalty for the crime of one of his relations. There was some social justice in this. The execution of Carton was the reparation of a sin.

But all this, whilst maintainable as a rationalization of the play, was not emotionally perceptible during its performance. The audience's sympathy was entirely for Carton and the cause he had undertaken to defend. What was remembered was not the wickedness of the St Evremonde, and by implication of their class, but the mob screaming for blood; not the death of a child crushed beneath the aristocratic carriage wheels, but the graceful insouciance of a man of rank who could go to his death with an elegant quotation from a foreign poet on his lips. If this feeling was true of *The Only Way*, it was a hundred times more so of *The Scarlet Pimpernel*. In that romantic tale there was no sympathy at all for the cause of the people. Its representatives were simply and wholly scoundrels, and stupid scoundrels at that, never able, despite their repeated failures, to perceive that the drunken, foolish fop, Sir Percy Blakeney, (played by Fred Terry with an irresistible air of vacuous enjoyment) was the man who, with the brain of a Sherlock Holmes and the nerve of a d'Artagnan, was foiling their simple-minded and villainous plots.

Fred Terry and Julia Nelson in The Scarlet Pimpernel *(1905) at the New (Albery) Theatre, London.*

It did not strike me as significant at the time that audiences of Sheffield teachers and tradesmen should take such delight in the idealization of the upper classes. In those days I passed at my school for an extreme Socialist. I subscribed to *Lansbury's Labour Weekly*, and told my headmaster that the best newspaper in the country was the *Daily Herald*. In the school's dummy run for the School Certificate (the predecessor, though of a higher scholastic standard, of our 'O' levels), my English Essay was awarded zero out of a hundred because of its alleged left wing bitterness, and when I went up to Oxford I was, I believe, the only member of the university who joined the Oxford City Labour party as well as the University Labour Club. In spite of these impeccable qualifications I saw nothing odd in a city of heavy unemployment being apparently devoted to the aristocratic cause, and its ethics and manners. If I had (as in fact was the case) a feeling that this devotion would not last much longer it had nothing to do with the development of politics. It was due rather to my recognition that Martin-Harvey and Fred Terry, in spite of the infatuation of the provinces, cut very little ice in London. The few new plays they presented there had only brief runs and unenthusiastic reviews. Newer stuff was being shown at the repertory theatre, where Donald Wolfit played in a quiet, naturalistic style that eschewed rhetoric, and was the exact opposite of the sort of thing he did when he became famous. This, I felt, was an indication that the old heart-throbbing eloquence and the presentation of emotions and heroisms larger than life were coming near the end of their long reign. The plumage was still magnificent, but the bird was dying.

But whether I noticed them or not, social changes were indeed taking place during my schooldays. The war had begun with the ecstatic verse of Rupert Brooke – a greater poet than is generally allowed nowadays because he expressed sentiments that are no longer fashionable – but after 1916 the spirit of 'If I should die think only this of me;/That there's some corner of a foreign field/That is for ever England' was dead; it had given place to the bitterness of a man no less brave than Brooke but far less romantic. Siegfried Sassoon had been decorated for his courage in the field, but he thought it a useless and a wasted courage, and wrote savagely in one of those revues which talked gaily of 'dear old tanks' that would flatten out the Germans:

> I'd like to see a Tank come down the stalls,
> Lurching to rag-time tune or 'Home, Sweet Home' –
> And there'd be no more jokes in Music Halls
> To mock the riddled corpses round Bapaume.

This new spirit of disillusion and hatred of one's own people did not penetrate to the theatre of my young days. Brave swords, pure love, and dastardly foreigners peopled the Sheffield stage till long after I went up to Oxford in 1924. But one felt the first faint stirrings of a new political outlook, tinged, it seemed to me when I first encountered it in our back garden, with Jacobinism. One heavy cloudy night, immediately after Lloyd George had won the 'khaki' election with a huge majority, my father stood talking to our neighbour over the hedge. Our neighbour was a grave, thoughtful, middle-aged man, and he said, with an absolute certainty that stamped his words on my mind for more than half a century, 'They may have won this election, but our time is coming. Everyone at the station is convinced of that, and dedicated to it.' Too much Martin-Harvey and Fred Terry had perhaps gone to my head, but I seemed to hear in these words the accents of the revolution, especially as they were pronounced by a policeman, by his profession engaged to protect the status quo. I felt uncomfortable, half afraid of vague things I knew nothing about. I watched the clouds scudding through the sky, uneasily.

My policeman, and his pals down at the station, were not alone. The people as a whole were beginning to discover themselves, and this was a disruptive feature of the national life, full both of promise and of menace. The workers were becoming organized. The historian A. J. P. Taylor remarked that the typical working man was no longer a shopkeeper but a shop-steward. In the summer of 1918 there was a wave of strikes, and these were concerned more with status than with wages. It is inconceivable but true that at a period when Britain was poised on the very edge of defeat there were strikes not only in the cotton industry, but also among the Coventry munition workers. Winston Churchill wanted to use force, and broke the strike by threatening to send the workers into the army. The workers were prepared to defy their country and their employers. But when the Germans were mentioned to them, they had second thoughts. So far had the country travelled, from the flamboyant folly of Rupert Brooke to the sober realism of Coventry. War is a terrible thing, and I have lived through it twice, and been very frightened. But somehow one admires the folly of Cambridge more than the wisdom of Coventry. Meanwhile, the police themselves went on strike.

Now all this did actually affect the theatre, but it did not affect my view of the theatre. While Martin-Harvey and Fred Terry were still exploring the romantic feelings of revolution in the past, no serious dramatist or actor was alive to the implications of the Russian Revolution of the present. One of my parents' most cultured friends mildly surprised us by remarking one evening that Lenin and Trotsky were great men, but I never heard either of them mentioned in the theatre, nor any reference made to the overthrow of the tsars. Barrie was writing *Mary Rose* (1920) and Shaw was contemplating Joan of Arc, but neither seemed to be influenced by the slaughter at Tsarkoe Selo. All that seemed very far away.

Strikes however were different. They influenced the daily life of everyone in Britain. Suddenly I was presented with a play that dealt, not with the romantic and costumed past, but with the events recorded every day in the newspapers. It was called *The Right to Strike*, and it asked the question whether, if industrial workers were justified in striking for higher wages, the same right to withhold labour did not extend to all classes, even those, like doctors and nurses, whose especial function it was to preserve life. It was a question that had not been answered more than half a century later, when a strike of hospital workers threatened the existence of at least two Governments, those of James Callaghan and of Margaret Thatcher. But though the question had not been answered, the attitude towards it had changed. In 1920, when I saw *The Right to Strike*, the Conservative answer would undoubtedly have been on the side of the striking health workers; in the 1970s and 1980s it would have been equally against them.

The Right to Strike did not create on me anything like so powerful an effect as might have been expected. There were scenes in it that in its London production had provoked howls of protest, and nearly brought the performance to a premature end. But in Sheffield these passed without making any visible impression. Yet the piece was, in its way, a portent. It was a clear and passionate forerunner of the sort of drama, closely bound to the political events of the day, which the English Stage Company was to produce some thirty or forty years later. It was an example of the drama of social relevance which it later became fashionable to pretend did not exist until the violent explosion of John Osborne's *Look Back in Anger* in 1956. Its young author, Ernest Hutchinson, died within a year of the production of *The Right to Strike*, or he might well have established a school of drama that antedated by nearly half a century the work of Osborne, George Devine, and Howard Brenton.

The Right to Strike was something of a *tour de force*. It was generally thought at the time, at the beginning of the twenties and even for some years afterwards, that it was impossible to interest the big theatre-going public in plays about the workers. Throughout the twentieth century the English drama has, in general, been about the ruling class. When the aristocracy dominated government, people of title besprinkled the cast list of West End entertainments, entertainments that then proceeded to tour the whole country without rousing any resentment. But when the aristocracy gave way to the middle class, then drama itself became middle class. In 1930 Somerset Maugham declared that it was no longer possible to introduce aristocratic characters into a play unless there was some special and compelling reason for doing so.

After the war of 1939–45 power passed gradually from the middle class to the trade unions and the workers, and in consequence the characteristic drama of the post-war period is, at least in spirit, proletarian. In the later 1950s and in the 60s, 70s and 80s it became inconceivable that a benevolent capitalist could be introduced into a play, or a vicious and villainous worker play an important or even an inconsiderable part, unless in fact he were a rebel against his class. The theatre is at all times socially relevant in that it is in general subservient to, or reflective of, the bases of power. It is towards realizing this fact, and watching this process that the whole of my professional career has been devoted. In defending the theatrical changes of the 1950s I did a little myself towards bringing about the proletarianization of the theatre. Whether this development has been a good or a bad thing, whether it has gained us more than it has lost, or vice versa, is a question that still remains open. On the one hand it has given us writers like John Osborne, David Storey, and Simon Gray; on the other it has led to the virtual destruction of high comedy, and to grave injustice being done by a coterie of critics to dramatists of the wit and theatrical skill of Terence Rattigan and William Douglas Home. Rattigan was for some years virtually a broken man because of the savagery with which he was attacked by the English Stage Company and its followers.

The author of *The Right to Strike* showed no awareness of the possibility of developments such as these. His play contains no endorsement of class hatred. The drama critic of the *Sheffield Daily Telegraph* in the 1920s described its chief character, Ben Ormerod, as 'the best type of Labour leader', by which he meant a man who touched his cap to his betters. Nevertheless, *The Right to Strike* was something of a revolutionary drama. In 1920 the workers were not in power, and in spite of the policeman in the back garden, showed few signs of ever becoming so. The authority of the aristocracy was rapidly diminishing, but it was not into the hands of the workers that it was passing. What Hutchinson perceived was that a movement of power was in progress, and that this movement was ultimately in the direction of the working class, though it was never actually to reach them in his brief lifetime. His imagination was fired by the social unrest of the aftermath of the First World War, and in particular by the moral issues raised when the withdrawal of labour threatened the community rather than the strikers' employers, a problem that became increasingly important as time went on.

What we in the provinces looked for in a play, though we were quite unaware of it, was the fulfilment of the Aristotelian doctrine that the most important thing is the plot. Many generations have associated Aristotle with the unities; many have considered that he was principally concerned with the Tragic Hero, the great man who falls from his grandeur because of some minor defect of character. But Professor John Jones, in *On Aristotle and Greek Tragedy*, has recently shown that Aristotle knew nothing of the Tragic Hero; what he insisted on was that the central and essential feature of a play was its action. Action was more important than character. The essence of a play lay in its change of fortune.

Instinctively this is what we wanted from a play when it came to Sheffield. We wished to be told a good story, culminating in a big scene in which some great reversal of fortune took place. This desire was only partially satisfied by *The Right to Strike*. One of the doctors who was bringing food to the people of the isolated village, whom the striking railwaymen were starving, was killed; and his friend Dr Wrigley vowed that so long as the strike lasted he would refuse to attend any railwayman. With remarkable promptitude the wife of the leader of the strike, Ben Ormerod, fell ill, and needed an operation which only this recalcitrant doctor could perform. He refused, as he had said he would; and this precipitated the big, the Aristotelian scene which we expected every play to provide. We were waiting for the change of fortune; and here it came. 'You killed my dearest friend,' said the doctor to the distressed and bewildered Ormerod. 'We wanted coal, food, medicine. Did you bring them to us? The Medical Association has struck me off the register because I struck. For the right to strike I have sacrificed my livelihood and lost my dearest friend.' Things looked very black indeed. Dr Wrigley was evidently a man who meant what he said. But then the tables were suddenly turned. The change of fortune, in the best Aristotelian manner, took place before our eyes. For up rose the widow of the dead doctor and spoke the words of peace. With more feeling than originality she reproved the doctors for having forgotten that 'We are all God's creatures', and the belligerent doctor, struck to the heart, donned his white overalls, and duly saved Mrs Ormerod's life.

This scene in London was a great success. The actress Marjorie Day, in one of her last performances before she retired, delivered her big speech (which moreover was said at the time to be exceedingly well written) in a way to touch all hearts. At the Garrick Theatre the Aristotelian trick seems to have come off. But in the provinces it did not. My mind, which is extremely retentive of details that move me, retains no memory whatever of this scene as it was played at the Lyceum Theatre, Sheffield.

So, on the whole, I remained dead to its merits. But however sentimental and melodramatic *The Right to Strike* seems after Priestley, Eliot, and Beckett, it was in its day a progressive and almost revolutionary play. It was strictly, almost literally, relevant to the problems of its time. It tried, if clumsily, to discuss them philosophically, and to consider their moral aspects. Ben Ormerod, bewildered and distressed by the unexpected development of the strike, was sympathetically portrayed and so was Dr Wrigley. Working men were shown, not as figures of fun, but as real people with real problems. Also it associated its characters with their work and their way of earning their living. The doctors in the play exercise (or refuse to exercise) their profession; they are not shown merely in their hours of relaxation, enjoying the profits that it brought them. *The Right to Strike* was more a play of the future than we in Sheffield realised in 1920.

If its big change-of-fortune scene struck me as less dramatic than actors like Matheson Lang and Martin-Harvey had taught me to expect plays to be, it nevertheless dimly made me aware that the real fundamental subject of theatre lay in the search for happiness. 'The pursuit of happiness' is an activity commended even in so grave a document as the American Declaration of Independence. The desire for happiness, or what is supposed to be happiness, whether it be in the form of eternal life or higher wages, intellectual dialectics or sexual intercourse, seems to me to be at the heart of all twentieth-century drama. My experience of theatre during half a century, from Buchanan and Jack Hulbert to Frank Sinatra and the Rolling Stones, suggests that all playwrights are looking for the same thing, though they look for it and sometimes even find it in different places. *Partage de midi* and *Oh Calcutta* both spring from the same desire.

In my lifetime of professional theatregoing I have never seen this desire expressed with such poignancy and succinctness as in the version of the American Clifford Odets's *Rocket to the Moon* which was played in London in 1948 under the direction of Peter Cotes. In this production there was a scene which has haunted my imagination ever since. There is little to admire in the characters of *Rocket to the Moon.* Most of them are dentists, and it would appear from this play that dentists are a gloomy lot of self-pitying weaklings, much given to moaning that they cannot make up their minds, or keep sober, or find customers, or desert their wives, or give their secretaries a real swinging night out at the Planetarium.

All this is very upsetting to Dr Stark, who is a mild, well-meaning fellow wanting only to jog along in a placid sort of way, without much excitement, but without dishonour either. Nor are his nerves soothed by the frequent incursions into his physically and psychologically simmering clinic of a neighbouring dentist who can neither get patients nor exercise patience, and who rails with a rasping and searing rhetoric against both what the universe gives, and those who, like himself, have not got what it takes. What with the heat and Dr Stark's fascination for women, the shouters and the failures, it is not surprising that before long Dr Stark's surgery becomes a psychiatrist's Paradise; the stage wriggles with neuroses.

Then, after two interminable acts of breast-beating, groaning, and Gummidgery, the thing of which the audience had almost given up all hope suddenly happens. Courage and optimism, cheerfulness and determination flood upon the stage, and we know that the world is a good place, and we are lucky to be in it. On that night in early spring of 1948, when Britain was still suffering from the austerities of war, it seemed nothing less than a miracle; and it was brought about by a travelling salesman, with only a few lines to speak; but with those lines – lines moreover that recorded yet another failure – the actor Laurence Naismith lit up the theatre. In a performance of brief, swift, guileless and unsuspecting heroism Naismith banished despair into oblivion.

Into the wretched collection of misery-mongers there burst this salesman of motor–car tyres, who had thirty times in one day failed to get a single order. Yet he came up fresh, resilient, and full of hope, and his face was radiant. And when he failed for the thirty-first time, his thought was not of himself, but of his wife, who, 'with a grin from ear to ear' would be waiting to greet him when he got home. 'A wonderful woman, the wife,' he said, and smiled as he thought of her. 'A wonderful woman,' he said, still smiling, still thinking of her as he went out after a day of total failure, never suspecting his own glory. After he had left the stage there was a moment's silence. Then Dr Stark's voice rang out. 'Whatever it is we are looking for in our lives,' he cried, 'that man's got it.' In those words desiring peace of mind Dr Stark spoke for the whole British theatre, such as I have known it. From before Hutchinson to after Brenton it has been looking for happiness.

In this search for happiness it has had some splendid moments of exaltation, and more of disappointment and disillusion. But my experience of twentieth-century theatre is that, whatever the circumstances of life, society, and international politics, it has never given up this search, though it has pursued it with a worsening temper and a diminishing hope. The turning-point came with Osborne's *Look Back in Anger* in 1956. Before that the theatre concentrated on establishing what seemed good to it; after, on destroying what seemed bad. The attitude changed from positive to negative. But always the same object was in view: the attainment, ultimately, of the state of mind of Odets's salesman.

In the 1920s, despite such plays as *The Right to Strike* and John Galsworthy's *Escape*, the search seemed frivolous and light-hearted. The theatre of those days appeared to find its ideal in delicate spectacles: the ravishing picture of the Fair at Neuilly: the airy figure of a Viennese dancer posed in front of a stained-glass window on a darkened stage – the sort of thing that Charles Cochran, the greatest showman of the century, whose taste stretched from professional boxing to Chaliapine, used to present at the London Pavilion in the days when after nightfall the theatres round Leicester Square seemed to glitter with fairy-lamps, and all the men and women to be seen wore evening dress.

In sharp contrast the theatre has at other times tried to find satisfaction for humanity's deepest needs in the impoverished, dedicated productions of the Fringe, beginning at one of the first Edinburgh Festivals in the late 1940s, and spreading to London pubs, garrets, basements and even to the streets. This was one of its experiments that, rightly or wrongly, I greeted with the greatest enthusiasm, soon coming to the conclusion that the dramatic heart of the Festival lay in obscure alleys rather than in official places. At other times the search led it to the world represented by the suave, modest, dancing, top-hatted, male-envied and girl-adored figure of Jack Buchanan, blithely dismissing all the cares of the universe with the grace of a trivial song and the nice conduct of an ebony cane: but more anxiously, and in a much more resentful mood, to the forward-looking and ambitious efforts of the English Stage Company under that stunning dynamo of social theatre, George Devine.

It has even, on occasion, found its ecstasy of joy in a Samuel Beckett demonstration that no joy is possible. It was at the moment of the revelation of *Waiting for Godot* that I felt the greatest confidence in the British theatre, which at other times had turned to religion or to anarchy for its consolation. But wherever it turned it was always looking for what that salesman had, to what was exhibited to us on the stage of the St Martin's Theatre in March 1948.

This will seem a woefully simplified account of the complex forces that have brought us in half a century from the supremacy of the commercial to that of the subsidized. There have been so many different theories, such a plethora of banners. Brecht's practice of alienation; the invention of agitprop; the sharp banishment from critical appreciation of the right wing theatre; the effort to create greater intimacy between players and audience by putting the audience all round the stage instead of in front of it; Peter Brook's experiments with strange languages and exotic actors and actresses in the most decrepit and broken-down, albeit romantic, theatre that he can find; the longing of countless small companies to destroy the state which gives them the funds which enable them to

---

Nicholas Hannen in John Galsworthy's Escape *(1926) at the Ambassadors Theatre, London (reproduced from* The Play Pictorial, *August 1926).*

continue their policy of trying to destroy it: all these may seem far from the idea of happiness. Yet they are the precise, though unconscious, manifestation of their desire for it. They are not ends in themselves; they are all means to an end, the perfect society in which happiness is universal and equal.

In 1925, when I saw John Galsworthy's *The Skin Game* at the Woodstock Road Playhouse, I first became conscious of the close connection between social questions and ideals and this search for happiness. Hillcrist, the country gentleman in the play, wishes for the happiness both of his tenants and of himself; and he believes that it can be attained if he and they behave decently according to their standards. Hillcrist is a gentleman, a gentleman in his book being 'a man who keeps his form, and does not let life scupper him out of his standards'. But Hillcrist does, alas, allow life to do just that, and under the influence of his ambitious and unscrupulous wife consents to something very like blackmail. He realizes that even gentlemen no longer behave like gentlemen, and his last regretful words are, 'What's the good of gentility if it can't stand fire?' These words express the tragic failure of the ethos of a whole social class which had hitherto been dominant. This is the end of the aristocratic philosophy of life.

It is a fine and noble ending – without recrimination, without blame of others, filled only with a sad regret that Hillcrist himself had proved unequal to the task of living up to the ideals of the best members of his class, without which his class had no right to the privileges it enjoyed. Hillcist's words mark the abdication of a whole order of society.

Somerset Maugham's plays dealt with the same class of characters as did Galsworthy's but with much inferior, even if wittier, specimens. Fortune-hunters, seekers after titles, and gamblers, whom one cannot help feeling he half admired, were the targets of his malicious wit. He derided Galsworthy, because he maintained that, by manipulating your incidents and choosing your characters differently you can alter your message. This is not true. It is not true that had Hillcrist been an even better man than he was, that if he had come out of the struggle with the capitalist Hornblower with clean hands, without question of giving in to the blackmail of his wife, that then the aristocratic order of things would have been saved – at least upon the stage if not in real life. An author's message, if it is to have any validity, arises out of the depths of his convictions, not out of his characters nor the incidents of his plays. They derive from it, not it from them. In the early 1920s Galsworthy was convinced that the age of gentlemen had passed, and that the result would have been the same even if he had made Hillcrist save his honour. What Hillcrist did to himself, the world would have done to Hillcrist.

However the incidents had been changed, however the characters been altered, the doom would have been the same, because the doom was in

---

Jack Buchanan in the musical Mr Whittington *(1934) at the Hippodrome, London.*

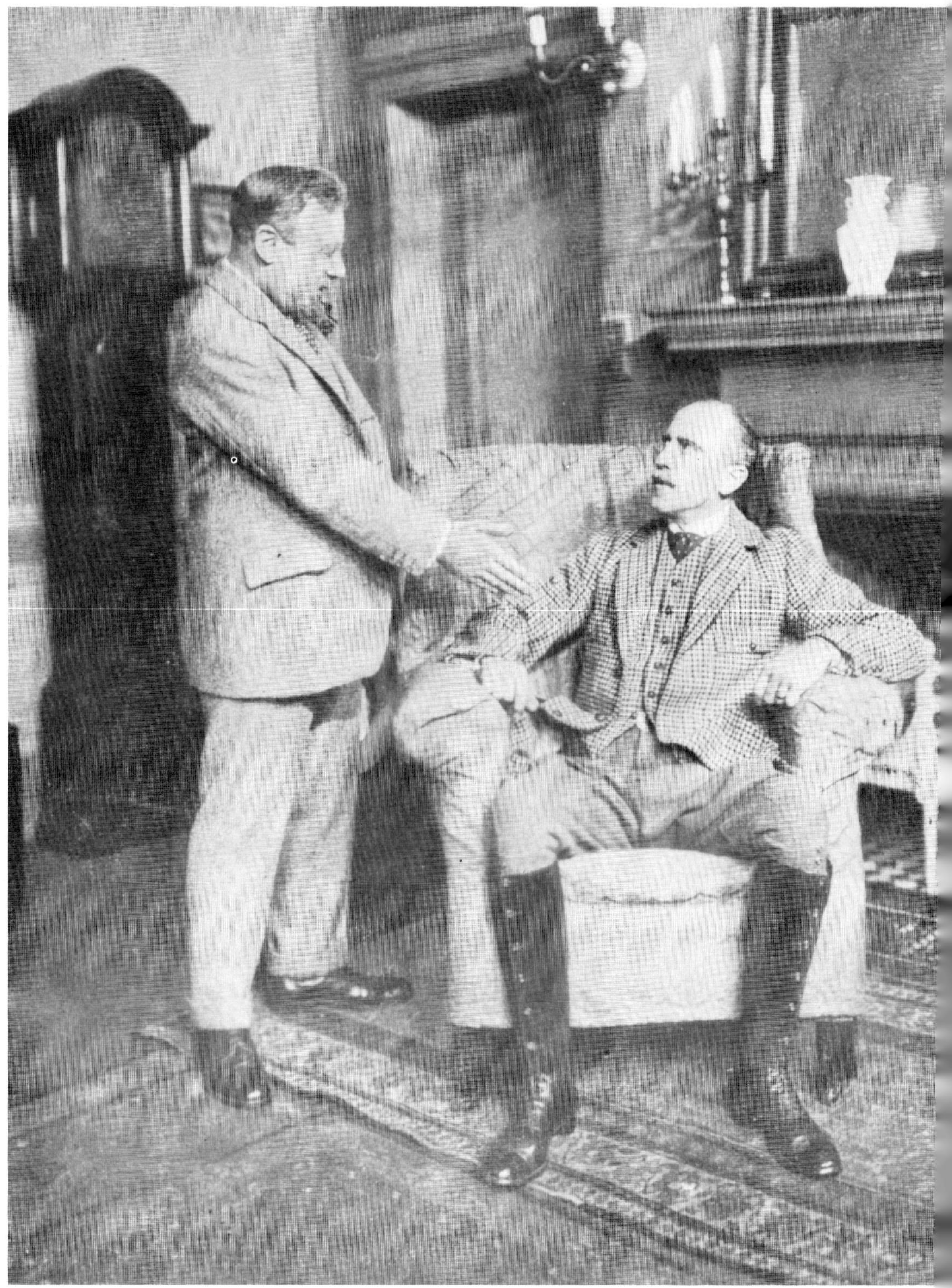

Galsworthy's soul. It might have been a more shining and brilliant doom, but it would have been doom just the same. The age of chivalry, of fine behaviour, of Sir Philip Sidney was over; such was the conviction that John Galsworthy expressed in his life and in his plays. In the days of business men, of multinational corporations, of the glorification of money, of wars, and of trade unions, with every man for himself – the days that make up the lifetime of those still living – Galsworthy's ideals seem snobbish, stuffy, and even were they attainable, probably undesirable. Yet there is still a lingering magic about them. The enormous popularity of the television version of *The Forsyte Saga* pointed to a nostalgic desire for a more gracious world than the one we are living in; and some years later the success (also on television) of *Brideshead Revisited* prompted one young actor – Nigel Havers – to exclaim that the age of the gentleman was returning.

Galsworthy's pessimism is seen in the fate that befalls Matt Denant. Matt Denant is the hero of Galsworthy's *Escape* (1926), and might have served as a direct answer to Maugham's criticism. It is a play that, unless it is seen in relation to Galsworthy's whole output, can easily be misunderstood. At least, that is what I felt when I first saw it, and still feel today. In this play, as in *The Skin Game*, Galsworthy's fondness for demotic language, for differentiating the language of the classes, greatly increased the sense of snobbery.

Galsworthy was a Socialist, a man with a sincere wish to better the world, not by specific policies, however, but by increasing people's qualities of compassion, tolerance, and mutual understanding. Matt Denant, having knocked down and accidentally killed in Hyde Park a man who was molesting a young woman, is on the run. Each episode shows him in a tight place, from all of which he escapes. The play still has much wit, and the story moves with a splendid swing, yet there was something not quite right with it. Even when seeing it for the first time, half a century ago, though I was carried along by the excitement of the tale and by the panache of Matt Denant, I felt slightly uneasy.

The case of Matt Denant, harassed, and at the end of his tether, vainly trying to escape the clutches of a harsh law, seemed designed to enlist our sympathies for all those who have had the misfortune to lose the world's good opinion. But in a play in which the hero is presented as Everyman in trouble, it struck me as unreasonable to put so much emphasis on the things that distinguish him from Everyman. One would like a plea to have been made for him as a man rather than as a gentleman. The scene with the shingled lady is one of the most amusing and delicate in the play; but would she, I could not help thinking, have lent him her husband's Burberry and fishing tackle if he had not been at school with her brother? And if his accent had not been stamped by Oxford, would the wife of the man in plus-fours have been so distressed by her husband's unsympathetic

Edmund Gwenn and Athole Stewart in John Galsworthy's The Skin Game *(1920) at the St Martin's Theatre, London.*

attitude? One fears not. And yet, if this is so, how can *Escape* have universal significance?

The answer is fairly simple. There is universal significance in *Escape*, not because it shows that when in danger all men are equal, which they are not, but that there come certain moments in the history of a nation when its governing class is finished. If it is not destroyed by forsaking its ideals, then it will be destroyed by remaining faithful to them. It will meet the fate if not of Hillcrist, then of Denant. The governing class in *The Skin Game* is doomed because the representative of the centre of power, Hillcrist, is flawed. His principles are right, but his action is weak. He falls at the last hurdle, and the principles of conduct and government which he tries, honestly enough, to embody, are seen to be things in which one cannot put trust. It is not so with Matt Denant. He is a snob; he is class-conscious; he is aware of his superior brains, mind, and body; he is not as other men are: he knows the difference that Eton and Oxford make, and the merits of belonging to an old family. He is everything that a few years later was regarded with suspicion and hostility. But whatever his disadvantages he had the supreme virtue, which Hillcrist had not, of being fearless, resourceful, and above all incorruptible. And it was because he was incorruptible that he fell. Once the hour has struck there is no escape.

The more frivolous side of the British theatre of the time provided some of the most brilliant entertainment the British stage has ever seen. This came chiefly from two sources. The first was Frederick Lonsdale, an amusing, epigrammatic, rather admiring satirist of the upper classes, a clever hand at a scandalous situation, superbly and insolently witty. *The Last of Mrs Cheyney* (1925) has a wonderful *coup de théâtre* at the end of the first act, when after all the guests have departed from a great party held by Mrs Cheyney, the servants take off their coats and lounge round the ballroom, and the audience suddenly realizes that they are a gang of thieves in league with Mrs Cheyney. It sprang a wonderful surprise on the first night, and it still manages to bring off a frisson whenever it is revived. Better still is *On Approval* (1927). In *On Approval* the cynical, selfish Duke of Bristol, impregnably protected by the impenetrable armour of his own self-conceit, is a creation worthy of Congreve. I saw it in Sheffield only in an amateur performance, but it made a strong impression on me, especially the actor who played the Duke (Roland Moorwood, a member of a well-known Sheffield family). It fascinated me to see that Moorwood (unlike other actors I have seen in the same part since) would not allow the Duke to have anything so common as a cold, but bestowed on him a frigor, which he made enormously impressive by pronouncing the 'i' long, as in tiger. 'There is no excellent beauty,' says Bacon, 'without some strangeness in the proportions.' And an excellent beauty of its own can sometimes be produced by a mere strangeness in

---

Gerald du Maurier and Gladys Cooper in Frederick Lonsdale's The Last of Mrs Cheyney *(1925) at the St James's Theatre, London.*

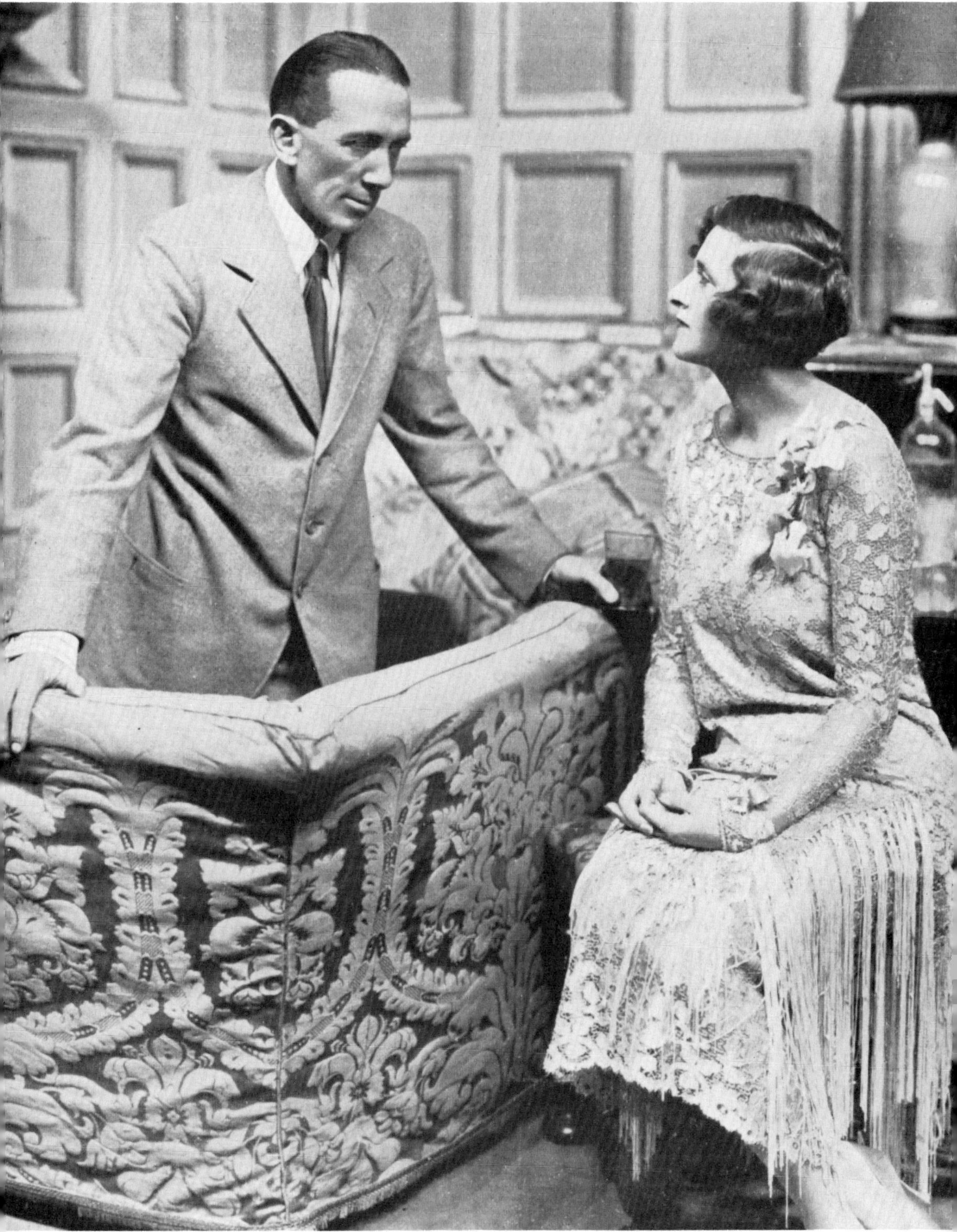

the pronunciation. It seemed to me that Moorwood conferred a certain distinction on our small provincial city by this tiny but stylish eccentricity. Unlike Maugham, Lonsdale was of a kindly disposition, and in consequence his satire and contempt are not as savage as Maugham's. One has a feeling that he liked those he castigated, especially perhaps the outrageous Duke. Some of Lonsdale's plays were shocking, but there was nothing about the man himself to arouse misgiving.

Similarly it was not until Noël Coward's diaries were published in 1982, after his death, that his wonderful patience, kindness, and generosity became properly appreciated by the general public, who had seen only the magnificent garments, and could not hear the heart beating beneath them. I certainly could not. Away in Sheffield, of course, I had no actual knowledge of the man, but I recognized him as being one with my local policeman, a threat to those established things that I liked. Compared to the copiousness of plot which I (indirectly supported by Aristotle) admired in *The Only Way*, Coward's plays seemed to me flimsy and lacking in action. They were not done at the Lyceum, the home of the old melodramas that I loved so much, but in the Repertory Theatre in South Street, playing to audiences composed in the main of schoolteachers, and other intellectuals of Sheffield. This was the sort of place from which the work of the future was to come, and it surprised me even then to find that Donald Wolfit after a season of delicate and advanced productions at the Repertory Theatre left it in the late twenties to join Matheson Lang in a trumpery piece in London called *Such Men are Dangerous*. But I suppose the lure of the West End was irresistible.

Sometimes I went over to Manchester by coach to the Palace Theatre, where the attractions were bigger and brighter than in Sheffield. It was there I first saw Sybil Thorndike and Jack Buchanan, Anton Dolin, and Anna Neagle (then called Marjorie Robertson). There too I had my first glimpse of the radiance of Peggy Ashcroft, also in one of Matheson Lang's melodramas, *Jew Suss* (1929). It was a memorable sight. After the interval the sun rose on a great medieval courtyard, empty but for the figure of a young girl sitting reading the Talmud. She was perfectly still, and the sun flooded her with great waves of gold. That was in 1929, and whenever I remember it (which is often) I am reminded of Burke's ecstasy on first seeing Marie Antoinette.

From this peace and tranquillity Noël Coward was altogether different. He was bitterly condemned by the greater part of public opinion, and even in Sheffield, where his uncle Sir Henry Coward was a distinguished musician of impeccable character, people did not regard him with approval. Our imagination found it impossible to disengage visions of his private life from the drug-taking, sexual excess, and perversion, flippancy and total irresponsibility which it was

---

Matheson Lang and Peggy Ashcroft in Jew Suss *(1929) at The Duke of York's Theatre, London, an adaptation of Lion Feuchtwanger's novel of the same name.*

uncertain whether he was advertising or denouncing in plays like *The Vortex* (1924), *Hay Fever* (1925), and *Private Lives* (1930). Even the highly respectable character of his partner in *The Vortex*, Lilian (later Dame Lilian) Braithwaite, did not save him from suspicion. It must be admitted that with his elaborate dressing-gown, his long cigarette-holder, and the bored paleness of his world-weary face the young Coward did nothing to dissipate the rumours that freely identified the customs of his plays with his own behaviour. Whilst at Oxford, one day in the Union Library, I read Beverley Nichols's *Twenty-Five*, which gave a most eulogistic account of Coward, and spoke warmly of his generosity and lack of pomposity in spite of his great success. But I was not convinced.

Coward's comedy lay chiefly in the carefully-calculated, well-bred, discourteous retort, in chic and cultivated bad manners. Then in 1931 he astonished everyone with his mighty patriotic pageant, *Cavalcade*. The fits of obstreperous and demonstrative patriotism which alternated with his satirical denunciations of gigolos and the aimless, pleasure-loving rich (those in fact who most admired him, and gave him his wealth, his cars, his extravagant holidays, and his exotic houses) here overwhelmed him: this unexpected patriotism, which ended with a moving speech hoping for those days to return when Britain had been rich and powerful, won him the admiration of those who had hitherto most vigorously denounced him as degenerate and immoral. A few believed that even in *Cavalcade* Coward was writing with his tongue in his cheek. But this was not so. In *Cavalcade* he was thinking of our Imperial splendour, of the Empire on which the sun never sets. And this he always loved. He did not give his devotion to deeply-loved parts of England: to the church clock at Grantchester, or to the stripling Thames at Bablock-Hythe. It was the Empire that he loved, far more than England, as he wrote to me in the last days of his life.

Coward's stories were banal, his satire barbed, bitter, and often brutal; his sense of fun exuberant, his characters caricatures, his attack sensational and merciless, his wit sharp and staccato, his heart kind and generous. He never forgot his friends. In fact, he urged their merits with a pertinacity which finally wearied Charles Cochran. When one of them achieved a success, as Graham Payn did in singing *Matelot* in one of his revues just after the Second World War, Coward took infinite pleasure in it. Cochran gave Coward his first chance, and was thereafter associated with him in a series of dazzling revues, which, in their grace, glitter, and good taste, and the brilliance of their casts – Gertrude Lawrence, Binnie and Sonnie Hale, Mimi Crawford, Jessie Matthews, and Jack Buchanan – epitomised the ephemeral splendour which was the mark of British theatre until the financial disasters of the second half of the 1920s. Coward devastated the character of a whole generation of young people, won the favour of royalty and of the socially exalted, did much private good and some public

---

Noël Coward in his In Which We Serve *(1942), one of the many successful films in which he appeared and which he directed (photograph: Cecil Beaton).*

Adrienne Allen, Noël Coward, Gertrude Lawrence and Laurence Olivier in Noël Coward's Private Lives *(1930) at the Phoenix Theatre, London.*

harm, and, with his contemptuous admiration, joined Somerset Maugham in destroying the reputation of the well-born, the well-to-do, and the well-educated.

Throughout the middle years of the century, Coward was a potent theatrical influence, but the proletarian dramatists of the post-1950s long and jealously derided him. Ineffectually and foolishly so, for in the end it was realized that he was fundamentally, and without knowing it, on their side. In the 1970s his reputation enjoyed a gratifying resurrection, for it finally dawned on the newest generation of the young that Noël Coward, despite his predilection for titled people, and the boiled shirts and ropes of pearls of his characters, was a revolutionary writer. He undermined, perhaps unconsciously, but nonetheless effectively for that, the authority of that ruling class upon whose deceived support he depended for the maintenance of the brilliant standard of his opulent living. Despite the difference of their temperaments he was at one with Galsworthy. Galsworthy showed that the virtues of the ruling class were insufficient; and Coward that what glittered in them was far from being gold.

The dominance of the upper class in the theatre, of fine manners and assured social position, was coming to an end. That was evident to me even before I left Sheffield for London in 1931. This great change in the theatre came about because a similar change was taking place in life outside. Especially was the upper class's sense of moral obligation deteriorating. For every Lord Hugh Cecil who devoted himself to serious issues, a hundred men and women of the élite classes and their rich hangers-on gambled away their wealth at the tables of Le Touquet. In the bleak and newly developed town that sprang up amidst the sand dunes of the north-west French coast, dotted here and there by white and glittering luxury bungalows shivering in the biting winds from which forests of trees barely protected them, and near the very door of the huge Westminster Hotel, there for a few years flourished mightily a casino (it is still there) in which the most splendidly gowned women in England threw away fortunes. In the mid-1920s Mrs Syrie Maugham was a frequent visitor; so was the resplendent daughter of the English secretary of a celebrated Paris club; and one of the Dolly Sisters fascinated all eyes. Her white dress, with three beautiful strings of pearls in her ears, became famous in *Vogue*. On her finger she wore a superb diamond ring. But even this was not the most striking thing about her. That was undoubtedly the piles of fresh banknotes wrapped in packages of ten thousand pounds which were on the table in front of her, and which she tossed carelessly, bound in their elastic bands, on to the roulette boards. Even the rich clientèle of the casino gasped at the nonchalance with which this star of the revue stage gambled what in those days were fortunes on a single casual throw. She and her twin sister appeared in London for the first time, at the age of twenty-eight, in *Jig-Saw* at the London Hippodrome (later the Talk of the Town, and closed down in 1982). Their other shows were *The League of Notions*, *The Fun of the Fayre*, and in 1921 *Babes in the Wood*. Subsequently they went to Paris. Who remembers them now, even though one of them died as recently as 1970? They represented nothing but the tinsel and glitter and reckless extravagance and ostentation of an age whose memory is preserved only in *Vogue* and *The Tatler*, for the envy and contempt of a censorious and hag-ridden later generation.

This ostentation, this flamboyant and vulgar splendour (as it was regarded by those who could not afford it), this glittering display, however, was in the mid-1920s being undermined – and in Paris, of all places – by a revolutionary change of taste brought about by a young woman then comparatively unknown, but world-famous for the next half-century under the name of 'Coco' Chanel. Chanel taught the wealthy not merely that they could not afford the meretricious Dolly type of magnificence, but that they actually did not want it. It was one of the great social lessons of our time.

This then little-known Parisian modiste (older than either of the Dolly Sisters, and outliving them both) inaugurated a wren–like fashion that made peacock glory seem out-of-date. As early as 1925 Chanel (who mischievously declared that her first name, Coco, was an abbreviation of 'cocotte') introduced the

The Dolly Sisters in de Courville's Jig-saw *(1920) at the Hippodrome, London.*

cardigan jacket. Like many revolutionaries and devoted enemies of superfluous wealth, she had her headquarters in luxurious surroundings in the rue Cambon and permanently kept a room at the Ritz, where she slept every night. But she sincerely felt the need for change and emancipation after the Great War. She fought long and hard and successfully against the flaunting splendour of pre-war women's clothing that still flourished in Le Touquet and other similar places, and by imitation on the musical comedy stage and in the elegant comedies of Lonsdale and Maugham. She started by freeing women from the corset and made the first chemise dress. This was the beginning of what became known as 'the poor girl look', which finally helped to eliminate evening dress from the theatre. She was the forerunner of the mini-skirt and of Yves St Laurent's beatnik collections. I was at Oxford at this time, and of course had no idea of the epoch-marking transformation that was being prepared near the Place Vendôme for the dazzling splendour and flashing silk stockings and sumptuous décor of the theatre which I loved. Chanel was a great woman; the spiritual mother of George Devine and all those in the world of entertainment who have a social conscience; and so long as she lived, unlike Garrick, she worked hard in the great work of eclipsing the gaiety of nations.

Opposite: Coco Chanel wearing a Chanel suit (1929).

(Left to right) Cedric Hardwicke, Diana Hamilton, Marda Vanne, Flora Robson, Marjorie Mars, Ralph Richardson, Louise Hampton, Phyllis Shand and S. J. Warmington in Somerset Maugham's For Services Rendered *(1932) at the Globe Theatre, London.*

At my college we had when I went up something called The Dramatic Reading Circle, but which was soon afterwards named the Newlands Society. This was because amongst its first members was an undergraduate named Anthony Newlands. He ran away from Oxford to become an actor. I understand that he joined the Old Vic, and I never discovered what became of him afterwards, though I presume that he never reached the highest ranks of his profession. Every Saturday night we met to read some play that was the talk of London. In this way even before I set foot in London I gained some idea of the characteristic metropolitan theatre. We read the work of people like Coward, Lonsdale, Galsworthy, and Alfred Sutro. But our main diet was Bernard Shaw and Somerset Maugham, whom we regarded (and we were not far wrong) as the principal dramatists of the age.

The great success of the National Theatre's revival of *For Services Rendered* at the beginning of the 1980s confirmed the impression the Newlands Society gained from reading Maugham's plays regularly sixty years earlier. His dialogue proved scarcely to have dated at all, and his cynical view of human nature, together with his conviction of the wickedness of war, was still in the mood of our time. But what is particularly interesting is that, though he hated it, what Le Touquet represented still seemed to him the focus of worthwhile attention, rather than the philosophy of Chanel. Were it not that he was on such bad terms with her, and treated her so shamefully, one might think that Maugham was interested in the type of person who frequented Le Touquet because his wife was an habituée of the place. It is however more probable that Syrie Maugham's presence in the gaming saloons was what made him – who, after all, was no great specimen of manhood – despise the people who filled them with their bets and spurious excitement.

Anyway, what we at the time perceived clearly enough was that a typical Le Touquet gamester, swindling, flamboyant, snobbish and uncultured, was the characteristic figure – more entertaining, alas, than a hundred Hillcrists – that Maugham, in his best plays, such as *Our Betters*, delights in presenting and abusing. Although written in 1915, *Our Betters* was not presented until 1923, and, well knowing that it had created a tremendous sensation in London, I made its acquaintance at the Newlands Society a year later. Even then, after all the obscenity and bloodshed of the trenches, amidst all the freedom given by night clubs whose proprietors were frequently in gaol but nevertheless married off their daughters into the peerage, despite the dazzling legs of girls in outrageously short skirts, Maugham's language still shocked and disgusted. At the first performance the word 'slut' used by one of the characters 'made the spectators . . . gasp with horror'. We have Maugham's own authority for this, and also for the fact that the play originally contained a scene that had to be altered in accordance with the instructions of the Lord Chamberlain. It all seems as futile now as the excitement caused fifty years or more later by Kenneth Tynan's sad little effort to shock by the use of 'fuck' on the BBC. I am glad to say that we adventurous spirits in the Newlands took Maugham's language without increase of blood pressure.

Seven years on, in *The Gentleman in the Parlour*, Maugham wrote of the decline and fall of the British Empire, and gave more than one good suggestion why that event was already coming about. His gloomy prophecies in this respect caused nothing like the sensation created by his freedom of verbal expression, for the very good reason that scarcely anybody believed him. Actually in 1923 Maugham himself seems to have been still confident that Britain was top nation. Astonishing as it may now appear, even foreigners at that date wished to be mistaken for Englishmen. Not, I am sorry to say, for Scotsmen, Irishmen, or Welshmen, but Englishmen. One of the chief characters in *Our Betters*, Thornton Clay, is a snobbish and wealthy American. His supreme ambition is to be thought English. He had been born in Virginia, but he claimed that 'of course, my home is London . . . I went (back) to America seven years ago. My father died, and I had to go and settle his affairs. Everyone took me for an Englishman. Of course, I haven't a trace of an American accent. I suppose that was the reason. And then my clothes.' And he looks down with satisfaction at their Savile Row cut. It is curious to remember that in my first days in the theatre pride in England was a ruling passion and an unshakeable conviction.

In *Our Betters*, as in his other work for the stage, Maugham's aim was to write a commercial, not a didactic play. But alas for human intentions. It in the outcome taught audiences something about British Imperial pretensions, and the subservient way in which those pretensions were regarded in the first quarter of the twentieth century even on the other side of the Atlantic. It taught something about the prudery of the language. Thus, as with Galsworthy, things turned out differently from what their author had envisaged. Maugham may have intended *Our Betters* (and *The Circle* and *The Breadwinner* and his other plays) to amuse. This they did, but they also did much more.

In their way they contributed to that fall of the Empire which Maugham, from 1930 onwards, foresaw. So did Galsworthy, though from different motives and a more exalted standpoint. For where Galsworthy killed hope Maugham encouraged contempt. In both performance and reading his best plays leave an overwhelming impression that the state of society is indeed scandalous. The theme, for example, of *Our Betters* is the invasion of the effete English aristocracy by American heiresses. This of course had been a familiar story with Henry James. But in James the American invaders are simple, disinterested, and innocent. They are deceived by the wickedness of Europe, but they do not add to it. In *Our Betters*, on the other hand, they are lascivious and corrupt. They are ready to do anything to obtain a title, and when they have got it to betray it, just as the English were willing to put up any title for sale. (It is the discovery of one of these American women in a compromising situation that provokes the word 'slut'.)

Maugham was a most effective propagandist without either intending or even perceiving it. He spread the idea that all the rich were morally worthless. He did not recognize the existence of well-born men of integrity like Lord Quickswood; and even Galsworthy, a fellow-author of high repute and blameless character as well as rich, was, as we have seen, a further subject for ridicule. To Maugham (whose talent was as immense as his character was contemptible) society and the governing classes were the people round the gaming tables of Le Touquet. Unconsciously he showed that the distinction between the drama of social relevance and the drama of entertainment is artificial, except that the drama of entertainment is often more skilfully written.

Both in Sheffield and in Oxford (which in the 1920s enjoyed one of the most illustrious periods of its history) we totally failed to appreciate either the artistic or the social importance of such a woman as Chanel. But we reacted strongly to certain developments on the political scene, and during the General Strike of 1926 hundreds of undergraduates volunteered their services to the Government. Oriel College was no exception to this rule, but for more than a century it had been a leader of anti-conventional thought. In the middle of the nineteenth century the 'Oriel heretics' – Froude, the Newman brothers and the rest who had participated in the Tractarian Movement – disturbed the tranquillity of the

OUR BETTERS," AT THE GLOBE.

Constance Collier, Margaret Bannerman and John Stuart in Somerset Maugham's Our Betters *(1923) at the Globe Theatre, London (reproduced from* The Sketch *of 10 October 1923).*

London street scene during the General Strike (May 1926).

Church of England by some of them rejecting the Thirty-Nine Articles and the beneficence of the Reformation, others by denying the doctrine of Baptismal Regeneration, and all of them by advocating Sunday cricket. A college whose most famous clergyman a hundred years ago had played cricket on Sundays was hardly likely to be upset when two of its undergraduates worked for the General Strike, and when A. J. P. Taylor and myself – still, perhaps frailly united by being today both of us Honorary Fellows of the college – threw in our lot with the strikers it preserved an amused calm at our eccentricity. Nevertheless, for all our advanced views, we accepted readily enough Maugham's thesis that the future (however disastrous it might be) lay with the riff-raff of the upper classes.

Galsworthy at least did not make that mistake, but so far as we ourselves were concerned our assumption led us wholly to misunderstand the situation of the highest class of all, and, more specifically and personally, the importance of Lady Elizabeth Bowes-Lyon, who even in our wildest speculations we never

Lady Elizabeth Bowes-Lyon, the present Queen-Mother.

guessed would become the prop on which British monarchy rested and the most significant woman of our age.

The very head of the State, royalty itself, had, without many people realizing it, found its position difficult at the end of the First World War. Before the war the royal family had had close relations with many kings and queens. They were bound together by blood and breeding, and were more closely associated with each other than with even the most illustrious of their subjects. But most of these royal families, the intimate friends of the British monarchy, had been swept away during the war. There was no longer a Tsar of Russia, nor an Emperor of Germany, nor an Emperor of Austria–Hungary. George V and Queen Mary had uncomfortably to look round for new friends, and to find them amongst their own people. Now, to the Prince of Wales, later King Edward VIII, this proved no difficulty. Things might have gone better with the nation if it had. But he soon found congenial companions amongst precisely the sort of men and women we encounter in the plays of Maugham, and with the general public he was enormously popular.

A greater problem faced a better but less glamorous man, his brother, the then Duke of York, who was reluctantly to succeed him on his abdication. The Duke was handicapped by a grievous stammer. Both at Dartmouth and at Osborne this prevented him from setting up any easy relationship with his fellows, and when he went up to Cambridge he made the mistake of living in a private house with his brother, the Duke of Gloucester. This again deprived him of any chance of becoming on friendly terms with his fellow-undergraduates at Trinity. It is a considerable historical irony that an unhappy fate was to call on this man, so little fitted by nature to perform the task, to make himself the leader of every class in the country in a memorable and (not through *his* fault) an ultimately disastrous war. But in this terrible crisis he acquitted himself well; and one of the chief reasons for this (if not the very chief) is that fate so far relented as to provide him with a potent defence in the person of his wife, the Lady Elizabeth Bowes-Lyon.

In writing about royalty one is beset by two opposite dangers; the grim possibility of becoming either fulsome or offensive. Therefore the less said about these exalted people the better. Nevertheless, one must not be prevented by unduly cowardly caution from recognizing certain self-evident truths which were of paramount importance to Britain and therefore to the sort of drama she came to produce. Lady Elizabeth's spontaneous gaiety as Duchess of York, as Queen, and as Queen-Mother, her natural kindness and sociableness, her capacity both for private and for public friendliness were for the next sixty years or so of vital importance in making royalty at one with its subjects. It was largely from her that the royal family learned how to adapt itself to a new, strange world in which most of its equals had been either killed or deposed. This adaptability proved to be one of the most stabilizing factors in a world otherwise given to insecurity, disruption and alarm.

In fact one of the few strokes of luck that Britain has had during the twentieth

The Queen-Mother (the then Queen) talking to Lord Elphinstone at the inspection of the Royal Company of Archers at Holyrood Palace, Edinburgh in 1937. King George VI is at the far right; in the centre the Princesses Elizabeth and Margaret Rose.

century has been the longevity of leading figures in its national life. The long and active life of the Queen Mother has given a continuity to the national ethos that it would otherwise not have had. Happily the stage has had similar good fortune. For within a very few years of Lady Elizabeth's marriage Ralph Richardson, Peggy Ashcroft, John Gielgud and Laurence Olivier began to attract attention, and remained prominently in the public eye as late as the 1980s, without the slightest diminution of fame during that whole huge period of time. This continuity was not broken until the sudden death of Richardson in 1983.

So small a thing as the inventions of a Paris dressmaker, so large a thing as the social decline of royalty both pointed in the same direction. Both were movements towards egalitarianism. Lonsdale may not have really believed that everybody could be quite as witty as the Duke of Bristol, but he did his best to make it appear as if he did. Galsworthy certainly aimed to make every man at least as good as Hillcrist, if not as gallant as Denant. But astonishingly the greatest dramatist of the time, a life-long socialist street-corner political left-wing orator, did not believe in equality at all. Shaw despised democracy. In Oxford and Sheffield we nevertheless considered him the eloquent, witty and dashing banner-bearer of the proletariat rousing itself from its slumbers, and enthusiastically applauded everything he said, did, and wrote. My first memory of John Gielgud is of a lithe, eager young man leaping on to the arm of Candida's chair, to pour out to her his torrents of adoration. But George Bernard Shaw in 1924 in the most famous and successful of his plays – *Saint Joan* – saw the salvation of nations coming from an individual, not a class, even though he was spiritually attuned to Trotsky's *History of the Russian Revolution*.

It was the essence of Shaw's vision, which strengthened as the years wore on, that Joan was exceptional. Shaw preached the doctrine of leadership. Moreover, the leader must be self-elected. A leader who is elected by others will not have superior qualities to his electors, since the mediocre are jealous of excellence, which they call élitism. Shaw therefore was not depressed by the breakdown of traditional mores: he looked instead for a Saviour. He found this Saviour in Joan. But that was 500 years ago. Even before all the furore created by *Saint Joan*, which gave to Sybil Thorndike (again a socialist and a supporter of the Communist *Daily Worker*) one of the most celebrated roles in English theatrical history, Shaw was looking for a replacement of a more modern kind.

He found this replacement in a king. Kings had, in Shaw's eyes, one enormous advantage over any other form of constitutional government. A monarch is not elected. Since he is not elected, since he is not a reflection of all the futilities of the wretched democrats who vote for Prime Ministers, Shaw argued that he had the chance of being a really remarkable man. Thus Shaw offered for us for our salvation an autocrat, King Magnus. This was in 1929 when the play was presented by Sir Barry Jackson with the soon to be prematurely knighted Cedric Hardwicke in the lead. At that time it was an astonishing prophecy, for it was then impossible to foresee any conceivable development in Britain that would make such a situation plausible. Yet within seven years a King's Party was a real possibility in England. But the central character in that bizarre and Ruritanian drama declined the challenge (no Titus he, and not even much of an Antony). So, the aristocracy declining, we never found out whether royalty could take its place. It is in large part due to the calming, confidence-giving influence of the former Lady Bowes-Lyon, in her marriage to the Duke of York, that royalty even survived.

It was not however only in politics that a need for leadership was felt. A

Poster advertising the 1915 production of George Bernard Shaw's Great Catherine.

VAUDEVILLE
Lessees & Managers
A. & S. GATTI
Vaudeville Theatre, Strand, W.C.
THEATRE, STRAND. W.C.
ALLINSON
BERNARD SHAW'S
GREAT CATHERINE
J. MILES & CO LTD

well-known drama critic, Archibald Haddon, unfolded the defects of the contemporary stage as he saw them. He maintained that the theatre had ceased to produce great actors. In 1922 he rhetorically asked how we could possibly compare the nonentities of his time – he mentioned John Martin-Harvey, Matheson Lang, Henry Ainley, Gerald du Maurier, Arthur Bourchier, and Godfrey Tearle as typical of the weaklings of the day – with such giants of the past as Sir Henry Irving, Sir Herbert Tree, Sir Squire and Lady Bancroft, Dame Madge Kendall, and Toole (poor, untitled Toole). In fifty years' time would such actors still be heard of, he demanded petulantly. But Haddon was unduly pessimistic and unjust where his contemporaries were concerned. All the names he mentioned with contempt rouse some sort of echo, however faint, more than half a century after he dismissed them so summarily. Moreover, there were newcomers, of whom the most breath-taking was Meggie Albanesi, that he appears never to have heard of. Yet Meggie Albanesi had already appeared with Fred Terry and Julia Neilson and played Hillcrist's daughter, and made one of the great sensations of the century in Clemence Dane's *A Bill of Divorcement*. She died in 1923, making things easy for Peggy Ashcroft.

Haddon, who worked for the *Daily Express*, must have been aware that his contemporaries were better than he represented them, for his knowledge of the theatre was extensive. Though not one of the greatest periods of theatrical history – not comparable, for example, with that between 1945 and 1960 – the 1920s had no need to feel shame. They presented many pieces which gave scope for fine and subtle acting, which were full of wit, were strong in the delineation of character, kept near to the social and intellectual problems of the day, and even suggested remedies for these which came closer to being realistically relevant to the problems of the time than anyone but Bernard Shaw supposed.

It is not however always the biggest things, nor the greatest actors that are most vividly remembered. Four ducks on a pond may have a significance that no towering cathedral may attain to, and to some readers the brief words with which Elizabeth Bennet refuses Mr Darcy's offer of marriage stir more poignant feelings than anything in *War and Peace*. Edmund Blunden says that 'Greatness can be identified, like the touch of a painter, in a detail'.

Like the touch of a painter, greatness can also be lost. Edna Best, though she had a long and fairly successful career, never after the 1920s did anything that embedded itself in the heart and mind of audiences. She was often embarrassed by the excessive enthusiasm of her admirers, the 'gallery girls' of the twenties, who thus tended to set the rest of the public and some of the critics against her.

In Frederick Lonsdale's *Spring Cleaning* (1925) she appeared as a girl who was no better than she should be, and was invited by a bright young spark to a formal dinner party. She had just finished partnering the purest and most beautiful of English actresses, Evelyn Laye, in *The Lilies of the Field*, and it came as a

Sybil Thorndike in George Bernard Shaw's Saint Joan *(1924) at the New (Albery) Theatre, London.*

tremendous shock to see her in a cloche hat and wearing a monocle. But in 1926 came her moment of glory when she played Tessa in Margaret Kennedy's *The Constant Nymph*; first with Noël Coward and then with John Gielgud. (In all my years of theatre-going there have been only two occasions on which the principal actor has failed to appear. On both occasions the offender was Gielgud.) In *The Constant Nymph*, in the midst of the tumultuous, raucous family called from its rowdy high spirits Sanger's Circus, Edna Best showed us the quiet centre of gravity in her portrayal of the grave, innocent Tessa, a child of infinite respose and pathos, saying little, feeling much, and understanding more as one by one the cruel arrows of life planted themselves in her heart.

In this, her greatest achievement, which she never afterwards approached, Edna Best showed those qualities of quietness, stillness, timing, dramatic lowness of utterance, and eschewal of the big voice and the heroic gesture which marked most of the highest levels of experience I have encountered in the theatre. (I shall have something to say about them in the next chapter.) But after that she became just like any ordinary actress.

CHAPTER TWO
An Age of Doubt
1930–1934

J. A. Froude in one of his lesser books vividly recalls a sermon which the future Cardinal Newman preached whilst he was still an Anglican priest and a Fellow of Oriel. It is a recollection which amply repays consideration by any theatre-goer who is at all interested in the motives that actually make him a theatre-goer. Newman had been describing, in an apparently unemotional way, the incidents of Christ's passion.

> '. . . He then paused. For a few moments there was a breathless silence. Then, in a low, clear voice, of which the faintest vibration was audible in the farthest corner of St Mary's, he said "Now I bid you recollect that he to whom these things were done was Almighty God." It was as if an electric stroke had gone through the church, as if every person present understood for the first time the meaning of what he had all his life been saying. I suppose it was an epoch in the mental history of more than one of my Oxford contemporaries.' (Basil Willey, *More Nineteenth Century Studies*).

This is one of the most brilliant descriptions of a great theatrical effect in all literature. Hazlitt on Kean's Othello did not make the reader more vividly aware of the actor's hold on his audience than did Froude in this passage by showing what a great speaker can do with those listening to him, when the preacher really believes what he is saying. Here Newman displays most of the qualities of a great actor. There is the incomparable timing; there is the careful preparation of the climax; there is the skilful employment of silence; there is the complete subjugation of the audience; there is the light suddenly thrown – in a moment, in the blink of an eyelid – on the course and meaning of an entire lifetime; there is the shock when, instead of the expected thunderous breaking of the silence, there is instead only something little more than a whisper, but a whisper which reveals a shattering dramatic fact, and that can be heard in every corner of the building.

It can be objected that the recollection of such an incident today is pointless. Newman preached in an age of deep religious feeling; today we live in a scientific age. But this means little, if what we are thinking of is intelligent audiences and not those whose wisdom comes from hasty perusal of colour supplements. All scientific theories are based on observation: that is, on evidence supplied at nearer or further remove by the senses. But the senses, which inform us by observation that the sun goes round the earth, are unreliable witnesses. Scientific theories are based on witnesses that cannot be trusted, or proved. Science depends on the assumption that effect follows cause, and this assumption is incapable of proof, as A. J. Balfour showed a century ago. In other words, in a scientific or a religious age audiences are in the same intellectual position: they believe where they cannot prove. No modern audience is justified in feeling superior at Newman's naivété in identifying a crucified criminal with God, who may not exist. Their eyes, watching a ship coming up over the horizon, tell them that the earth is not flat. Those same eyes, watching the sun progress from east to west, tell them that the earth is stationary. A modern audience will say that in the first instance their eyes can be believed in, and in the second that those same eyes cannot be believed in. And they will contradict themselves, not out of knowledge or reason (in any case fallible) but simply because they have been told so on authority. Audiences today are in exactly the same case as those of a century ago: they act on faith, not on proof.

There are many other explanations of the power of the theatre as well as that indirectly and unintentionally offered by Froude. Racine, one of the greatest of dramatists, on one occasion maintained that the merit of a play was determined by the length of its run; on another, on the pleasure it imparted; on yet another on the efficacity of its moral instruction. Aristotle judged a play by its plot, Maugham by its power of amusement. Shakespeare seems to have attached greatest importance to character and rhetoric, and Ibsen to ingenuity and elaborateness of construction. Shaw insisted on wit and stimulation of thought. The most modern criterion applied to judging a play has been its contemporary social relevance. The sensible critic should hold most or all of these criteria in mind when judging a play, but it is likely that some will influence him more than others; and one must admit that in the theatre experiences such as Froude had when hearing Newman, are comparatively rare. Nevertheless it is they that to me make the theatre worthwhile.

Whether the theatre is democratic or not was not discussed at that time by any considerable dramatist but Shaw. Democracy was something, as we have seen, that Shaw, as a socialist, despised. Certain other dramatists also shared his more than considerable admiration for royal rule. Clifford Bax, a somewhat precious yet nevertheless graceful and highly cultured writer, deeply interested in Eastern philosophy, wrote in 1932 his most successful play, *A Rose without a Thorn*. It deals with Henry VIII's fifth wife, Catherine Howard, and harks back from the businesslike view of royalty to the romantic. There is an awe about Bax's royalty. You would admire Magnus's acuity of mind, but you would not be afraid to speak to him. He had no aloofness of bearing. But in *A Rose without a Thorn*

John Henry Newman (1801–90).

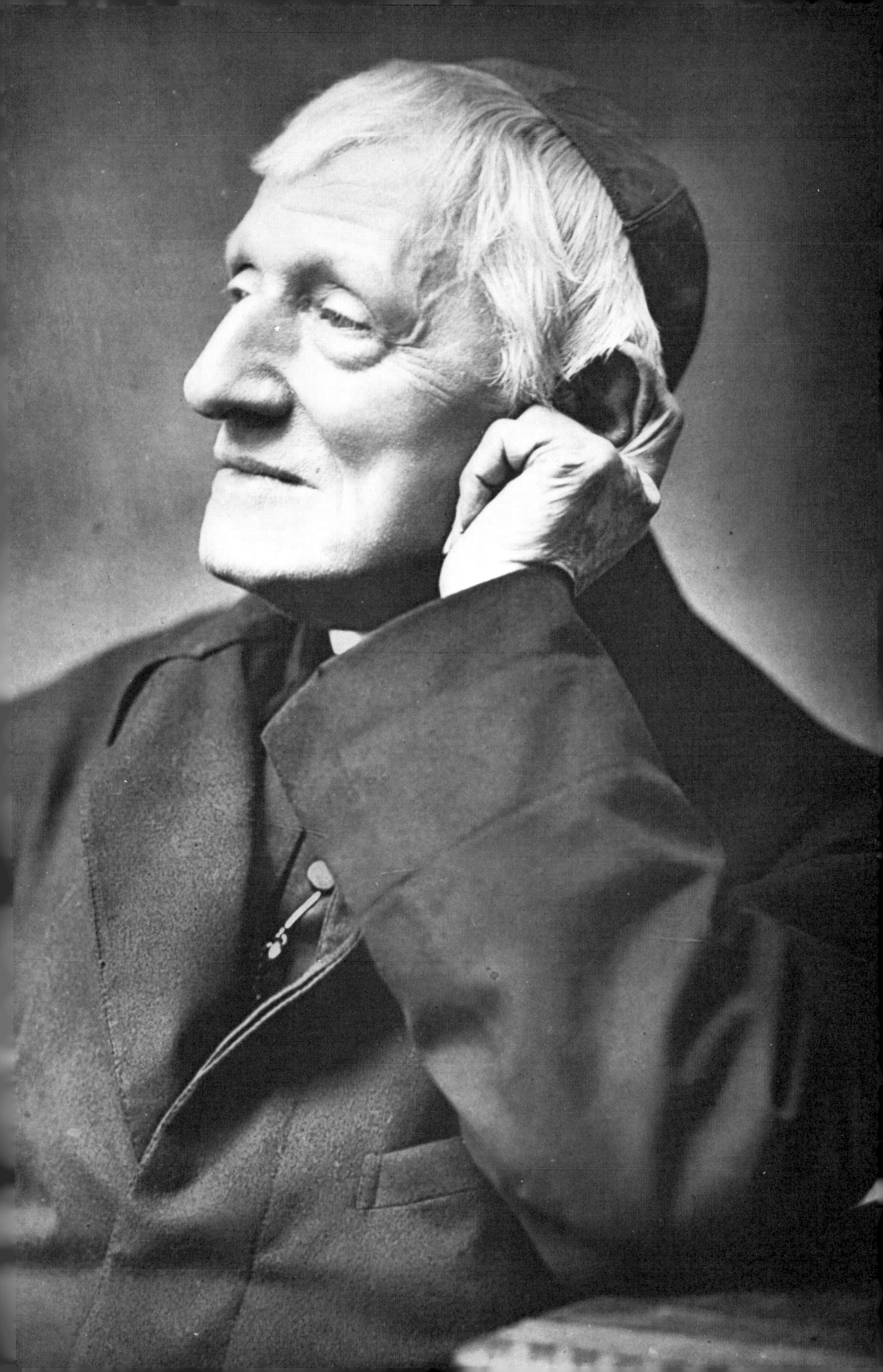

Frank Vosper's Henry VIII had a magnificence about him. He looked like a Holbein who had just stepped down from the canvas, and you instantly felt that a casual, uninvited word might well cost you your head. Angela Baddeley's Catherine was dazzled by the prospect of queenship; especially she brought a lovely, pathetic peace to the solemn scene in which the Archbishop announces her doom.

Not everything however was gloom and despondency in the British theatre in the perilous days of the early 1930s. In 1932, at the New Theatre, the London public discovered in John Gielgud a star, in Gordon Daviot's *Richard of Bordeaux*, of the first magnitude. This was the greatest success of Gielgud's early career, and I do not think that any British actor has ever surpassed it. There were queues round the New Theatre from dawn until the evening performance began. It was not a great play, but it enabled Gielgud to show the other kind of kingship from Henry VIII and Magnus, both strong men, knowing their own minds and of iron will. Gielgud's Richard was aesthetic, vacillating, roused to irresponsible anger by the slightest rebuke, and immediately subsiding into petulant despair. There was one passage when he was attacked by his uncles in which, with a voice of high-pitched, almost hysterical rage, he gathered his swirling cloak round as if to protect him from assassination. It was a truly sensational effect.

These years were also the period of the great Ben Travers farces at the Aldwych, when Tom Walls came very near (though not so near as he supposed) to being the Perfect Man-about-Town, and the dithering, amiable Ralph Lynn, infinitely funnier than Walls, blundering into the furniture, stammering to the girls, developed into high art the gentle dropping of a monocle at the critical moment. Audiences knew well enough that the tension of a performance would never lead him to drop it wrongly. But what we were not to learn for another ten or fifteen years was that not even the most frightening terror yet invented by men would make him do so. But that was when the flying-bombs came.

One by one the great farces rolled on. *A Cuckoo in the Nest* (1925); *Rookery Nook* (1926); *Thark* (1927); *Plunder* (1928); *Turkey Time* (1931); *A Bit of a Test* (1933), and so on. Travers, the tiniest bundle of light-hearted frolic for the ladies the twentieth century has seen, and a man who prayed on his knees every night before he went to bed, lived to an immense age: and his last days were even more famous than his first. In 1976, when he was ninety, he had three plays running simultaneously: *Banana Ridge* (1938), *Plunder*, and *The Bed Before Yesterday*. *The Bed Before Yesterday* Travers had written when he was eighty-nine, and *Plunder*, when produced at the National was unexpectedly perceived to be a precursor of the so-called Black Comedy which a few years before had been thought quite erroneously to be a new discovery. For *Plunder*, all the way back in 1928, had two murderers as heroes, and both of them got off without as much as a caution.

John Gielgud in Gordon Daviot's Richard of Bordeaux *(1933) at the New (Albery) Theatre, London.*

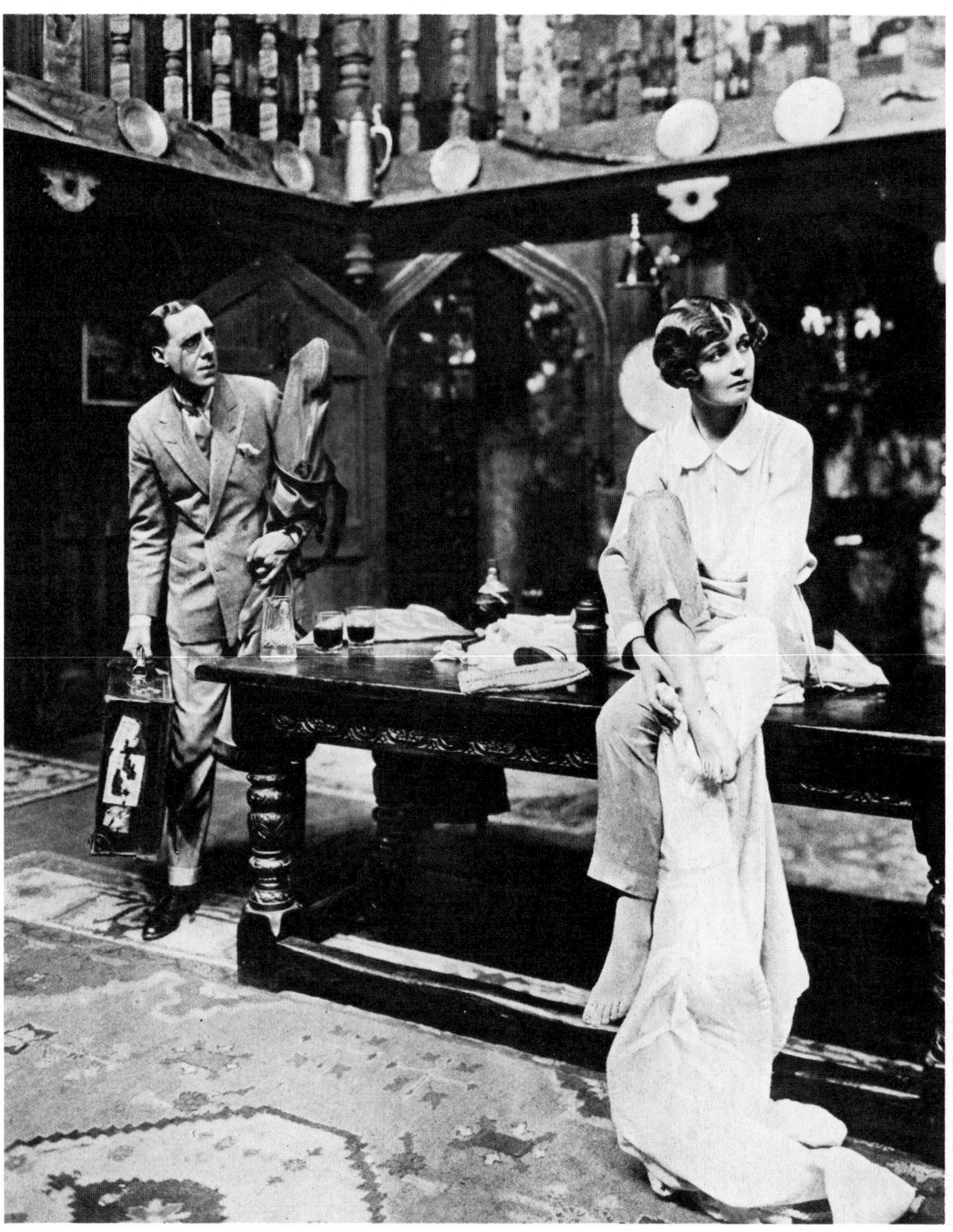

Above: Ralph Lynn and Winifred Shotter in Ben Travers's Rookery Nook *(1926) at the Aldwych Theatre, London.*

Opposite: Poster advertising the 1926 production of Rookery Nook *at the Aldwych Theatre, London.*

"ROOKERY NOOK"
BY BEN TRAVERS
NERMAN

But despite the Travers gaiety and the emergence in John Gielgud of a great star, the Carlyle theory of the salvation of humanity by Heroes was growing less and less acceptable. It would have been rejected even more quickly than it actually was had it not been that democracy and the mediocre were despised even more than élitism. An air of apprehension set in over the country, and by reflection over the theatre, and the blazing portent of the R101 airship, which crashed, in flames at Beauvais, was rendered all the more disquieting by the arrival and progress of Hitler on the German scene. Therefore mediocre writers like Phyllis Morris, Lionel Britton, and even C. K. Munro made little noise in their time, and soon became quickly forgotten. They are like that great mass of unknown, unremarkable people, little noticed when they were alive, and unrecorded, who make up the populations of the past.

These used not to be mentioned in the history books, which confined themselves to kings and queens and the activity of the great: their pomp, their victories, their defeats, and their great speeches. But half a century after *The Apple Cart* the atmosphere was changing, and more and more the common people were superseding the rich and famous. This had dangerous as well as salutary aspects, but it is something to be taken account of in histories of the theatre. Obscure plays and players deserve their small memorials as much as the Ashcrofts and the Pinters their stupendous mausoleums. And the forgotten plays had their merits. In Phyllis Morris's *A'Hunting We Will Go*, the last words of its principal character, Clive Morley, have a certain melancholy in their beautiful falling close. So indeed had her life. I saw her play about 1932, when she was nearly forty years old. She was very active for many years in small parts on stage, screen, and television, and she had been educated, no doubt with great hopes, at Cheltenham Ladies' College. But none of this prevented the fall at the end. As I am writing these lines I hear that she has died, at over eighty, in a charity home.

A'Hunting We Will Go was in many ways an unimportant play, and was presented for one performance only on a Sunday night at the Savoy Theatre. It was an attack on certain sections of the upper class, and I write on it at greater length than might be expected simply because I must be one of the few people still alive who actually saw it. Yet for the people that it finds itself called on to condemn its brief epilogue shows some sympathy. The old days were passing, but not without regret. More surprisingly it was one of the first plays to show any sympathy for Communism. Its objection to the well-born and the well-to-do was that they hunted. Its hero, Clive Morley, was a Crusader against hunting, and the author gave to him as his only ally a Communist who thinks not that blood sports are cruel, but that fox-hunters are parasites.

This, presented before a middle class audience, was loading the dice against Clive, but here Phyllis Morris made one of her rare hits. For she gave to the Communist a speech which Reginald Purdell delivered with such fire that the audience was quite won over. At the end of the play there is a riot in which the MFH, to whom, by the way, Morris was not unsympathetic (for she had the important dramatic quality of seeing her opponents' point of view) is killed, but the hunt still goes on. 'They have always hunted,' says Morley with a despairing half-admiration. 'They are hunting now; and I think they will hunt till the crack of doom.'

This trifling and unsuccessful play was not as negligible as its fate suggests. It showed several significant things: that at that time the stage responded to feelings of humanitarianism; that its attitude to Communism (we knew nothing of the treachery that was brewing at Cambridge), in response to generally changing public opinion, was less automatically condemnatory than it had been, for example, in Arnold Ridley's *The Ghost Train* (1925); that the ethics of the upper classes were not quite as exemplary as Galsworthy had revealed them to be in *Escape*, yet nevertheless their passing was enveloped with a certain regret.

Little of the theatrical lightning that was in the international atmosphere passed into the serious theatre, but some of its electricity illuminated the lighter stage. Charles Cochran was more responsive to the heightened tension that had invaded public affairs since the establishment of Adolf Hitler as Chancellor of the German Republic in early 1933 than was the Old Vic. It is not that he dealt with, or was even deliberately conscious of, the problems which the advent of Hitler implied. But the unrest that they brought with them ran like a disturbing current through the whole of his twenty-first revue. *Streamline*, in which the debonair Peter Graves made his first London appearance, was put on at the Palace in 1934 and was a very glittering affair. Its electrical atmosphere reached its height in the final scene, in which the whole company, which included then famous names like Florence Desmond and Naunton Wayne, danced faster and faster, rushing madly hither and thither, progressing ever more furiously under gyrating spotlights, in a direction that led nowhither to a goal that no one envisaged, impelled only by a wild incapacity to remain at rest and at peace. That is what Europe and Britain were like, that was their disturbance of temper in 1934.

In the cast was the celebrated music-hall artist Sherkot, a small man whose pale face incarnated the same anxiety of the times as was more frenziedly expressed by the dancers. Sherkot was not celebrated as a leader of his profession; he was no George Robey. He was not in the front rank, nor did he top the bill. Nevertheless, his talent was considerable. He had the unique faculty of being able to create an entire football match as seen through the eyes of an agile but easily alarmed goalkeeper. He would stand alone and aghast in the goalmouth, without a single prop besides the goalposts. His roving eyes, bursting with anxiety as they watched the flying, treacherous ball (which existed only in their own creation of it); his sickening despair when the ball beat him, and his simple joy when he managed to stop it on the goal line were memorable features of the light entertainment of the 1930s. They represented also the passage of power from one class to another. It is true that at Eton and at Westminster soccer is played, and not rugger, but rugger is the game of the class that was still ruling in the 1920s, and Sherkot's soccer that of the class whose hour was about to strike.

Cochran was a brave man, and a man of fine taste, and it was in one of his shows, *Helen*, that we had seen, a year before the melancholy and apprehensive gaze of Sherkot, the last glorious blaze of the setting sun of the great spectacular musicals which combined splendour with a proper sense of the aesthetic. As we watched *Helen* in 1932, we did not realise that we were never again to see such an array of talent as graced this, the most ambitious of all Cochran's shows. It was an *opéra bouffe*, based on *La Belle Hélène* (by Meilhac and Halévy), with music by Jacques Offenbach, directed by Max Reinhardt; the dances and ensembles by Léonide Massine; the scenery, costumes, and other accessories by Oliver Messel, with Evelyn Laye (almost unbelievably beautiful and divinely fair), W. H. Berry and George Robey.

Never again was so much taste to be allied on the musical stage with so much splendour. No British (nor, for that matter American) producer of musicals has had in modern times an aesthetic sense as ambitious and yet so delicate as Cochran's. With the genius of Reinhardt and the decadent fancies of Messel, to say nothing of the beauty of the young Evelyn Laye to help him, he produced in *Helen* the most perfect jewel of its kind that the English stage has seen. Homer never directly describes the beauty of Helen, as, for example, Shakespeare describes the beauty and wonder of Cleopatra's barge; it is the difference between the classical and romantic methods. The only passage in which Homer approaches this subject is the famous scene where the Trojan elders, watching Helen walking along the battlements beneath which the Greek and Trojan armies are fighting, observe to each other that it is no wonder that young men go to war for her.

It is this scene which Reinhardt chose for his final and loveliest stage-picture. The Greek and Trojan soldiers, clad in a brave array of green and yellow and grey, with red-splashed plumes in their helmets, raised their spears and swords in salute to Helen, clothed in white, as she stood with arms uplifted, against a background of blue sky, whilst Achilles sang a version of the words of Homer. This was the apotheosis of *Helen*, the last time the English stage attempted pictorially to rival, even though in a romantic spirit, the beauty of classical art.

It is however not possible to understand the development of the British stage during the 1930s unless we examine the economic and political situation of the country. Of this situation the theatre was a reflection. An anti-élitist spirit was gaining ground as aristocratic influence declined. The movement that began in the house of a Parisian couturière had made so much progress by the year that Cochran presented *Helen* that a well-known actor, Eric Maturin, who specialized in playing well-bred cads, wrote to *The Times* complaining that except at first nights audiences in the stalls no longer wore evening dress. He argued that white ties and tails were decorative, and added that he preferred playing to audiences that were clean, but his appeal had no effect, though aesthetically it had something to be said for it.

Meanwhile some scientific progress was being made. Just as women moder-

A first night audience in 1932 at the Palace Theatre, London (attending Dinner at Eight *by George Kaufman and Edna Ferber).*

ated their notions of dress, so the disaster of the R101 taught men to become less ambitious in their efforts to improve transport. They turned their attention from the air to the ground, and on 30 December 1932 the first electrified train in Britain reached Worthing station from London. It was raining, and the only person to greet its arrival was a policeman, whose figure, as he marched masterfully towards it, was vividly reflected in the rain-soaked platform. Great hopes were entertained of this somewhat inauspicious beginning: more frequent trains, first-class treatment for commuters, increased comfort, and luxurious rolling stock. Fifty years later few of these hopes had been realized.

The idea of scientific improvement was as active in the theatre of the early 1930s as it was in the mighty brains of those who ran the railways. Every enterprising manager in London seemed to be busy installing revolving stages. Cochran used one to excellent effect in the song 'Dancing on Your Ceiling' in

Ever Green (1930), and both the Coliseum and the Alhambra, at that time devoted to huge musical entertainments, had them.

Then suddenly all this lavish expenditure ceased, not so much because theatres could no longer afford it, though that was an important factor, as that it was found to be useless. It was noticed that two of the most popular plays in London, Merton Hodge's *The Wind and the Rain* and Emlyn Williams's *Night Must Fall*, – the first a gentle romance between two undergraduates of Edinburgh University, played with quiet passion by Celia Johnson and Robert Harris, and the second a terrifying story of murder in a cottage in Epping Forest – had only one set each. Neither set was of much importance in itself, each being the living-room of an ordinary middle-class house, and of course they had no need of a revolving stage. Yet *The Wind and the Rain* (1933) ran for 1,001 performances, and *Night Must Fall* (1935) for 435. *Lady Precious Stream*, a Chinese play at the Little Theatre (which was destroyed during the war), had practically no scenery at all.

Nevertheless, scenery was still on occasion employed effectively. But it came more and more to be used to emphasize the drama rather than in itself to dazzle the eye as the great set-pieces, such as the Neuilly Fair, had done in the Cochran revues of the 1920s. The crowds in Komisarjevsky's production in 1933 of Louis Golding's *Magnolia Street*: the crooked, narrow road, the squalid bay windows, the gaudy shops all made a deep impression; and the way in which a small child eating an apple held together the elaborate picture of Regency Brighton which Noël Coward built up in *Conversation Piece* in 1930 was very striking. In one episode in *Cavalcade* Coward worked scenery into the very warp and woof of his drama: it was a scene in which a girl, talking on board ship to her young husband of the bright future they would have, moved her shawl, which was seen to be covering the name of the boat, SS *Titanic*.

The economic problems of the theatre were only a reflection of the much worse economic problems of the country, and of the western world in general. In 1933 the *Berliner Illustrierte Zeitung* published a disturbing cartoon showing the top half of the globe, with representatives of the leading nations staggering across it under the weight of large boxes filled with coins that represented the cost of unemployment (*Illustrated London News*, April 1933). America led the unhappy procession with 12 million unemployed, but with no estimate of the cost. After America came Germany, with 4,600,000 unemployed; the cost being RM 3,000 million; Britain was third with 2,850,000 unemployed, the cost being two-thirds that of Germany; Italy had just under a million unemployed, whilst even so small and customarily prosperous a country as Switzerland had 25,000 people out of work. Unemployment relief in England amounted to 3.7 per cent of the national income, and in Germany to 5.2 per cent. World production had declined by 38 per cent.

(Left to right) Robert Harris, Mackenzie Ward, Ivan Brandt and Celia Johnson in Merton Hodge's The Wind and the Rain *(1933) at the St Martin's Theatre, London.*

Unemployment in England in the 1930s.

In London many great town houses were dismantled; on 13 August 1931 it was learned that the Dowager Marchioness of Curzon, widow of the proudest of former Foreign Secretaries, was heavily in debt. Naturally, large sections of the population, wondering how to eke their next meal out of the dole, were appalled to hear that this unfortunate woman had had to sell her racing stable, and her residence at 1 Carlton House Terrace. Most startling of all was the sight of Prince Aly Khan reduced to running to catch a bus in Piccadilly (Andrew Barrow, *Gossip*).

A group of the unemployed lay down in the foyer of the Savoy Hotel, and the upper classes themselves became politically conscious; many became socialists. A tremendous furore broke out when the Oxford Union voted that it would not fight for King and Country. But a more sinister development was little heard of until several years after the war, during which the Oxford Pacifists proved even more belligerent than most other people. A clique of Soviet informers was established amongst Cambridge undergraduates.

In spite of the national distress the first great Royal Ball for many years was

Chesterfield Road, Sheffield, c.1930: the main road from Sheffield to London.

given at Buckingham Palace on 16 July 1931, but with conditions being so obviously bad the King cut short his holiday at Balmoral in the late summer and returned to London. Queen Mary was angry at not being allowed to take part in the crisis. 'I will not be left sitting on a mountain,' she declared with picturesque gallantry. But Charlie Chaplin and the Prime Minister, Ramsay MacDonald, took things more casually. After luncheon together at Chequers both these great men fell asleep.

The economic conditions of the western world, coupled with the rise of Hitler, naturally affected the nation's self confidence. No man or woman, no intimate deed could be separated from a background of horror. 'The re-occupation of the Ruhr, Hitler's blood-purge, the war with Abyssinia – the crisis age was beginning . . .,' wrote Jocelyn Brooke. 'Yeats died, Housman died, Kipling died: death was in the air. "The king is sinking rapidly" – Sir John Reith's sepulchral tones seemed to usher out a tribal scapegoat, the Dying God. My own father died. The whole background of my life, which for so long had seemed immutable, was rapidly disintegrating; the Gods were dying – an epoch was drawing to its close.' In millions of homes throughout the country, these sad words of Jocelyn Brooke – the words of a defeated spirit – were dully echoed.

Defiance was rare and ineffectual. Churchill repeatedly warned the nation of the dangers surrounding it, but always in terms that frightened people out of their wits, so much more powerful than ourselves did he represent the enemy. The Labour Party ardently wished to oppose Hitler, but only so long as we remained disarmed and without military power. Many British Communists spoke up valiantly against Hitler, but were subsequently discovered to have been traitors.

It is no wonder that all this futility of spirit, this collapse of national confidence and courage, actuated, either in acquiescence or rebuff, the most notable developments of the stage. Anxiety penetrated deep into the consciousness of the theatre. This was vividly revealed in a play called *Strange Orchestra* (1932), by a new dramatist, Rodney Ackland, the son-in-law of Frederick Lonsdale. Ackland was a man of great promise and even achievement, but later he unfortunately lost heart when he became convinced that one of the drama critics had savagely mishandled one of his plays. But for *Strange Orchestra* there was nothing but praise.

It showed a discontented, aimless, and disillusioned world; in the commonplace setting of a Chelsea flat it revealed (in addition to a few pleasanter qualities) tragedy, boredom, cruelty, and jealousy. It reminded audiences of Chekhov in style, though it was less humane in temper. All Ackland's characters – Jenny, who is disappointed and deserted; Peter, the professional scamp; Freda, the chorus-girl, ill-tempered and jealous; Jimmy and Laura, the idyllically happy young couple whose courage fails; George, the Philistine; Esther, sensitive to the world's cruelty; and Val, who has the temerity not to think much of D. H. Lawrence – all these were vital and real.

It seemed that a dramatist of considerable stature had emerged when *Strange*

Orchestra captured so exactly, and with such a sense of life and variety, the temper of his time. Ackland's ability to form a coherent whole out of so many different characters, each with his or her special individuality, roused general admiration. It was enthusiastically said that Ackland 'drives half a dozen horses at once, keeps them abreast, and gets them past the winning-post without any suspicion of disorder'. Ackland did indeed reflect the pessimism of the period, but paradoxically the fact of this reflection was not altogether one of despair, for in itself it held the seeds of great hopes. It suggested that if the world was sliding into ruin, the theatre at least was rich in promise. Not only did it bring into public notice a new dramatist of exciting potentialities, but it marked a distinct stage in the progress of one of the country's leading young actresses.

At the beginning of the 1930s the rising hopes among the theatre's younger actresses were Jessica Tandy and Jean Forbes-Robertson, with Peggy Ashcroft not far behind. Jessica Tandy went on to a prosperous career in the United States, and Peggy Ashcroft reaped honours both official and aesthetic. But Jean Forbes-Robertson died comparatively young, and never realized the tremendous expectations that were held of her. She was frail and grave, and there was something about her not quite of this world. As Jenny Lyndon she gave a haunting performance, as of a girl striving to seize hold of some fundamental explanation of things that could resolve the apparent discords of life, an explanation that always just eluded her grasp. She was like someone who had been forsaken, and was forlornly looking for what she had lost.

If it is possible, by some casuistical process, to find something to rejoice about in *Strange Orchestra* (even if disaster comes it is a good thing for the theatre to produce new dramatists of talent), there was no satisfaction to be gained from A. A. Milne's *Other People's Lives* (1932). Milne was celebrated not only as the creator of Winnie-the-Pooh, and as the author of immensely popular, deft, and affectionately playful light verse about his young son, Christopher Robin, but as a witty dramatist who had entertained large audiences (but not in Sheffield) with such plays as *The Truth about Blayds* (1923), *The Dover Road* (1923) (in which Henry Ainley had been extremely fine), and, most famous of all, *Mr Pim Passes By* (1919).

These plays were rather flimsy and whimsical; they suggested a carefree temperament, a Fenners-on-a-sunny-afternoon outlook on life; they were the very soufflé of drama; they brought into the theatre a touch of the romance of musical comedy, the spirit of the Côte d'Azur. But Milne now felt that the gravity of the age called for something more serious; and it is this feeling, manifesting itself in such a master of the bright decorations of life, which makes *Other People's Lives* perhaps even more important, in spite of its imperfections, than many works still vividly remembered and spoken of with reverence. Milne however was at a disadvantage compared with Ackland, for Ackland was at that time a young man, in accord with the temper of the age. Milne, on the other hand, middle-aged, had to adapt himself to a new world, and he did not do so very effectively.

But that makes *Other People's Lives* all the more significant, if not as a play, then as a social document. *Strange Orchestra* suggested that there was something wrong with society; *Other People's Lives*, still dragging after it the flimsy remains of an old optimism, rather limply took the view that there was nothing much to complain about in the lives of the poor, and that any effort to improve them only made the situation worse. It accepted the proposition that man was helpless in the face of reality. Galsworthy in *The Skin Game* had assumed that if people behaved decently towards each other (not that there is any chance that they will), then society might be just and happy. Six years later in *Escape* (six years before *Other People's Lives*) he had adopted a gloomier outlook. But Galsworthy was a man of grave disposition, whereas Milne had, at any rate hitherto, given the impression of being a man who took life and its problems gaily. His pessimism, therefore, his conviction that things can never improve, no matter how hard we try to improve them, shows all the more impressively the national collapse of will in the 1930s before the onslaught of unemployment, the disastrous effect of the country's lack of leadership, and the growing terror of events abroad, even though as yet Hitler was only a feeble shadow of what he was soon to become. It is a striking example of the fact that the plays which are most socially relevant and revealing are not always those whose authors present them with the most portentous air. Let us therefore look at *Other People's Lives* in some detail.

The most dashing characters in Milne's play, the Waites and the Bellamys, were four Bright Young Things who take to works of mercy as a diverting alternative to parties and dances. By trying to improve the lot of their humble neighbours, the Tillings, in the flat below, who are perfectly happy as they are, they ruin them. They make Mr Tilling realise that the novel he is writing about lords and ladies is preposterous; Miss Tilling is packed off to Canada with the hope of peopling the Dominions with sound British stock; and unwanted medical attention is forced on Mrs Tilling, from which she dies. Yet the Waites are not wicked; they just blunder.

So did Milne. He felt that the world round him was depressed and discouraged, and in *Other People's Lives* he tried to assure people that really there was nothing much wrong after all, if only they would leave things alone. But in 1932, with nearly three million unemployed (for whose welfare no such provision was made as was the case in later days), and with Hitler on the verge of being elected German Chancellor, it would have needed a more powerful propagandist than Milne to convince the nation that things were less bad than they seemed. There was little vital force in his arguments, and even his famous sparkling wit was dull. When poor Mr Tilling made dreadful puns like 'Sir John – surgeon' the audience was both embarrassed and saddened – embarrassed at the feebleness of the joke, saddened that one of the cleverest and gayest of dramatists should have sunk to such a level.

Harold Warrender (left) and Maurice Evans (right) in A. A. Milne's Other People's Lives *(1933) at the Wyndham's Theatre, London.*

Extra Quality
Very Dry

Yet in one respect *Other People's Lives* was notable in its own right. It gave the British public one of the last opportunities it was ever to have of seeing an actor whose potential greatness it quite failed to recognize. One of the Bright Young Things was played by Maurice Evans, an eloquent and impassioned actor of the highest merit. But John Gielgud had already given the first of his brilliant performances in Gordon Daviot's *Richard of Bordeaux* (1932 and 1933), and in the way of emotional acting Gielgud already held the monopoly which he was to retain for the next decade. Even the brooding fear and determination with which, in the last act of the 1934 production of Harley Granville-Barker's *The Voysey Inheritance*, Evans resolved to face the consequences of the embezzlements of the hero's father failed to hit either the public attention or critical appreciation, which was vastly unjust. Giving up the British theatre for lost, Evans went to America, where he toured with Katherine Cornell in *Romeo and Juliet*. He followed this with remarkable success as Hamlet, Falstaff, and Richard II. In New York, Evans found a more perceptive public than the one he had left behind him in London, and soon after his arrival in America he was recognized as one of the world's great theatrical stars. From 1935 he whom Britain had overlooked became celebrated all over the theatre of the English-speaking world.

Milne was not the only one among the older writers to perceive that the theatre needed something of deeper implication than what they had hitherto been giving it. In *Our Betters* and *The Circle*, Somerset Maugham had shown that many of the upper classes were worthless and selfish. On the other hand they were witty. It had always been good fun. But it was good fun no longer. In a world slithering into poverty the aristocracy was no longer a suitable subject for the sort of entertaining, half-admiring satire which Maugham's plays aimed at them. It needed reforming, and in *Sheppey*, Maugham, a man as worldly as Coward or Ivor Novello, and considerably less good-hearted than either, set about the task. It was astonishing that a man such as Maugham should have these altruistic impulses, and more astonishing still that he should attempt to accomplish them through an examination of the possibilities of Christianity in modern life, which is what he did in *Sheppey* (1933). It was about a hairdresser's assistant (played by Ralph Richardson) suddenly converted to doing good to his fellow-beings, much to the understandable resentment of his family, who were called on to sacrifice a great deal for his philanthropy. It utterly bewildered the public, which could not make up its mind whether Maugham was lampooning Christianity or prescribing it as a sort of universal patent medicine. Despite Richardson's performance, in which there were moments of beauty, the play was a failure. Maugham withdrew from the theatre enraged, vowing never to write for it again.

Other People's Lives and *Sheppey* both in a way, however ineffective, showed their authors' feelings about unemployment and the tragedies it induced transmuted into other terms. But C. L. Anthony (later better known as Dodie Smith) faced the problem that has been one of the two great banes of our century in a more direct manner, armed in the full panoply of the commercial theatre. Her *Service* (1932) was a sentimental play about a big store at a time of recession.

Its staff (their attitude difficult to understand half a century afterwards, but realistic enough then) were as loyally devoted to it as a soldier to his regiment. Timothy Benton, a hardworking but not very enterprising employee was particularly devoted to his chief, Gabriel Service, who was distressed at the necessity of sacking Benton. These parts were played by two very competent actors, J. H. Roberts and Leslie Banks.

At that time the characteristic feature of British acting was understatement, and there was an incident in *Service* in which understatement achieved a memorable effect. As Service begins to tell Benton of the economies the firm is making, Benton stands fingering a few business papers, with a timid smile on his face. One could tell the exact moment at which Benton realises that he is to be one of the 'economies', for at that precise moment the smile vanished – completely, suddenly, in a flash.

The Brechtian technique which dominated the 1970s was to put things like unemployment figures or statistics of those killed in war streaming across the back of the stage in electric lights. They were a dazzling sight, like the Blackpool illuminations. But I could never remember what the figures were for more than a few seconds, and in any case they gave no impression whatever of what it feels like to be out of work. But I have remembered the vanishing of J. H. Roberts's smile for fifty years, and know exactly what the dreadful feeling in the pit of his stomach was.

Whilst Dodie Smith's *Service*, though worthy enough in its way, was little more than a magazine story, J. B. Priestley's *Cornelius* (1935) marked an epoch. Both plays were what would later have been called 'commercial', but whereas *Service* was not really seized with a *conviction* of unemployment, Priestley gave the audience a sense of mass unemployment (without adequate maintenance) as a horror too dreadful to be believed. This was the first time that the stage grasped the full magnitude and terror of unemployment, and Priestley made the audience realise it simultaneously with Cornelius himself, who was played with heroic and poetic panache by Ralph Richardson. The scales fell suddenly from Cornelius's eyes, and what he saw we saw too.

The scene in which this happened is still vividly before me. Raymond Huntley played the small but effective part of an ex-officer reduced to being a door-to-door office salesman of office ribbons, stationery, carbon papers, and so on, and in the course of his dreary rounds, which have brought him to a state of stoic dullness, he calls on Cornelius, who, as it turns out, is not in a much more prosperous condition himself, though as yet (he is a man of romantic imagination) he has not brought himself to realize it. Cornelius is one of two partners in the firm of Briggs and Murrison, which is on the point of collapse. It can be saved from bankruptcy only if Murrison, who is scouring the country, returns with a full order book.

Cornelius strives with humour and courage to keep up the morale of his tiny staff, but though he is efficient in his business methods he is too flamboyant and resilient in his temperament to perceive the full gravity of the situation. He sustains hope in Murrison's success, but at the same time dreams of some lost city in the clouds. So it is with some briskness that he sets about the drooping and discouraged salesman. 'Be original,' he says, 'Strike out for yourself. Come round with fresh lobsters or pipe cleaners or dirty postcards. Think of some new way of earning a living. There must be dozens that nobody's ever tried.' To which the officer replies wearily, 'No doubt. But don't you see, if I was capable of inventing a new kind of job, I should never have been in this fix at all. I'm not clever enough. Don't pretend to be.'

Cornelius, in spite of his own situation, whose seriousness has been hidden from him by the happy fertility of his fancy, turns to a subordinate, Biddle, and asks incredulously, 'D'you think that's true, Biddle – that here's a fellow, willing to work, fairly intelligent, who not only can't get anything to do here – I can understand that, – but who finds the whole world closed to him, bolted and barred.' To which Biddle replies, 'I'm afraid it might be.'

Cornelius becomes very agitated. 'I can't believe it. If you're willing to work hard, willing to take risks, ready to be scorched or frozen, drowned or sent half-mad with thirst, there must be openings somewhere for you in the world. They can't have closed everything up, so that we're all like bees in a glass case. It's unthinkable, Biddle. I've always had at the back of my mind a little open door, with plantations and jungles and pampas and quartz mountains just outside it – with the sun on 'em. Don't tell me that all that time that little door's not been open, has been locked from the outside, screwed fast.'

At a time when unemployment in Britain was nearly three million, this speech had made a great effect. It even roused hopes that a great spirit might conquer all obstacles. Now we must not suppose that it was only in the 1930s that a grim vision of the miseries and inexplicabilities of life faced mankind. Nor does such a vision arise only from material conditions. It is a horror that is constantly recurring. A century before, it had haunted the mind of Newman, though for quite other reasons than those which distressed Cornelius. And yet not altogether so. The vision that Biddle's words opened up before Cornelius had striking similarities with, as well as differences from, those that taxed the powerful and elegant mind of Newman. In a sense the disasters that Newman saw looming ahead, disasters which the nineteenth century made 'the condition of England question' so anxious a subject of debate, were purely spiritual, whilst those of Cornelius seemed to be entirely material. But in fact the problems that almost paralysed Britain's will to live a century after Newman were also spiritual; though this did not become evident fully until a year or two later.

It is however interesting to note that the leading actor in *Cornelius* and Cardinal Newman both started from the same outlook, and maintained it throughout their lives. Three decades after his performance in *Cornelius* Sir Ralph (he had become Sir Ralph then) Richardson remarked to me quite suddenly, and without reference to anything either of us had said before, 'I know that God exists. I am as certain of it as I am of my own existence.' He took up a vase of flowers. 'There may be some people', he went on, 'who do not know

Ralph Richardson (left) and James Harcourt in J. B. Priestley's Cornelius *(1935) at the Duchess Theatre, London.*

within themselves that God exists. But that gives them no right to deny his existence.' He looked again at the flowers he was holding in his hand. 'There are some people who have no sense of smell. But that would not justify them in saying that these flowers have no scent.' He put the flowers down, and changed the subject to something else.

Professor Basil Willey (*Nineteenth Century Studies*, p. 87) quotes Newman using almost exactly the same words as Richardson, and then going on to analyse the condition of England in terms which Richardson himself would have fully recognized as not irrelevant to what it was in the days of Priestley's early plays. This is Professor Willey's summary of a famous passage in *Apologia pro vita sua*. 'Starting then with the being of a God (which, as I have said, is as certain to me as the certainty of my own existence) I look out of myself into the world of men, and there I see a sight which fills me with unspeakable distress. The world seems simply to give the lie to that great truth, of which my whole being is so full; and the effect upon me is, in consequence, as a matter of necessity, as confusing as if it denied that I am in existence myself. If I looked into a mirror, and did not see my face, I should have the sort of feeling which actually comes upon me, when I look into this busy living world, and see no reflexion of its Creator.'

Newman went on that to think of 'the disappointments of life, the defeat of good, the success of evil, physical pain, mental anguish, the prevalence and intensity of sin, the prevailing idolatries, the corruptions, the dreary hopeless irreligion, that condition of the whole race, so fearfully yet exactly described in the Apostle's words, "having no hope and without God in the world" – all this is a vision to dizzy and appal; and inflicts on the mind a sense of profound mystery, which is absolutely beyond human solution.'

This is the conviction against which Cornelius fought so hard and long. He did not easily surrender the idea that somehow, somewhere there must be a human solution. We all know that eventually, after much travail, Newman found comfort in a spiritual answer in which not everybody can agree with him. But alas, scarcely anybody at all can believe in the solution to England's distressful problem of a hundred years later which Cornelius discovered and acted upon. What Cornelius does is to smash down his office door, and march triumphantly through it to – of all romantic illusions – 'find . . . the lost city of the Incas'. *Cornelius* is a moving play of a business man boldly facing danger, but it ends in Cloud-Cuckoo-Land. One feels that even the stationery-peddling officer had more grasp of reality than this. Richardson gave his usual fine and inspiring performance and Priestley says that the play had an enthusiastic first night, and some of the best reviews he ever received, but that audiences never quite took to it. It may be that it seemed finally to shirk the issue. After all, Cornelius not only marched out to an unbelievable fantasy, but he deserted his colleagues as well. Biddle was more real than any lost city of the Incas, and what, in the crash of Briggs and Murrison – for Murrison returned without any orders – would become of Biddle? Exalted in his imaginary Andes, Cornelius did not think of Biddle. The problem in this play begins by being a material one – the problem of unemployment; it ends as being as spiritual as Newman's. Spiritually Cornelius, gallant and generous man that he was, failed.

Generally speaking, there was throughout the 1930s a failure of spirit, an inner malaise, in Britain. But there were now and again touches of a finer kind. Cornelius's kicking down of the door of what had become his prison and his magnificent stride into the great open spaces was a giant gesture. But it is not the big things like this, the defiance of the threatening skies, that return to the mind during a sleepless night, or at a moment of great joy or sorrow, or in moods of tranquility. There is no poignancy, however great the credit, in Boycott's record number of runs in a Test match, but the heart stirs at such a single line as 'My Hornby and my Barlow long ago', even though one may not know who Hornby and Barlow were. What Thackeray remembered all his life was the theatre of his schooldays, and the quality of a certain actor – Charles Kemble. 'The yellow fogs didn't damp our spirits and we never thought them too thick to keep us away from the play: from the chivalrous Charles Kemble, I tell you – my Mirabel, my Mercutio, my princely Falconbridge.'

It is of no princely Falconbridge, of no elegant Mirabel that I think on the nights when I lie awake, but of an unpretentious little actress called Betty Ann Davies. In one of Herbert Farjeon's revues Betty Ann Davies gave a very touching and poignant sketch of a young schoolgirl, behindhand with her homework, who knows with a dreadful apprehension, and a horrible certainty, that the next day she will be made the laughing-stock of her class by a sarcastic mistress, because she cannot repeat her lessons. The abbreviated gym-dress, the pig-tails, the puffed-up face, the trembling on the brink of tears, the thin little voice that arraigns the monstrous injustice of the universe – these are things that trouble the memory more than do the noise and bombast of a Wolfit, or than the acrid irony with which Joyce Grenfell, making her first appearance in the same revue, chastized with immense success the social pretensions of middle class ladies who had the misfortune to be less well-born than herself. I am afraid that Joyce Grenfell would have made cruel fun of Biddle, but I do not think that Betty Ann Davies's little girl would have deserted him.

But even when charity was present, there was not always hope. In *All God's Chillun Got Wings* (1924) Eugene O'Neill showed, on a grander scale, and with a more piercing sorrow, touched by that spiritual despair which engulfed the western world in general, the same compassion that rendered Betty Ann Davies's trivial little sketch so moving. *All God's Chillun Got Wings* was not a masterpiece of consistency. In the woman of the later scenes, who marries the black Jim Harris because no other career seems open to her, and whose irrational loathing of his colour is overcome only through the the unseating of her reason, it is hard to recognize the little girl of the first episode who had for the big black boy so naïve an admiration. At times the play is sentimental, crude, and even hysterical. Yet it is one of the memorable pieces of the century, and one of the plays which, with *The Ice-Man Cometh* (1946), makes it difficult to deny that O'Neill is the most powerful dramatist of our time.

Jim Harris's colour is the generating force of O'Neill's drama. It is this characteristic that, despite its comparatively happy ending, made it to some people a gloomy play. For when Jim's devotion to his wife, his kindness and patience, his unselfishness and courage avail nothing against her revulsion from his colour, audiences perceived that here, in O'Neill's opinion, was a problem that no amount of nobility is sufficient to solve.

But there were also audiences with whom other things weighed more than this despair. Jim's affection for Ella is a star that shines all the brighter for the gathering darkness round it. This aspect of the play was brought out by Paul Robeson with an almost unbearable poignancy. It was seen in the passionate outburst in which he laid his devotion at Ella's feet; and again in a most moving moment on the church steps. On one side of the steps was stationed a row of negroes. When the bridal couple appeared through the church door, the negroes

uttered a long, low hiss. Ella, almost overpowered by this manifestation of the hatred and misunderstanding that will hedge about their married life, shrinks on her husband's arm, whilst he, slowly descending the steps, tries to lift up her heart by talking of the blue sky and love and courage, and all those things which will enable them to hold their heads high, whatever the world may do to them.

Here Robeson's resonant voice, his suppressed excitement, and his translucent sincerity, showing a man essaying the heroic task of putting confidence into another when his own hopes are at zero, was unforgettable. Flora Robson too gave a very fine performance in its revelation of conflicting emotions, and the memory of that church door opening, Robeson's strong, straight body emerging, and on his arm the trembling figure of a frightened woman remains vivid after fifty years have passed. To these two performances, and to O'Neill himself, is due the fact that perceptive audiences were left with the feeling that neither misunderstanding nor betrayal nor racial bitterness can destroy human affection. Many waters cannot quench love, neither can the floods drown it. But when *All God's Chillun Got Wings* was concluded one was forced to admit that love – at least individual love – however splendid and moving, did little or nothing to solve the sort of problem that faced Cornelius, and had faced Newman before him, and has faced other generations since.

The general mood still remained one of hopelessness. Even so vital and unbreakable a spirit as Laurence Olivier – an actor who, some few years afterwards, was to rouse all Britain with his soaring and tremendous delivery of the speech about St Crispin's Day – made his first mark on the London stage in a mood of sadness. This was in *The Rats of Norway* (1933), by Keith Winter, a young Oxford dramatist from whom great things were expected which in actual fact, for some reason or other, never happened. *The Rats of Norway* was about a decaying private school torn to shreds by overweening ambition and the tumult of passion. The leading players, the headmaster and his wife, were Raymond Massey and Gladys Cooper, whilst Olivier himself, then a virtually unknown actor, took the relatively small part of an assistant master. He had come to the school with high aims and lofty thoughts, but he was left at the end disillusioned and defeated. Memorably he stood before a great window looking out over the desolate school garden. In a voice of infinite sadness and quiet he recited the seven heartbroken lines of William Allingham:

Four ducks on a pond,
A grass-bank beyond,
A blue sky of Spring,
White clouds on the wing;
What a little thing
To remember for years –
To remember with tears!

Flora Robson and Paul Robeson in Eugene O'Neill's All God's Chillun Got Wings *(1933 performance) at the Embassy Theatre, London.*

Laurence Olivier as Mercutio in the 1935 performance of Shakespeare's Romeo and Juliet *at the New (Albery) Theatre, London.*

This was the first time that I had seen Laurence Olivier. After *The Rats of Norway* – long after, for it took critics a long time to recognize genius when they saw it – Olivier achieved fame such as has come to no other contemporary actor. He is celebrated on the stage, in films, and on television. He is the only player who has divided fame into three parts, and, like Caesar, taken them all. He is the finest, most graceful, poetic and powerful of our Othellos; he is our most moving Hamlet, our saddest and most conscience-stricken Macbeth, and the most thrilling speaker of Shakespearean verse that living audiences have ever heard. Yet in his early career his speaking of verse was utterly condemned. He spoke verse for the emotion to be found in it, and by his leading up to an emphatic isolation of a single word he repeatedly swept away the house in a flood of feeling only the next morning to find himself critically reviled for not having treated poetry as though it were a kind of ever-flowing brook or ceaselessly-ticking metronome. This objection was brought to his delivery of the lines of William Allingham. He gave a singularly quiet performance, and was accused of shouting and histrionics. There was no dramatic pause such as so thrilled Froude before Newman spoke his carefully prepared climactic words. He did not speak of tremendous things: he had no 'Almighty God' with which to stun and shock his audience. His words could indeed be heard to the remotest parts of the theatre, but they were only words about a pond and a few ducks to whom, as was not the case with Christ upon the Cross, nothing was happening. But in their resigned speech they revealed such a regret, such a profound sorrow, such a recognizedly hopeless longing for a happiness lost and irrecoverable as Britain herself was feeling in the darkening night of the 1930s. When I think of the preaching of Newman I think of the heartbreak of the young Olivier.

CHAPTER THREE
Threat of War
1934–1938

It is extraordinary that the mood of depression should have settled upon the country with such speed. Whatever misgivings and sense of departed honour may have haunted Galsworthy, the mood of 1920 had been one of almost offensive and unfeeling confidence. The power of the West, embodied in its technological efficiency, seemed invulnerable. Even in so restrained and wise a writer as Joseph Conrad the West's capacity for conquest appeared unlimited. This infinity of strength may have given him more a feeling of sadness than of pride. Nevertheless it existed in this romantic and pessimistic genius as strongly as it did in any jingo. He expressed it with melancholy but unquestioning confidence in the opening words of *The Rescue*, published two years after the end of the Great War of 1914–18.

In the first years of the 1920s Conrad, so widely travelled, so imbued with a sense of history, could yet regard the East as inevitably destined to be the helpless prey of the West.

> The shallow sea that foams and murmurs on the shores of a thousand islands, big and little, which make up the Malay Archipelago has been for centuries the scene of adventurous undertakings. The vices and the qualities of four nations have been displayed in the conquest of that region that even to this day has not been robbed of all the mystery and romance of its past – and the race of men who had fought against the Portuguese, the Spaniards, the Dutch and the English has not been changed by the unavoidable defeat. . . . Their country of land and water – for the sea was as much their country as the earth of their islands – has fallen a prey to the Western race – the rewards of superior strength if not of superior virtue. Tomorrow the advancing civilization will obliterate the marks of a long struggle in the accomplishment of its inevitable victory.

After the defeat of the most technologically efficient and powerful of Western nations in Vietnam, the difficulties the Russians encountered in Afghanistan, and the total loss of the British Empire these confident words about the inevitable victory of the West have an ironic ring. Their melancholy triumph was threatened, and more than threatened, within fifteen years.

Before *Cornelius*, Priestley, with *Dangerous Corner* (1932), *Laburnum Grove* (1933), and *Eden End* (1934), was already an established dramatist. He had rivals like Keith Winter and Rodney Ackland, as well as Merton Hodge, but they came to little in the end. The man who came nearest to approaching Priestley in talent and in stamina was another doctor (this time from Scotland). Osborne Henry Mavor (1888–1951), better known as James Bridie, impressed many critics with his *The Anatomist* (1931) and *A Sleeping Clergyman*. Of the rising new dramatists Bridie alone had something of the energy, intellectual curiosity, and above all that courage which hitherto we have been finding (except in Priestley) so lacking in a country despondent and spiritless. Amongst them, only Priestley and he showed that courage was not entirely dead, and, in a time of increasing fear and depression, sent audiences home feeling braver and more confident than when the evening began.

The Black Eye (1935) is typical of Bridie's work, and it has an affinity of spirit with *Cornelius*. Bridie's George Windlestraw was as irrepressible as Cornelius; like Cornelius he was ready to step out into a new world when the old one failed. George (Stephen Haggard, an actor of immense promise who was killed in the Second World War) has for the fourth time failed to pass his Chartered Accountant's examination, but his father is willing to give him another chance. George, however, is not prepared to take it. Having made the mistakes marked out for him by other people, he feels himself ready to make a few of his own.

He begins by forgetting to keep the appointment which Elspeth, his brother Johnnie's fiancée, has arranged shall get him a good job with her shipowner father. Just as he is about to set out for London to seek his fortune (as Cornelius had dreamt of scaling the Andes) his father meets with a mishap, and George has to take his place at the head of the business, of which Johnnie is a shining light on the technical side. Very soon, again like Cornelius, he finds that the business is on the verge of collapse, but his plans to deal with the situation are interrupted by a ruinous quarrel with Johnnie over Elspeth, which results in his leaving home.

Taking cover in a cheap lodging-house, he earns £20 by free-lance journalism, wins £740 at a game of chance from his ex-convict fellow-lodger, and turns this into £8,500 on a single bet. He is found by Elspeth and Johnnie making a fool of himself in a hotel lounge, is taken home in disgrace, has a fight with Johnnie in the back garden (where he gets his black eye), makes it up with his family, saves the business, and settles down to a life of quiet respectability. Elspeth, however, will have nothing to do with brothers who behave towards each other in this extraordinary way, and flings out of the house in a temper. The last line of the play is spoken by Johnnie, as he sinks contentedly into a large arm-chair, 'I wonder if people who get married live happily ever after?'

The Black Eye, like *Cornelius*, was admirable in its character-drawing and the vigour of its writing. But its faults were glaringly obvious. The play is not all of a piece: the plot preposterous, even if full of action. George's examination failures, his masterly skill in grasping the essentials of his father's business at about two hours' notice, his gambling follies, and his subsequent financial astuteness do not belong to the same person, and Johnnie's position in the commercial world is never made clear or credible. Like the over-fanciful and romantic ending of *Cornelius*, these things indicate that the author of neither play had yet reached the best that he could do. Bridie in 1943 wrote a play of the supernatural, *Mr Bolfry*, which was a great improvement on *The Black Eye*, and the superb striding out into the bitter cold of space after death which concludes Priestley's *Johnson Over Jordan* (1939) achieves everything that the ending of *Cornelius* failed to do: and with the same actor, Ralph Richardson, too.

But I do not mention either play as a contribution to literature. They are important for social reasons. They throb with a spirit of which the despairing Britain of the 1930s was sorely in need. The theme of *The Black Eye* – that a man who faces life boldly, without too careful counting of probabilities, who is willing to follow his bent without misgivings, is quite likely to turn out a success – is the lesson of all the fairy tales that advise you to leap before you look, and as such is not likely to meet with the approval of the followers of Samuel Smiles. But it had in it a fine zest that was salutary for a theatre and a country dominated by economic anxieties.

For in war, or in times that threaten war, the thing that counts is national morale. The immense strength of Russia and Germany is their morale, which risks all things and endures all things.

For this reason it is a serious mistake to regard the lighter theatre (such as *The Black Eye*) as irrelevant to contemporary social problems. Happily therefore for the country the theatre of entertainment continued to prosper well into the 1950s. Stanley Lupino, Dorothy Dickson, Evelyn Laye, Ivor Novello, Peter Graves (and later his beautifully singing wife, Vanessa Lee), Phyllis Monkman, Bobby Howes, Laddie Cliff, Leslie Henson, Anna Neagle and the mighty Buchanan strove to amuse and entertain their audiences. And then there was Terence Rattigan, whose comedy *French Without Tears* (1936) ran for more than a thousand performances, with a cast that included players then unknown but later famous – Kay Hammond, Roland Culver, and Rex Harrison.

A quarter of a century later the theatre of entertainment was continuously and contemptuously attacked by those who were the luminous spirits of the age. Since these produced work which for a time made the British theatre the most important in the world their opinions cannot be dismissed lightly. But there is something to be said for frivolity, even though it left the great economic and political problems of the day undiscussed. Its escapism did much to keep the British nation fairly sane, just as *A Midsummer Night's Dream's* escapism had done for the country in the darkening years after the defeat of the Armada.

The supposition that escapist theatre appeals only to shallow minds is a mistake. Lord Blackett was one of the greatest scientific minds of the century, but he was fond of recalling that, in the days of his brilliant Cambridge youth, he went nineteen times, not to plays of the order of *Saint Joan* or *The Skin Game*, but to the effervescent, pierrot-like revue, *The Co-Optimists*. Furthermore, dismissing serious problems from one's thoughts is often the best way of solving them. When the mathematician Poincaré was baffled by some intricate mathematical process it was his habit to take a bus or metro ride, since he found that the hitherto elusive solution would flash into his mind as he dodged the traffic.

But though escapist actions may lead to immense practical consequences, they do not need these consequences to justify them. Sitting in a garden has its own value even without watching apples fall. It is the indispensable nature of the artist (without which he is not an artist at all) to fulfil himself in his work. Shakespeare fulfilled himself in *A Midsummer Night's Dream* and Wilde in *The Importance of Being Earnest*, even though to the superficial glance that demands an immediate connection with current events neither is of the slightest use. Rattigan fulfilled himself in *French Without Tears*, just as nearly forty years later William Douglas Home fulfilled himself in *The Secretary Bird* with Kenneth More and Jane Downs, and *Lloyd George Knew my Father*, with Peggy Ashcroft and Ralph Richardson.

Even before the work of Rattigan, Cyril Connolly indirectly emphasized the importance of what they were doing by the black pessimism he saw around him in Britain. 'This, then, is the conclusion; everywhere the individual seems doomed; it matters not whether he loves life or letters; individualist though he may think he is, his leaders will betray him, abandoning that longed-for equilibrium of mind and body, that poise of Aristippus, for Buddha, for Quetzalcoatl, for Communism, for the Pope of Rome. We live no more in the heroic age' (*Life and Letters*, Vol. 1).

There was, however, an artist, soon to make a significant mark in the theatre with *Murder in the Cathedral* (1935) and *The Family Reunion* (1939), who passed through the intellectual despair of men like Connolly and Jocelyn Brooke, and came out on the other side. In a remarkable essay, Dilys Powell showed T. S. Eliot emerging unexpectedly as the most practical of men of letters, since he not only perceived the defects and dangers of society, but discovered for them a remedy in which, unlike Maugham, he believed. In his early poems society is mouldering away, and *The Waste Land* (1922) gave 'a panoramic vision before the crash'. Dilys Powell went on to remark that 'here the abrupt transition from one set of emotions to another . . . combines with the varied metres to give an impression of instability appropriate to the main theme, the decadence of Europe and the despair of the individual.' Then there comes the decisive utterance, the profound perception. 'Finally, we have seen him sum up the desperate situation of a Europe facing life and death without the spiritual and intellectual certainties which sustained an earlier generation.'

Eliot thus became the wisest and most far-seeing of our poets and dramatists. He did this remarkably early, and with a philosophical breadth and both a Christian and a Pagan learning beyond the reach of other creative writers of his time. Dramatists like Beverley Nichols, W. H. Auden and several lesser-known and less talented men recognized the dangers besetting Britain some years before the general public, the Labour Party (which consistently opposed re-armament) and the National Government. But Nichols and Auden wrote in the 1930s, whilst Eliot perceived the untenability and lack of virtue of Europe as early as 1922, the year of *The Waste Land*. What is more, though in a somewhat runic manner, he took the bold step of suggesting the remedy. This was no other than a return to those 'spiritual and intellectual certainties' we had abandoned.

What Eliot proposed was what he himself with much pain and travail had come to in his own life: that is, religion. It was a brave thing to do. I have already said that there were in the theatre men of some distinction who openly professed the Christian religion. The man who subsequently became the most famous of British actors, Laurence Olivier, did at this time scrupulously observe all the ceremonies of the Anglican Church. Nevertheless, the stage is mainly a pagan place; those who are there do, I think, embrace; but in general what they embrace is not the Christian religion. Politics, certainly; pleasure – perhaps; but religion, no.

For a few years after the war this situation seemed to be, perhaps permanently, ending. Shaw had failed in his efforts to substitute a royalist and intellectually superior form of government for the political world, but in the theatrical Christopher Fry, John Whiting, and the influence of Jean-Louis Barrault and T. S. Eliot almost succeeded in making an intellectual civilisation dominant on the stage. Laurence Olivier greatly helped in this movement by presenting Fry's *Venus Observed* (1950); the popularity of Claudel and Racine was outstanding; and Henry Sherek's production of Eliot's *The Cocktail Party* at the Edinburgh Festival in 1949 appeared to open a new era in the theatre. *The Cocktail Party* was expected to be merely a *succès d'estime*. But against all foreboding the public flocked to it in such numbers that it was soon afterwards produced both in London and New York, and altogether it made a profit of £25,000, a great figure in those days – the exact amount, in fact, that Jack Buchanan left when he died. It was Eliot who, amongst his many other claims to fame, successfully opened the campaign to make religion and philosophic aestheticism the driving force of the theatre. How that campaign was defeated by able and socially strongly motivated people is the principal story of the drama after 1955.

The generalized alarm expressed by Eliot with a noble obscurity had been canalized into specific dramatic channels by Beverley Nichols in *Avalanche* (1932) and by Robert Nicholls in *Wings Over Europe* in the same year. The name of Hitler had as yet scarcely been heard of by the general public, but these two writers felt the throb of war was in the air, and deserve credit for their prescience. *Avalanche* and *Wings over Europe* complement each other in that the first play began well and finished disappointingly, whilst the second did precisely the opposite. Both were melodramatic, both dealt with serious problems, both fulfilled Aristotle's insistence upon the importance of dramatic action and the turn of fortune, and both were somewhat underestimated by public and critics alike.

The fears that *Wings over Europe* and *Avalanche* expressed were, at the end of 1932, only latent. But within a few months they sprang into vividly and frighteningly active life. On 30 January 1933, less than a year after the production of Robert Nicholls's vision of atomic destruction, the news was announced of Adolf Hitler's accession to the German Chancellorship. There was in Germany a wild jubilation whose frenzy can still be appreciated from the photographs of the time. Thousands of Nazis flocked to the New Palace built for the German Chancellor, and for hours the square resounded to shouts of 'Heil, Hitler'. Many gave the Fascist salute, which Hitler returned from a first-floor window, his figure illuminated by a floodlight behind him. President von Hindenburg, with what thoughts running through his aged mind we do not know, watched the demonstration from a window of the Old Palace on the other side of the Wilhelmstrasse.

Despite the fears and premonitions of *Wings over Europe* and *Avalanche* there were still people in Britain who, closing their eyes to Hitler's sensational rise, and, ignoring his *Mein Kampf*, pretended to themselves and to the public that there was really nothing to bother about. Nor were they all stupid and ill-informed people. G. K. Chesterton was one of them, and though he had failed to fulfil the brilliant promise of his youth, he was still by no means a negligible figure. Perhaps he felt that a man who had been a labourer and a house-painter was not to be taken seriously. At any rate he treated Hitler with contempt. 'There was a time', he wrote, 'when England was very rich; unemployment has put an end to that. There was a time when, as in 1870, Germany was very powerful; the Great War ended *that*. But Hitler has started up the old boasting that Germany is invincible. The English do rather better. We are beginning to let it dawn on us, in a dazed way, that we are not in a position to patronise the whole world in the matter of money, and we shall put up with our poverty in as manly a manner as we may. But at least we do not all go mad, and rush into the streets screaming that we are all millionaires; we do not recognise the general ruin by shouting that all our own pockets are stuffed with pearls and diamonds; we do not tell an astonished world that we are still as rich as when Consols were at their highest. And that would be the commercial parallel to the madness of Mr Hitler' (*Illustrated London News*).

Yet for those who took an interest in the Continental theatre it should have been obvious for some time before the accession of Hitler to the Chancellorship that the atmosphere of Central Europe was becoming dangerously favourable to the ideas he was trying to propagate. At this period Viennese light opera was enjoying a tremendous vogue. (Hitler himself was a devotee of *The Merry Widow*.) It spread even to England, and the delightful Viennese actress Lea Seidl, who became a naturalized British subject, had an outstanding success at the Coliseum in an Austrian musical, *White Horse Inn*, which was highly spectacular, and gave an enchanting nostalgic picture of Austrian life in a mountain village in the days when the Emperor Franz Joseph, of whom it drew a very sympathetic portrait, was an old and benevolent man, much beloved of his people.

White Horse Inn was charming and sentimental, but there were other Viennese operas of greater significance, sharper intellectual bite, and more cognizant of aesthetic and political trends which neither the Coliseum nor any other English theatre presented to the public, though the success of Lea Seidl must have drawn their attention to what else the Viennese stage had to offer. The most significant of these was *Johny Spielt Auf* (*Johnny Strike Up*), which was staged at the Vienna Opera House shortly before *White Horse Inn* appeared at the Coliseum in April 1931.

Johnny Strike Up was one of the innovations of the century, and its fate was charged with ominous political potentialities. It was by a then ultra-modern young composer, Ernst Křenek (b. 1900), and, after it had been rejected by several German opera houses, it had been staged with sensational success in Leipzig in 1927. It was performed in more than a hundred cities, and its book was translated into twenty languages. It made Křenek's name and fortune and was a work of astonishing virtuosity. At the age of 43 it introduced the great Mozart soubrette Elisabeth Schumann into the flirtatiousness of musical comedy, and in her teasingly short skirt she looked surprisingly piquant for a star of grand opera.

The *Illustrated London News* for 18 February 1931 said that in its introduction of jazz idioms *Johnny Strike Up* foreshadowed both the future cultural importance of the non-western world and the free atonal technique that Křenek employed in later works, after he had become an American citizen. But in another sense it was traditional, for it was staged with a realism that recalled the great old spectacular productions of Drury Lane, especially in the final scene, which was set in a railway station whose gleaming trackway was dominated by a huge clock with a vast white face. Its heavy fingers showed the time to be three minutes to midnight.

It was its innovative tendencies rather than its grandiose scenic reminders of plays like *The Whip* or even Reinhardt's *The Miracle* that concentrated the public's attention on *Johnny Strike Up* and made it a subject of angry controversy. Herr Schalk, the musical and administrative director of the Vienna State Opera, said that jazz was a 'relapse into barbarity', but Dr Scheiderhan, the director-general of the state theatres, took the more practical view that opera must pay some regard to the taste of the public and to box-office returns. These quarrels might have been dismissed as no more than the disagreements that greet any successful work that has in it elements of the unconventional. But what was really alarming about the reception of *Johnny Strike Up* in Vienna was that hundreds of Nationalist students demonstrated in front of the Opera House, demanding the abandonment of the performance, on the ground that the piece had been put on under Jewish influence. They were dispersed by the police. This was one of the earliest examples of anti-Semitism manifested by the

---

Hitler addresses a crowd of 20,000 gathered in the Sportspalast, Berlin, at the inauguration of his Winter Relief Plan of 1938.

Ein Volk hilft sich selbst!

Continental theatre. It is an ironical circumstance of the whole disturbing affair that Křenek was not a Jew, but a Christian.

The importance of Nazi hatred of the Jews was soon recognized by a young Oxford graduate. W. H. Auden, then 28 years old, made it a dramatic climactic feature of his play, *The Dance of Death*, which was staged by Tyrone Guthrie and Rupert Doone, with music by Herbert Murrill, and decor and masks by Robert Medley. It was presented at the Westminster Theatre in October 1935. The suggestion implicit in it was that totalitarianism must be defeated, and that for this task democracies like Great Britain were completely unfitted.

Unlike the far more lavishly produced *Johnny Strike Up*, *The Dance of Death* succeeded in doing what Daniel Rops in his study of the medieval French cathedrals says is essential before any creative advance can be made. This is the discovery of a new technique. What made Amiens and Chartres possible was the invention of the ogive, the pointed Gothic arch. In *The Dance of Death* Auden flung aside the old traditions as surely as did the builders of Evreux or Rouen, Chartres or Amiens. The consequences of Auden's technical experiments have not been as momentous as those of the adventurous cathedral builders who created (dangerously, as it turned out, for it collapsed more than once) the lofty nave of Beauvais; but they have been considerable. Auden shook the foundations of realism which dominated the theatre of the twenties and thirties, and thus prepared the way for Beckett and Pinter, the two most notable of modern European dramatists.

Now *The Dance of Death* was an attempt to work out for the theatre a new, significant art-form, and there were those who found the attempt successful. The theory of drama evolved in *The Dance of Death* expressly forbade the search for new and unaccustomed ways of thinking. The proper subject of drama, Auden maintained, is the commonly known, the universally familiar stories of the society or generation in which it is written. The audience, he declares, ought, like the child listening to the fairy tale, to know what is going to happen next.

This is, of course, a thesis that most people would disagree with. It entirely destroys the pleasure to be gained from the plays of, say, Agatha Christie, or from a philosophic detective novel like E. C. Bentley's *Trent's Last Case*. John Gielgud says that *Hamlet* is somewhat spoiled for him because he knows the ending. But Auden despised the element of original story. To make sure that his audiences got no surprises, he included in his programme for *The Dance of Death* a short analysis of the theme of the drama. But he not only told us what was going to happen before it took place; on the stage he put an announcer (John Allen) who told us what was happening whilst it was happening.

Auden's conception in *The Dance of Death* was the decline and fall of the middle class. According to the strictest sect of his economics Auden was (though not in quite such an avowed sense as Rupert Doone) a Communist, and his play ended with the triumphant storming of the stage by a band of Bolsheviks who erupt out of the audience singing the *Internationale*, and waving a Red Flag of truly magnificent proportions.

Jack Hulbert and his wife Cicely Courtneidge, an outstanding musical partnership.

It was not however what Auden said, but the way he said it that was (within the scope of our knowledge at the time) supremely interesting. He took the most frivolous of entertainments, the musical comedy, and transformed it so that it became an instrument of serious drama of which the potentialities, in his skilful handling, seemed illimitable. It was a memorable achievement, as though one were to see *No, No, Nanette* taken, without incongruity, as the mouthpiece for a twentieth-century *Contrat Social.* Now in the realm of musical comedy it is universally supposed that an enormous improvement has been brought about since the end of the Second World War. This is a delusion. After 1940 the light musical stage produced no personalities so striking, positive, and powerful as Jack Buchanan, Jack Hulbert, or Stanley Lupino, nor so talented as Cicely Courtneidge, Dorothy Dickson, or Anna Neagle. It was therefore driven back on telling stories more coherently than did the productions of those great stars, whose personal genius made a story superfluous.

But *Oklahoma!* (1947), *Guys and Dolls* (1950) or *West Side Story* (1957) are children's entertainment when compared with the issues tackled by *The Dance of Death*. In the heady excitement of first seeing it one was tempted to think that when Scott took the flimsy, sensational pasteboard romances of Mrs Radcliffe and 'Monk' Lewis and turned them into the vast panorama of the *Waverley* novels, he hardly did a more remarkable thing than Auden accomplished in *The Dance of Death*. The play, which is a short one, is continuous in its action. It opens on a bathing beach, where young representatives of the bourgeoisie are pursuing the current cult of sun-bathing and athletics. To them, and to their songs and games, enters a dancing Figure (Rupert Doone) which symbolizes the dissolution of their class. Sharply cutting into their uselessness come cries from the audience demanding a workers' revolution, which the Announcer quickly takes up, and uses as an excuse for fomenting a rising which will be suited to English conditions. Meanwhile the Theatre Manager suavely begs the audience to be quieter, and a budding Fascist organization begins to form upon the stage. As soon as it is established, this organization, with an effect at once surprising and extremely vivid, turns upon the Theatre Manager, and beats him up. We are back with the Nationalists hooting *Johnny Strike Up*.

From then on, the transitions from one phase of sociological development to another are cunningly and smoothly arranged, whilst the dramatic effect is elicited and pointed by a skilful use of all the instruments of theatrical expression – song and dance, speech and action, mime and decoration and grouping. The central Figure of Rupert Doone is always dramatically adequate in holding the piece together, and it becomes an early example of what later came to be hailed as total and participatory drama.

When *The Dance of Death* was published it received poor reviews. But the Group Theatre performances at the Westminster were loudly acclaimed. The *New Statesman* called it 'a return to reality and to mystery (having) nothing in common with the degenerate theatre of the present age'. The *New Statesman* admitted that it was not a masterpiece, but concluded that 'it is of greater importance for the future of drama than all the "masterpieces" of Mr Noël Coward, Mr Somerset Maugham, and the pseudo-realistic school'.

In *The Dance of Death* Auden was preoccupied with what he considered the degeneracy of the bourgeoisie, which he felt would bring about a revolution. (The Group Theatre was a communal organization.) Terence Rattigan, castigated and reviled years later by the adherents of the English Stage Society as a provider merely of candyfloss and trivial amusement, did not go so far as Auden. The thought of revolution did not, so far as his work reveals, enter his mind. But he agreed with Auden in his assessment of important sections of the middle class. This assessment he embodied in *After the Dance* (1939), a play that he did not include in the volumes of his collected works. His reason for doing this is obvious. *After the Dance* is not a very good play, and it failed to please the public. But it was a serious play, exactly the kind of play which the later critics who broke his spirit and for a long time ruined his reputation, said that, because of his supposed adulation of the well-to-do, witty dilettantes of the middle class, he would not want to write. By implicitly disowning *After the Dance* Rattigan deprived himself of one of his most effective answers to his critics.

In *After the Dance* Rattigan writes of the post-war Bright Young Things

Terence Rattigan's After the Dance *(1939) at the St James's Theatre, London.*

twenty years later, when the garishness of night clubs has given way to the fogs and gloom of common day. The action of the play takes place in the flat of David Scott-Fowler, a wealthy man at the end of his youth, who is ruining himself with drink but clinging desperately to some shreds of self-respect in his casual interest in the fringes and tassels of history. After twelve years of marriage he is bored with his wife, Joan, whose constant unrealizing gaiety begins to tire him. She, in her turn, is afraid of showing any real feeling because she thinks her husband will despise her for it. These people Rattigan chastises with whips, for his humour in this play is mordant and censorious.

David's younger brother belongs to a different generation and a different code of behaviour. In his role of secretary he is intensely serious, and intensely dull. He is engaged to Helen Banner, who in turn is in love with David, whom she wishes to rescue from his present way of living, caring little that in doing so she drives into a weak despair her own fiancé and into suicide her intended husband's wife. Rattigan approaches Peter Scott-Fowler and Helen Banner with scorpions, for, if driven to strike a reluctant balance, he would apparently prefer people who waste their own lives to people who try to improve the lives of others against their will, being of the same mind as A. A. Milne in *Other People's Lives*.

After the Dance is astringent, and Rattigan is genuinely disgusted with his characters, but his craftsmanship is less sure than was usual with him.

Moreover, his first play, *French without Tears*, had had a brilliant cast of young people who were then comparatively unknown, but who showed all the sparkle and brilliance that subsequently brought them fame. The players in *After the Dance* were probably more familiar to the public than their predecessors in *French without Tears*. Yet they did not give the play as much help. Robert Harris, who had been such a rock of security in *The Wind and the Rain* (1933), was not happy as David Scott-Fowler. Gaiety has never sat easily on this fine actor, who on the stage seems more given to brooding over the sins of the world than to enjoying them. Try as he may, seriousness will keep breaking in but within the limits of his temperament he gave a sensitive performance.

This is one of the many complex emotions aroused, not only by Terence Rattigan's *After the Dance*, but by a play by Auden and Christopher Isherwood, *On the Frontier*, which was given by the Group Theatre for one performance at the Globe Theatre in 1939. One performance only, but to many at the time this one performance seemed desperately to be playing with the future on its side, in contrast with apparent ephemera like the Cochran and Charlot revues. Its relevance to current events (the accord of Munich had been signed between Hitler and Chamberlain only a few months previously) was inescapable even to the dullest eye. Unintentionally its dedication (to Benjamin Britten) carried an indirect rebuke to the Rattigan play I have just been considering.

> The drums tap out sensational bulletins;
> Frantic the efforts of the violins
> To drown the song behind the guarded hill:
> The dancers do not listen; but they will.

Actually, when Rattigan did unmistakably hear, he took action, not perhaps more decisive, but certainly more gallant, than either Isherwood or Auden.

What *On the Frontier* did directly and beyond question was to make the theatre aware of the terror of the threat of imminent war. For this, and for the excitement engendered by their excursions into then unexperienced areas of new technique, they provoked in some quarters a rather hysterical enthusiasm. I myself, brought to the boiling point by *The Dance of Death*, wrote of the authors of *On the Frontier*, 'These two young writers are the most daring experimental workers in the English theatre today, pioneers in a form of drama whose consequences, great, small, or even non-existent, cannot yet be foreseen' (*The Christian Science Monitor*, 4 March 1939).

Shaw had fought (in fact, he was still fighting) the battle of politics in the theatre. Auden and Isherwood carried on the same battle, but they extended it to wider fields. The interest of the early pioneering Shaw lay in strictly national politics, in such questions as the relationship between social classes, the place of religion in the theatre, the institution of marriage, and the morality of private ownership. But the subject-matter of *On the Frontier* – like that of his *Geneva*, but treated much more seriously – is international politics, the stress and strain between sovereign states, the clash of ideologies over continents and oceans, and the havoc thereby wrought in private lives. Important scenes take place in the Ostia-Westland room, showing the living room in two private houses in these hostile countries. Later scenes are set in the study of Valerian, the biggest armaments manufacturer in Westland, while the interludes are short musical episodes played in front of a curtain. They form a kind of chorus commenting on the action.

The peoples of both nations deceived by the same calumniating propaganda; rival wireless stations shrieking out the same lies; the young men of both countries marching in the same temper, singing similar songs, to the same battlefield; and a youth and a girl separated for ever by the folly and misunderstanding and bellicose credulity of their rulers – these are the things that Auden and Isherwood attempted to put upon the stage with a combination of Expressionism, musical comedy, poetic drama, and realism.

The vitality of their conception and the inventive skill of their technique were admirable, but their reach exceeded their grasp more evidently than it had done in *The Dance of Death*. It was clear that they were academics. They came from the seclusion of the universities, and showed little acquaintance – far less than Eliot and Fry were to do a decade later with work equally experimental – with the commercial theatre, with its compelling necessities, its disappointments, and its rewards. Their stagecraft was not as certain as their intellectual integrity and daring. Yet in one important respect – in the sense of making social and political relevance obvious instead of implicit – theirs was the drama of the future.

In general the play gave the impression of being a discussion. But some of its scenes were theatrically vivid and true. Not many things could have been more effective than the smooth, self-possessed capitalist of Wyndham Goldie faced with the revolver of the mutinous soldier; and Ernest Milton's harsh, declamatory dictator moved one to pity as well as to exasperation and anger. (Wyndham Goldie, a contemplative and reflective actor, always genuinely thought that he was a much finer player than either the public or the managers and critics recognized; for all his intelligence he did not realise that his acting, though that of a very capable thinker, was achingly dull.) Ernest Milton, with his virtuoso exercise of the remarkable instrument of a voice which he played on as if it were a Stradivarius, and the elaborate, formal employment of gestures which reminded one of those of an eighteenth-century dancing master at a small German court, was much more exciting than Goldie; but as his mannerisms and affectations increased with the years and also the realization that he was never going to attain the rank that he had expected his performances became exaggeratedly ridiculous.

In retrospect, Lord Radcliffe's report on the security services (1981) put the whole theatre into a somewhat anomalous position. No one is now any longer certain how far the band of intellectuals who supported the Spanish Government in its battle with Franco (1936–9) and shared in the 1930s theatre's propaganda against Fascism was actuated by motives of genuine patriotism and devotion to the cause of freedom and how far they were direct or indirect agents of Soviet

Russia. The ideas propounded by the liberal and professedly democratic young intellectuals of the 1930s are now in many cases suspected of being only a cloak for treachery. Those who admired them most then are amongst their most bitter critics today. Coats have been turned with unrivalled celerity; the ideas of youth have been abandoned root and crop without any recognition, still less admission, that this is what has happened.

Sir Anthony Frederick Blunt, later Professor of Art in the University of London and, from 1952 to 1972, Surveyor of the Queen's Pictures, was precisely the sort of adventurously intellectual thinker who was most fervently admired by the opponents, for example, of Neville Chamberlain. Yet when it was revealed in 1981 that Blunt during the thirties had been recruiting agents for the Soviets amongst Cambridge undergraduates (Blunt was at that time a Fellow of Trinity) none of those who had championed the very causes which Blunt had fought for either said a word in his defence or admitted that they for a long time had been travelling in very dubious company. Of the scores of thousands of progressives who in the 1930s thought that if honours were justified at all they should be given to men who were like what Blunt appeared to be, not a single voice was raised in protest when he was stripped of his knighthood. Personally, though I had a great admiration for their artistic achievements, I never agreed with the politics of the Left between 1930 and 1940. But if I had so agreed I hope that today I should not run for cover so hard as those who belonged, or who were deceived into appearing to belong, to his way of thinking.

It should be held in mind that the Group Theatre was a communal organization, and that its motives were not always necessarily what they professed to be. But we should not be too depressed by the thought that many parts of British society in the 1930s were riddled with Communist agents. We speak of our failures freely enough, and this leads us to suppose that we had no comparable successes. But this is not so. Neither the Soviet nor the German secret services were any cleverer than the British, if indeed, as clever. It is only in the last few years, for example, that it has been revealed that the Russian counter-espionage system is extremely vulnerable. It has had in it many British agents like the naturalist Frederick Marshman Bailey, the discoverer of the renowned blue poppy in Tibet. Bailey had a price set on his head in the USSR. Nevertheless, while the Russians were searching for him as diligently as ever the French Revolutionary forces searched for the Scarlet Pimpernel, Bailey got himself recruited into the Russian counter-espionage service, and was given the special task of tracking down a British agent named Bailey, whom naturally he never found (see *Dictionary of National Biography*, 1961–70). The clever fellows are not all on the other side, though this is often concealed in plays like *Another Country* and *The Old Country* (1977), both of them works of some excellence. In *The Old*

Anthony Blunt faces the Press (November 1979) after the disclosure of his involvement in the Burgess/Maclean/Philby spy scandal of the 1950s.

Alec Guinness in Alan Bennett's The Old Country *(1977) at the Queen's Theatre, London.*

Country Sir Alec Guinness, with a nostalgic melancholy and regret, played the part of a British traitor who, in his dacha near Moscow, missed almost unbearably the characteristic sights and sounds of his native land; the ringing of church bells; the sonorous psalms of the Prayer Book; the old Victorian hymns and the harvest Festivals. *The Old Country* was one of Alan Bennett's finest plays.

The atmosphere of *The Old Country* was one of resigned calm. The war that Auden and Isherwood so much feared had come and gone, and left behind it a devastation of a different kind from that which they had expected. The disillusioned hero accepted it with a weary and patient endurance, in a state of equilibrium between the distrust of those whom he had betrayed and of those for whom the betrayal had been committed.

CHAPTER FOUR
The Search for Peace of Mind
1938–1939

In 1938, however, the year of Munich and of the greatest alarm and tension of all the thirties, the theatre, for a miraculous moment, turned to another Russia, and found comfort there. This was due to the initiative of John Gielgud. Even before the war the theatre had become a worrying financial problem. A Cochran revue would cost as much as £20,000, at that time an immense sum. Gielgud adopted a personal method of dealing with such questions. He took over the Queen's Theatre for a definite, pre-arranged period, which meant that he could secure the lease at a lower rate than would be given to a manager who proposed to put on a play that might be taken off at the end of a fortnight. He gathered round him a regular company, guaranteeing them employment for at least two-thirds of a year. Whether the financial calculations worked out correctly is doubtful, but artistically the Gielgud season of 1937/38 was one of the rarest blazes of theatrical light of the century.

It began with a very successful production of *Richard II*, one of Gielgud's finest parts. The royalty of speech, the tension of nerves, the overriding of all rational emotion by the torrential or elegiac beauty of words and images which are more evident in Richard than in any other of Shakespeare's characters, was exactly suited to Gielgud's temperament. It was with a terrible majesty, charged with an anger controlled only by a superhuman effort, that Gielgud spoke Richard's rebuke of outraged majesty when Northumberland did not kneel to him:

We are amazed; and thus long have we stood
To watch the fearful bending of thy knee,
Because we thought ourself thy lawful king;

and with a terrible self-pity, revelling in the sensual pleasure of excessive grief, that he showed Richard's moments of despair. This superb production, which lifted the theatre out of the cold terrors of reality that were beginning to overwhelm the British people into the loftiest realms of self-indulgent poetry, was followed by the lighter diversions of *The School for Scandal*, and subsequently by Chekhov's *Three Sisters*.

John Gielgud in Shakespeare's Richard II *(1937) at the Queen's Theatre, London.*

Gielgud at Oxford in 1925 had appeared in the first successful production of *The Cherry Orchard* in Britain, and when it was transferred to the capital James Agate called it in a memorable review the best play in London. Chekhov, however, is not an author who is natural to the taste of leading actors, for he does not indulge in star parts. He excels in a distributed, not a concentrated, glory. The strength of his plays was only just coming to be realized in 1937/38, for he inserts into his texts none of the isolated purple patches that leading actors of the pre-war period loved. But he was a favourite dramatist of Gielgud's, partly because of Gielgud's excellent taste, partly because of his unselfishness as an actor, and partly because of the old and unexpected Oxford triumph. Not long before *Three Sisters* Gielgud had also played in *The Seagull*.

In *Three Sisters*, he took the part of Colonel Vershinin, the philosophizing soldier who is made anxious by the thought of his wife and children. His performance was completely in the temper of the play, whose atmosphere of ineffectual yearning after an elusive happiness (less familiar to theatre–goers then than it became later) was summed up in Vershinin's exclamation, 'How sad it is that youth should pass away.' Gwen Ffrangcon-Davies also was exquisitely suited, as the eldest of the sisters, to this regretful mood, but the most moving performance of all was Michael Redgrave's Baron, awkward, absurd, ugly, yet oddly attractive.

Redgrave was even more studiously intellectual than Gielgud, and he had given a powerful performance as Bolingbroke in *Richard II*. He and Peggy Ashcroft, as the youngest sister, made a very poignant thing out of their shy, embarrassed parting on a note of forced cheerfulness in the last act, just before the duel; and the fading music of the marching regiment, dying away into silence at the end of the play, was a sadly sufficient comment on the vanishing hopes of the entire Russian bourgeoisie before the sky darkened into revolution.

This was the last evening of tranquil beauty that the British theatre was to know for many years, if indeed it was ever to know such a thing again. There was, as Scott said of *The Antiquary*, a kind of salvation about it. For one magical evening we could suspend disbelief in Wordsworth's

> The holy time is quiet as a nun
> Breathless with adoration.

When a little of it was recaptured one afternoon in 1949 the same players were principally concerned, and Alec Guinness nobly aided them. It was at Burlington House, where the British Drama League arranged a matinée performance in honour of Jacques Copeau, the founder of the Vieux Colombier. Guinness spoke with a sad and lovely peace Shakespeare's 116th sonnet. When he came to the line, 'Oh no, it is an ever-fixéd mark', he smiled gently, reassuringly, like a mother comforting a frightened child; perhaps always the world's scepticism should be rebuked in this way, with faith and without anger.

Peggy Ashcroft and John Gielgud read the scene between Viola and Orsino in which Feste sings 'Come away, come away, death'. At first, bearing in mind

Peggy Ashcroft and Michael Redgrave (far right) in the Gielgud production (1937–8) of Chekhov's The Three Sisters *at the Queen's Theatre, London.*

such dynamic performances as his Richard II, one was tempted to think that Orsino could not be among Gielgud's best parts. As we have seen already, so highly charged an actor is peculiarly fitted for characters of great nervous tension. If you shut down all the power stations in Britain, you could hardly lose more electricity than went out when he stopped playing in Gordon Daviot's *Richard of Bordeaux* in 1934. But his brain is as active as his nerves. His is not the dry intellect of an Aristotle, but the poetic intellect of an Eddington. Angrily declaiming the pictorial rhetoric of Christopher Fry's *The Lady's Not for Burning* (1948), every long speech of which is like a tour of the crooked alleyways of a medieval town, past churches and alchemists' kitchens, and the chimneys of astrologers, he came out of each twisted jennel, with bells ringing and the involved meaning crystal clear.

Orsino is not for such a player. This Duke, though he talks a lot about love, is staid enough to woo by proxy, and blind enough not to perceive passion standing by his side. Gielgud began his speeches with an impetuosity the fellow does not

Christopher Fry's The Lady's Not for Burning *at the Globe Theatre, 1949: (left to right) Claire Bloom, Nora Nicholson, John Gielgud, Pamela Brown, David Evans, Harcourt Williams, Richard Burton and Richard Leech.*

deserve; but he gradually subdued his temperament to the character's self-control, and spoke the 'Mark it, Cesario' lines with all the excitement of his nerves died down, and the only thing left the music of his voice.

Perhaps he was invaded by the exquisite calm of Peggy Ashcroft's Viola. The first thing one noticed then (and always noticed) about Peggy Ashcroft was her quietness. She seemed stiller than the moon itself, for all its eternal silence. But, unlike the moon, she was alive; and, in parts like the Duchess of Malfi, where her heart is laid open to the precise, accurate stabs of a cruel world, she can convey, by a quivering of the corners of her mouth, by the cold aching of her splendid voice, a suffering deeper and more hard to be endured than is within the scope of screams and tortured shrieks.

Her Viola, of course, was not of this sad, hopeless order. Viola is not, like the persecuted Duchess, laid upon the rack. Nevertheless, in this scene, with all its imminence of unrequited affection, she is brought within sight of it; and Dame Peggy's capacity for suggesting endurance of torment without rebellion, and of a patience which illumines it with beauty, laid on the bare room of Burlington House an absolute magic and fetched out of sorrow an emotion happier than happiness itself.

The serenity the theatre, like the nation, was now desperately seeking, and indeed found in Dame Peggy and Sir John, it sought increasingly in philosophy, in J. B. Priestley's *I Have Been Here Before* and *Time and the Conways* (1937) and *Johnson over Jordan* (1939) and in Charles Morgan's *The Flashing Stream* (1938). This last play was one of the most profoundly disillusioning aesthetic experiences of my career. It startlingly exposed what had hitherto been thought to be sheer gold as a shoddy imitation of whose worthlessness its manufacturer was ludicrously unaware. Its author, Charles Morgan, was a writer who not only had built up an enormous reputation amongst people of taste and knowledge in his novel *The Fountain* a few years earlier, but had seemed not able to write even the briefest criticism in *The Times* (of which he was the drama critic) without producing an essay whose cool lucidity of judgement and phrase gave every perceptive reader a thrill of pleasure.

Unfortunately he took himself to be the Plato of dramatists and novelists. He felt that he understood love and philosophy with a profundity beyond the comprehension of common men and women. He denounced people with a sense of humour with extraordinary venom, for, after *The Flashing Stream*, people with a sense of humour tended to laugh at him. The play dealt portentously with passion, for passion was what Morgan thought he understood better than did men and women of coarser clay. Passion of intellect and passion of the flesh, desire of the body and desire of the higher mathematics – it was of these that he was confident he had made *The Flashing Stream*. But in his elaborate preciosity, his almost sublime pretentiousness he succeeded in giving only the impression that he was in love with his leading lady, which for all I know he may have been, for she was very attractive.

Insofar as the theatre has any national influence at all, in the late 1930s (despite the fact that some good plays were being written, and there was an abundance of outstanding acting) little of it seemed to be being exercised to any effective degree. Contemporary observers found nothing to suggest that the fraught nerves of a country distracted by Hitler's reoccupation of the Rhineland, the burning of the Reichstag, and later the hysteria over the Munich agreement were being brought back to normal by the impact of the warnings of Auden, the preciousness of Morgan, or even the sad serenity of Chekhov, the tranquility of Peggy Ashcroft, the golden eloquence of Gielgud, the humanity of Ralph Richardson or the dynamic force of Laurence Olivier.

It was in these unsatisfactory circumstances that one of Britain's most forthright and common-sense dramatists, St John Ervine, a man who hated the esoteric and the pretentious, was brought back, like Galsworthy, to consider the question of class. Ervine believed in aristocracy; that is, strictly speaking, government by the best. Where he differed from most people who held such beliefs was in discovering where aristocrats were to be found. He did not look for them in the public schools and the older universities, still less in Debrett and the peerage. In *People of Our Class* (1938) there dwelt in Dorset an impoverished county family called Marsh. The elder daughter, Shena, played by Ursula Jeans, horrified her father, Sir Gregory Marsh, by declaring her intention to marry the son of the local butcher, Henry Hayes (Bernard Lee), a fellow of rather shambling appearance and uncertain accent, who was earning £3.10s a week as assistant in the village chemist's shop.

Now, just because Ervine was a believer in salvation by aristocracy, he approved of Shena's decision. He knew that class distinctions exist in England, and he was glad that they existed, because it was precisely this conviction that put him wholeheartedly on the side of Shena and Henry. For a class is not a caste. People are constantly moving up and down the social scale. The personnel of any class is always changing. The Marshes are continually falling, and the Hayeses rising.

In *People of our Class* Ervine said just that, that and no more. He did not assert that the middle classes are declining, and that the working classes are the salt of the earth. He confined himself to saying that one particular working man was better for Shena Marsh than the two or three potential husbands of her own class. In fact in a very important speech, he made it clear that Shena would have preferred a man in her own order of society rather than Hayes. But she had decided that such men, if they were of value, were beyond her reach. Obviously, since she was a high-spirited girl, not at all likely to underrate her chances, she could have come to this conclusion only after considerable experience. Thus Ervine could not make her a very young woman. He fixed her age at 28.

This was the great weakness of the play, for, though nothing was said on the point, Shena's age gives a rough indication of Henry's. It is as a man of 30 that Bernard Lee played him, and so made nonsense of Ervine's whole thesis. It was essential to represent Hayes as a young fellow of outstanding ability, in contrast with the futility and weakness of the Marshes. So a great deal was said about Hayes's energy, his determination to succeed, and the exceptional nature of his education. A man of this type, who at the age of 30 has got no further than being an assistant in a village shop, hardly answers to Ervine's conception of an aristocrat, though Ervine himself did not seem to see it. The play is not significant as a contribution to dramatic literature; but it is undoubtedly symptomatic of the frantic eagerness with which the theatre at this time was seeking for some place where it could find a solution to the nation's distress, and in its forecast of what was to be the ruling class of the future.

But in the face of the towering might of Hitler and the flamboyant boasts of Mussolini, faith in the aristocracy (whether Debrett or deserved) and in the belligerent young poets from the universities collapsed. Wherever salvation was to be found, it was not located either in *People of Our Class*, *Avalanche*, *Wings over Europe*, *Strange Orchestra*, *The Dance of Death*, or *On the Frontier*. As a last resort J. B. Priestley turned the theatre-goer's attention to the common man and woman. He found that there might not be much hope there, but at least there was plenty of courage. And then Robert Sherwood, in *Idiot's Delight*, showed that there was neither.

Priestley was greatly encouraged at this time by Sir Barry Jackson. Jackson was the last rich businessman to become an open-handed and enlightened patron of the theatre. He founded the Birmingham Repertory Theatre in 1913, and it was there, in the mid-twenties, that Laurence Olivier, Ralph Richardson, and Cedric Hardwicke gave some of the finest of their earlier performances. In 1929 Jackson established the Malvern Festival, and ran it until 1937. He was also prominent in the London theatre, and in the thirties the strain of so much work began to tell on him. He continued to live at Colwall, within a few miles of Malvern, but in a broadcast address in 1937 he announced that he would be unable to take part in the following year's Festival. With the departure of Sir Barry went the scheme of programme-building which had made each annual Festival in some sort a historical review of the development of British drama, from the medieval moralities to the latest productions of Bridie and Shaw. It was thus that Jackson created a summer Festival which in 1938 gave a home, indeed a birthplace, to Priestley's *Music at Night*.

Malvern was one of the greatest theatrical refuges from the heat and bustle of the world that have been created in my time, and, in the anxieties of 1938, the changes brought about by Jackson's departure seemed minimal. At a first view, at any rate, all seemed to be as it had been for a decade past. The setting, obviously, remained unaltered. Malvern then as always enjoyed the enduring charm of its unique situation, which arises from its being a mountain town built in the centre of a plain. Its hillsides were criss-crossed with streets meeting at an angle and an elevation that made driving a motor car a hundred yards a feat of high adventure. That at least is how it seemed to the innocent motorists of 1938, ignorant of the perils of the road which the future held in store for them.

Nor, in its beginning, did the 1938 Festival appear much different from its predecessors. In fact the new Director, Captain Roy Limbert, laboured hard and successfully to preserve the traditions established by its founder. To find Professor Boas delivering a morning lecture in the cinema that adjoins the Winter Gardens and the theatre was a delight that might have occurred at Malvern in any August since 1931. Dr Boas was still wearing that MA gown which, as he himself used to say, added a pleasant touch of formality to the proceedings, and, at the same time, hid any deficiencies of clothing. The same impression of continuity from previous Festivals held throughout the afternoon, when Limbert set up a large garden party on the lawns of the County Hotel beneath the shadow of the hills and the noble bulk of the great Abbey, whose bells rang out in the blazing sunshine a joyous peal that for a long time drowned the less robust noises offered in unequal competition by the hotel orchestra.

The characteristic feature of the Malvern Festival in the 1930s did not lie in its dramatists, though these included Bernard Shaw, Rudolf Besier, and J. B. Priestley; nor yet in its players, although it had such stars as Ralph Richardson and Cedric Hardwicke, who was at the height of his fame when he played the

(Left to right) George Bernard Shaw, Granville Bantock, Sir Barry Jackson and Sir Edward Elgar at the 1934 Malvern Festival (from Arts Monthly, *August 1934).*

Bishop in *Getting Married*, Captain Shotover in *Heartbreak House*, Lickcheese in *Widowers' Houses*, and Edward Moulton-Barrett in Besier's *The Barretts of Wimpole Street* at Malvern in 1930. More systematically studied work has been given at the Stratford-upon-Avon Festivals during a much longer period of years; and there are occasions when the Chichester Festival has a brighter air of fashionable gaiety. But the Malvern Festivals had two features which neither of the other famous Festivals has even tried to emulate. They were comprehensive, they had plays, music, dances, and academic lectures; and also Sir Barry Jackson invested them with great social appeal. In this they have only been rivalled – and that on a smaller but nevertheless attractive scale – by the Pitlochry Festival; at least, until the Edinburgh Festival came along after the war, and in its ambition, resources, and achievements topped all others.

In the gloomy decade that preceded Hitler's invasion of Poland in 1939 the Malvern Festival was the annual event to which theatre-goers most eagerly looked forward. In those miserable years, to come to Malvern each August was like joining a club. For three weeks it became the Garrick of the Midlands. It made the theatre-goer sure of the friendship of nine hundred others like himself, and of a dozen or so more distinguished. Roy Limbert entered upon this heritage with great éclat. He was determined that the lustre of Jackson's reign should be at least equalled, perhaps even eclipsed; and after his afternoon party he gave an even more ambitious evening reception. Here the theatre-goer who had paid for his modest seat in the stalls at each of the six productions of the Festival could gaze with awe and admiration upon the imposing brows of James Bridie, J. B. Priestley, C. K. Munro, and Lord Dunsany, four of the dramatists represented on the Malvern stage in a single week.

If, in its social aspects decorous, quiet, and friendly, the Malvern Festival represented a world that was passing away, some of its later plays also showed that the electric spirit of the times had not yet affected their complacency. In 1938, between the reception and the garden party, there was a play written by the only man in the world who would dare to lift the curtain upon his last act as late as 9.58 p.m. and not let it fall till 11.40 p.m. *Geneva* was a play on which it was known that Shaw had been at work for several years. This was in fact apparent from internal evidence, for it satirized the League of Nations at a period when Hitler was only an apprentice at dictatorship compared with his Italian brother-in-arms of the Berlin–Rome axis. Nowhere did it show any recognition of the fact that the relative importance of Mussolini and Hitler had changed.

In *Geneva* the two dictators, Mr Battler and Signor Bombardone, are portrayed as an enormous, a titanic joke. The hysteria and sentimentality of Mr Battler are grossly overdone, but the magnificent bumptiousness, which was not without an engaging grip upon realities, of Signor Bombardone (superbly played by Cecil Trouncer) on that still careless evening made the preposterous length of the third act not only bearable, but actually pleasant. There is also in *Geneva* a British Foreign Secretary (Ernest Thesiger) who, like most of the upper-class

Englishmen of Shaw's imagination, is incapable of thought, but who can nevertheless, in his vague, amateurish, and absurdly self-confident way, draw rings round all his diplomatic opponents. But *Geneva* was poor stuff all the same.

C. K. Munro's *Coronation Time at Mrs Beam's* also, like *Geneva*, showed that Malvern was a last refuge of an age that was passing away. Munro was reckoned to be one of the most intellectually daring of British dramatists, scorning the restrictions of the well–made play, and relying instead on the amusing interplay of lower–middle–class characters. But in *Coronation Time at Mrs Beam's* he was, as he said, content to try to repeat an old triumph. Nearly a score of years before, he had introduced delighted audiences to the wonders of Mrs Beam's middle–class boarding establishment; and memories were still fresh in 1938 of the cantankerousness of Mrs Bebb and the garrulous facility of Miss Shaw in the discovery and examination of mares' nests. Now here they were all again, no older, no wiser, no richer, no poorer than they were before. It seemed as though the passing years, with all their excitements, terrors and disasters, had held nothing for them.

Munro was here trespassing upon a theme which his 1938 partner, J. B. Priestley, had, after *Time and the Conways* (1937), made his own especial property. In *Cornelius* Priestley had tried to show that a gallant man can triumph over material ruin; but all he had done was to end up with a fairy–tale of a man setting out on an unbelievable and impossible journey. It seemed (though he was in 1938 on the verge of changing his view) that courage was not enough, and he became absorbed in the philosophical problem of time as a comfort during the dark days through which we were passing. Moreover in 1937 Keith Winter, who a few years earlier had given signs of immense promise, also dealt, in *Old Music*, with the effects of time.

It was in a play of Winter's that I had first seen the young Laurence Olivier. He had, as I have recalled already, played the small part of a junior master in a decaying prep school in *The Rats of Norway* (1933).

Keith Winter was never to write so well again as he had done in *The Rats of Norway*. But, like Priestley, the passing of time absorbed him. In *Old Music*, which was at the then-existing St James's, he obtained from it a certain familiar effect of pathos. The Victorian uniforms, the play's constant references to the Crimean war as an event of enormous contemporary importance, its peculiar atmosphere of Austenish middle-classness dashed with Thackerayan aristocracy, gave to it a half–sad feeling of a tale that is told and has long since vanished into nothingness, and Winter accentuated this impression by making the drama itself a play within a play. It all seemed rather remote, rather unreal, like the pages of a family album turned in a mood of nostalgic reverie.

Old Music was typical of much of the drama of the thirties, in that, being of no outstanding merit in itself, it was beautifully staged, this time by Rex Whistler (1905–44). Celia Johnson added greatly to her already considerable reputation by her lovely performance of a gentle governess who married disastrously in order to escape the misery of economic dependence.

At the Duchess, in *Time and the Conways* Priestley took a much keener and more perceptive interest in time than was evident in *Old Music*. For practical purposes one might say that all English plays present an argument. Until the beginning of the century this argument – as the word is used in the foreword to each book of *Paradise Lost* – was a plot. Then Shaw transformed the meaning into a dispute, and the most intellectually fashionable dramas became conversational dog-fights in which half a dozen diverse types got round a table and tore one another's opinions to tatters.

In *Time and the Conways* Priestley must have been greatly tempted to produce one of these pseudo-Shavian disquisitions, for the germinating seed of the play is a devouring interest in the philosophical rather than in the emotional implications of the passing of time. But happily the interests of the dramatist triumphed over those of the intellectual, and Priestley gave an argument in the Miltonic rather than the Shavian sense.

Nevertheless, Priestley did not abandon his philosophic pretensions. Priestley is convinced (or at least he was at that time) that time itself is an illusion, that it cannot rob us of affection, wealth, ambition, hopes, as it sometimes seems to do. In five minutes of set speeches at the end of the second act he made his intellectual position quite clear; but the story he devised to illustrate his theme does nothing of the kind. Time does not fail to rob the Conways; it would appear to defeat and ruin them. As a thinker Priestly firmly denies the defiant Victorian mood of the lines,

> I long have had a quarrel set with Time,
> Because he robbed me. Every day of life
> Is wrested from me after bitter strife.
> I never yet could see the sun go down,
> But I was angry in my heart,

but as a dramatist he illustrates it perfectly, in a play that is never less than good.

The first act relied too much on the fun of charades for its effects, but the second was (and remains) magnificent. It proves, like the last act of *The Voysey Inheritance*, how a profoundly realistic technique in the hands of a master when inspiration is running high can move and impress an audience. This scene, which shows the sorry pass to which the Conways have been brought after the great hopes and ambitions of twenty years earlier, was superbly played by a cast that included Jean Forbes-Robertson, Barbara Everest, and Raymond Huntley.

Throughout the thirties Priestley showed an enquiring and an experimental mind. However small, in Taylor's opinion, the influence over the nation's thought the poetry of Auden may have been, Priestley did a great deal to keep the imagination of the theatre-going public alert and active. People never quite knew what to expect when they went to see a new Priestley play. It might be loosely picaresque, like the musical adaptation of *The Good Companions* (1931), or with a plot as tightly organized as *Dangerous Corner* (1932); a light-hearted romp like *When We Are Married* (1938), or a glimpse of the mysterious heroic, like *Johnson over Jordan* (1939); a philosophy like *I Have Been Here Before* and *Time and the Conways*, or a theatrical experiment like *Music at Night.*

Music at Night, though few or no people guessed it at the time of the 1938 Malvern Festival, foreshadowed a great deal of what the drama of the future was to be. It resembled a piece of music more than it did a realistic play, and for that reason pre-war audiences were baffled by it. They found its story either confusing, or non-existent, and its characters shadowy and ill-defined. They could not of course know how much there was in it that prefigured the work of Samuel Beckett, or a play like David Storey's *Early Days* (1980). Malvern was accustomed to judging the past, not to foreseeing the future. It applied the rules of the established, and did not attempt to assess the value of what might happen if these rules were ignored. It was therefore unjust in its relative lack of appreciation of *Music at Night.*

This play was about the performance of a new piece of music, an 'attempt to dramatise the mental adventure of a group of persons listening to it'. Priestley himself summed it up in these words: 'It is assumed that the mood of the music more or less controls their moods. The progress throughout the play is from the surface of the mind to deeper and deeper levels of consciousness. The strange happenings in Act 3 arise from my belief that at these depths we are not the separate beings we imagine ourselves to be.' The critics of 1938 no more understood this kind of drama than the first public did *Waiting for Godot* (1955). But they were civilized enough in the tone of their complaints.

Obviously *Music at Night* was a play that led to peculiar technical experiments. Since nearly all of it, to the audience's consternation, was taken up with a revelation of the private thoughts, memories, and longings of people who, in actual speech and action, did not give themselves away at all, it was composed almost entirely of soliloquies; of soliloquies which, just to make things more difficult, reacted on each other.

The third act, which used a kind of choir, an 'antiphony of the living and the dead', as Priestley himself indicated, challenged some of the deepest problems of philosophy and metaphysics, and seemed more likely to confirm or affront the audience's fundamental attitudes than to change them. But there were things in it that in performance were profoundly moving. At this time the British theatre was unusually rich in players who, whilst not being quite in the front rank, had distinctive merits that sometimes enabled them to carry off the best moments in a play. This happened in *Music at Night* with Ernest Thesiger's aged Balfourian statesman's momentary recovery of his youth when, in memory urged by the slow movement of the music, his old servant brought him a young man's straw boater. This was most beautifully done, the years sliding off the tall, frail, highly mannered Thesiger like a garment that is thrown aside. Very touching also was the gossip-writer's conscience-stricken talk with his accusing mother, and the Communist poet's apostrophe (finely spoken by Alec Clunes) to Queen Nefertiti; whilst the last time that Mrs Amesbury (Jean Cadell) saw her son before his accident in the air was extraordinarily dramatic.

Whilst Priestley philosophized and experimented, the European situation grew steadily more critical. Both the British and the Americans lost confidence day by day. Yet the Germans themselves still maintained a fairly high opinion of the British strength. According to the *Illustrated London News* of 1 July 1939, Count Pückler, formerly the London correspondent of the *Deutsche Allgemeine Zeitung*, estimated that Britain, despite the decay of its shipping and shipbuilding industries, and the decline of its agriculture, was still the richest country in the world. Its foreign investments were less than they had been, but Pückler believed that Britain had an unequalled command of raw materials, and the nucleus of an excellent army.

Priestley himself showed a very robust spirit. For by 1939 he was ready, in *Johnson over Jordan*, to face the worst unflinchingly. The ending of this day seemed beyond description magnificent. *Johnson over Jordan* begins with preparations for Johnson's funeral, and then merges into a scene showing Johnson's first days in an office. Each of the three acts opens naturalistically with the funeral and then develops into fantasy, revealing Johnson as *un homme moyen sensuel*, seeking pleasure in night clubs and such places, and then in memories of the purer part of his nature: his joy in Don Quixote and quotations from the Bible, and the memory of his first meeting with his wife. At the conclusion of each act a mysterious hooded figure appears (played majestically by Richard Ainley), and his third appearance heralds the play's apocalyptic close.

The actual impact of the last few moments of *Johnson over Jordan*, when Johnson, now dead, is distracted by parting from the fading echoes of his still living wife's voice, and is afraid of the unknown future, was tremendous. In his script Priestley made great demands; and in the performances of Ralph Richardson and Richard Ainley, and in the illimitable stage setting, they were wonderfully met. I cannot refrain from putting them down here; partly because I am unable to write with such inspiration as Priestley, and partly because, almost for the only time in the thirties, and just before the great ordeal was about to begin, the British stage knew a brief moment of exaltation.

THE FIGURE [*gravely*]. Robert Johnson, it is time to go now.
[*And here is the Porter, standing just behind Johnson with his hat and overcoat and a bag.*]
PORTER. Your things, sir. [*Helps him on with his coat.*]
JOHNSON [*now with his overcoat on, holding his hat and bag, with an echo of childish accents*]. For Thine is the kingdom, the power, and the glory . . . and God bless Jill and Freda and Richard . . . and all my friends – and – and – everybody . . . for ever and ever . . . Amen.
[*He puts on his hat and is now ready to go. He looks up at the Figure, doubtfully.*]
JOHNSON [*hesitantly*]. Is it – a long way?
THE FIGURE [*suddenly smiling like an angel*]. I don't know, Robert.
JOHNSON [*awkwardly*]. No . . . well . . . good-bye.

[A majestic theme has been announced, first only by the woodwind. As

Johnson still stands there, hesitating, the light on the Figure fades, and then the whole staircase disappears leaving Johnson alone. He looks very small, forlorn, for now the whole stage has been opened up to its maximum size, and there is nothing there but Johnson. The music marches on, with more and more instruments coming in. Johnson looks about him, shivering a little, and turning up the collar of his coat. And now there is a rapidly growing blue light; the high curtains have gone at the back, where it is bluer and bluer; until at last we see the glitter of stars in space, and against them the curve of the world's rim. As the brass blares out triumphantly and the drums roll and the cymbals clash, Johnson, wearing his bowler hat and carrying his bag, slowly turns and walks towards that blue space and the shining constellations, and the curtain comes down and the play is done.]

In this fairly lengthy passage which I have quoted Priestley uses very exciting words. They are exciting because they are exact and precise, and yet describe something that, in its grandeur and terror and exaltation, is strictly immeasurable. They are of a vastness of conception that would loose the bands of Orion, and are not unworthy of guiding Arcturus with his sons. The music of the spheres rises in them in the most thrilling of crescendos, and on a small, circumscribed stage Priestley asks for the presentation of nothing less than infinity and eternity. And in the midst of this huge, utter emptiness of brightness and cold he places the tiny, unprotected spectacle of one undistinguished man, with no more protection against the whole universe than his coat, his hat, his bag, and his courage. Marvellously the scene-setters and the actor responded to the author's tremendous challenge. When all that I have seen and heard upon the stage, visions and inspirations, the noble actors and the lovely ladies have vanished from my mind I shall remember this one thing: Richardson, after a moment's hesitation, turning up the collar of his coat, and by that single, simple action creating round him a temperature of absolute zero, through which he walked with resolute step into the unknown, comforted by the faint sound of his wife's vanishing voice, and no longer afraid.

Johnson over Jordan was produced in the early part of 1939, by the end of which year Britain was at war with Germany. I wish I could say that the British people marched into that war as bravely as Richardson marched into the great emptiness of the universe. (By the way, Richardson himself did: without hesitation he threw away his career, and joined the RAF as soon as the war started.) But the people as a whole were very much frightened, and the intellectuals who had been clamouring for months and even years for the destruction of Hitler now began to have surprising doubts. After Stalin had expressed his whole-hearted support for someone who up to that moment had

---

Ralph Richardson in J. B. Priestley's Johnson over Jordan *(1939) at the New (Albery) Theatre, London.*

been regarded as the reincarnation of the devil, some of them seemed to think that Britain should, like Russia, be on the side of Nazism. Or even that Nazism and Russia should be encouraged to destroy Britain. It was not a period on which we can look back with pride.

There was a general sense of fear throughout the land. The people wildly exaggerated the country's supposed helplessness. They did not realize that till 1940 the Luftwaffe had made no direct preparations for war against England. Germany, says A. J. P. Taylor, 'had no battle fleet, no landing craft, very few submarines. . . . The German Luftwaffe had no plans or training' for bombing English cities, 'despite Hitler's threats of indiscriminate destruction'. The British air staff, without discussion, took these threats seriously, and greatly overrated Germany's air strength.

In 1939 British air production overtook German, but still the British people continued to be afraid. They enormously exaggerated the effects of bombing. 'In 1937 they expected an attack continuing for sixty days, with casualties of 600,000 dead and 1,200,000 injured.' The Ministry of Health calculated in 1939 that from one to three million more beds would be required in hospitals immediately war started. Compared with what actually happened this panic appears ludicrous. In nearly six years of war civilian casualties amounted to only 60,000 killed and 235,000 injured.

Robert Sherwood's *Idiot's Delight* (1938) therefore more accurately reflected the spirit in which the British went to war against Hitler than did the determined courage with which Priestley's Johnson marched out into the unknown. *Idiot's Delight* put into an effective dramatic form the irritated incomprehension and fear with which the British people watched the inexorable progress towards war, and its final scene, in which a man and a woman attempt to drown the thunder of bombs by banging on a piano and singing 'Onward Christian Soldiers' made a tremendous effect on the opening night. The audience left the theatre in a mood of slight hysteria, never before having been brought so close to a realization of the terror of war. A few flakes of snow were falling, and an old man was selling newspapers at the door of the theatre. I looked anxiously at his poster to see if war had already been declared. But it was not to come for another year.

The long period of suspense during the late 1930s came to an end with the formal declaration of war on 3 September 1939, and Sir George Reeves-Smith, the managing director of the Savoy Hotel, duly marked the importance of the event by the next morning appearing in the front hall of the hotel in a lounge suit and a bowler hat. It was the first time in forty years that he had failed to wear a frock coat and top hat. This, though it threw the hotel staff into consternation, was a ceremonial gesture rather than a sign of collapsing morale.

Sir George's imaginative and symbolic action left the country in no doubt that a new era had begun, and among many sections of the population the event that

Bomb damage near St Paul's Cathedral, London.

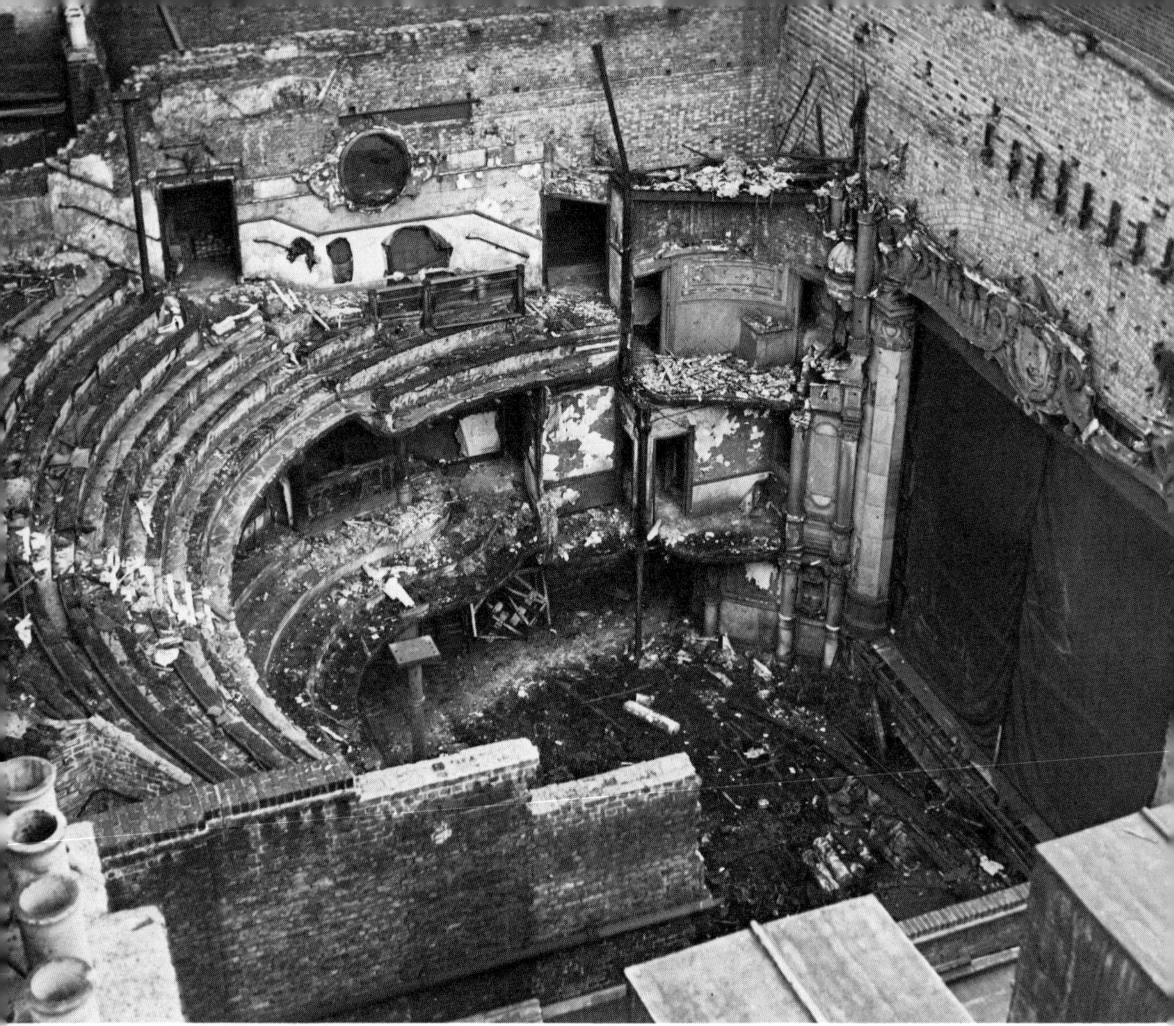

The Holborn Empire, one of London's most successful music halls, in October 1948, its ruins hardly touched 8 years after a devastating air raid.

had inspired it came as an emotional relief. There was none of the bravura and the gallantry that greeted the opening of the war of 1914–18; there was no rejoicing. Nevertheless, there was a general feeling that it was better to know the reality of war than to wait month after month in vain apprehension.

This relief of tension, however, was accompanied by a certain amount of caution. Queen Mary set an example of prudence by withdrawing from London to live with the Duke and Duchess of Beaufort at Badminton. But even in the crisis of war she did not desert her household staff. In fact, she took them with her, and her arrival at Badminton with sixty-three servants caused her hosts some alarm. The Aga Khan went to his palace at St Moritz. Eleven thousand children of the well-to-do were despatched overseas by their parents. But evidences of alarm were classless. They were spread equally amongst all sections of the population, and hundreds of thousands of the children of the poor fled to the rural solitudes and the refuge of big (and little) country houses thrown open to them. But millions of people remained steady, though quaking, waiting in London for the bombs to fall. Even at the height of the Blitz in 1940 and afterwards, sixty per cent of Londoners continued to sleep at home instead of in the huge communal air raid shelters provided by the authorities.

Ralph Richardson, along with many other actors, joined the forces. The Duke and Duchess of Windsor returned to England, and David Niven returned from Hollywood, wishing to follow Richardson's example. Cecil Beaton worked on the night shift in a telephone exchange, and two American acrobats, the Two Valors, refused to be evacuated to the United States. They said that they preferred to face bombs rather than the New York critics.

The theatre, in fact, stood up well to the apprehension, and, when it came, to the endurance of bombing. Immediately after the declaration of war the theatres were closed by official decree. War came at a moment when commercially the stage, despite its high costs, was exceedingly prosperous. Jack Hulbert's revue *Under Your Hat* at the Palace Theatre, for example, had just made a £30,000 deal with the libraries for the third time. It was taking £4,200 a week, a huge sum for London at that time. As soon as permission was given theatres began to reopen one by one. The first of these was the Little Theatre (subsequently destroyed by bombing), where Herbert Farjeon's *Little Revue* was a great success. At first the Government forbade theatres to remain open after 6 p.m. So the Little began performances at a quarter past one, and its example was quickly followed by other playhouses.

When the authorities lifted their ban on evening performances the first theatre to take the risk of playing after dark was the Westminster, which imported J. B. Priestley's *Music at Night* from the Malvern Festival. Street lighting had been suspended from the beginning of hostilities, but theatre–goers found that the darkened city was much easier to move about in than they had expected. Policemen with torches were ready to pilot pedestrians across the road in the neighbourhood of the theatres. Motor buses, like huge, dim, blue apparitions, glided to and fro. Private cars groped through the gloom, helped only by shaded sidelights. Everything had a rather charmingly conspiratorial air about it, and the feeling inside the theatre, whilst the performance was going on, was that of some secret (and probably illegal) society. All this soon began to make theatre–going an even more attractive adventure than it had been before the war.

As a result the morale of the theatre soon became very high, and remained so throughout the war. It withstood the shock of events even better than it had done in 1914. Between 4 August 1914 and Christmas of that year sixteen new plays were produced; of these only six were still running in January 1915. But in the last four months of 1939 there were at least thirty-three major productions, of which twenty-nine were still playing at the beginning of 1940.

The theatre thus did a great deal to keep the morale of the British people high. One intellectual play had an enormous effect in keeping alight a spirit of hope at a time when it was nearer to extinction than it had ever been, either before or after. This was *Thunder Rock*, by Robert Ardrey. Little is heard of this play now, and Ardrey is not one of the great literary names of the century. Nevertheless, what he accomplished for the British people at a moment of almost supreme despair (everywhere but on the lighter stage) merits their lasting gratitude.

The contribution to the welfare of their country made by British intellectuals was, however, somewhat different from Ardrey's. Where he inspired, they depressed. Where he told us never to give up hope, they moaned that all hope was extinguished. Where he, more quietly than but as equally effectively as Churchill, urged us never to surrender, they either ran away or told us that our cause was evil. If there were in the thirties any writers in the theatre on whom we felt that in time of trial and crisis we could absolutely rely for strength and support, those writers were W. H. Auden and Christopher Isherwood. They, and they alone, had consistently warned us that we were on the very edge of disaster. Their plays, *The Dance of Death* and *On the Frontier* (1938), had faced the prospect of the holocaust more frankly and boldly than had those of any other dramatists. It is ironic that *On the Frontier* had specifically warned the frivolous-minded and the irrational optimists:

> The drums tap out sensational bulletins;
> Frantic the efforts of the violins
> To drown the song behind the guarded hill:
> The dancers do not listen; but they will.

But when danger became really imminent, these men went to the United States. What the progressive theatre had to offer to the British people during the war came from a single intellectual, and he an American; and from the despised entertainers. When the bombs dropped the violins redoubled their efforts, and the dancers went on dancing more or less unperturbed. But Auden and Isherwood listened only from the other side of the Atlantic. Their departure had profound effects upon the intellectual world. It was so controversial that it prevented for several years that taking over of the theatre by intellectuals which was effected after the war by Christopher Fry and T. S. Eliot.

The confusion consequent on Auden's leaving England can best be charted in the pages of the magazine *Horizon*, which the well-meaning but bewildered Cyril Connolly started in 1940. Both Stephen Spender and T. S. Eliot tried to tackle the problems of relating the theatre to world events. Spender, disapproving of Auden, said that he was weary of events being dealt with in a public manner in verse plays, and yet attracted, too. Eliot agreed that the problem was to write about a smaller theme – family life, for instance – in which there would be implications of what was going on in the world outside. Some audiences would take and enjoy the play at its face value, whilst others would understand its deeper meanings.

Eliot and Spender were almost alone in their particular intellectual circles in maintaining some sense of purpose and direction. Connolly himself, tepidly patriotic and gloomily ironical, wrote wryly of the emigration of Auden and Isherwood:

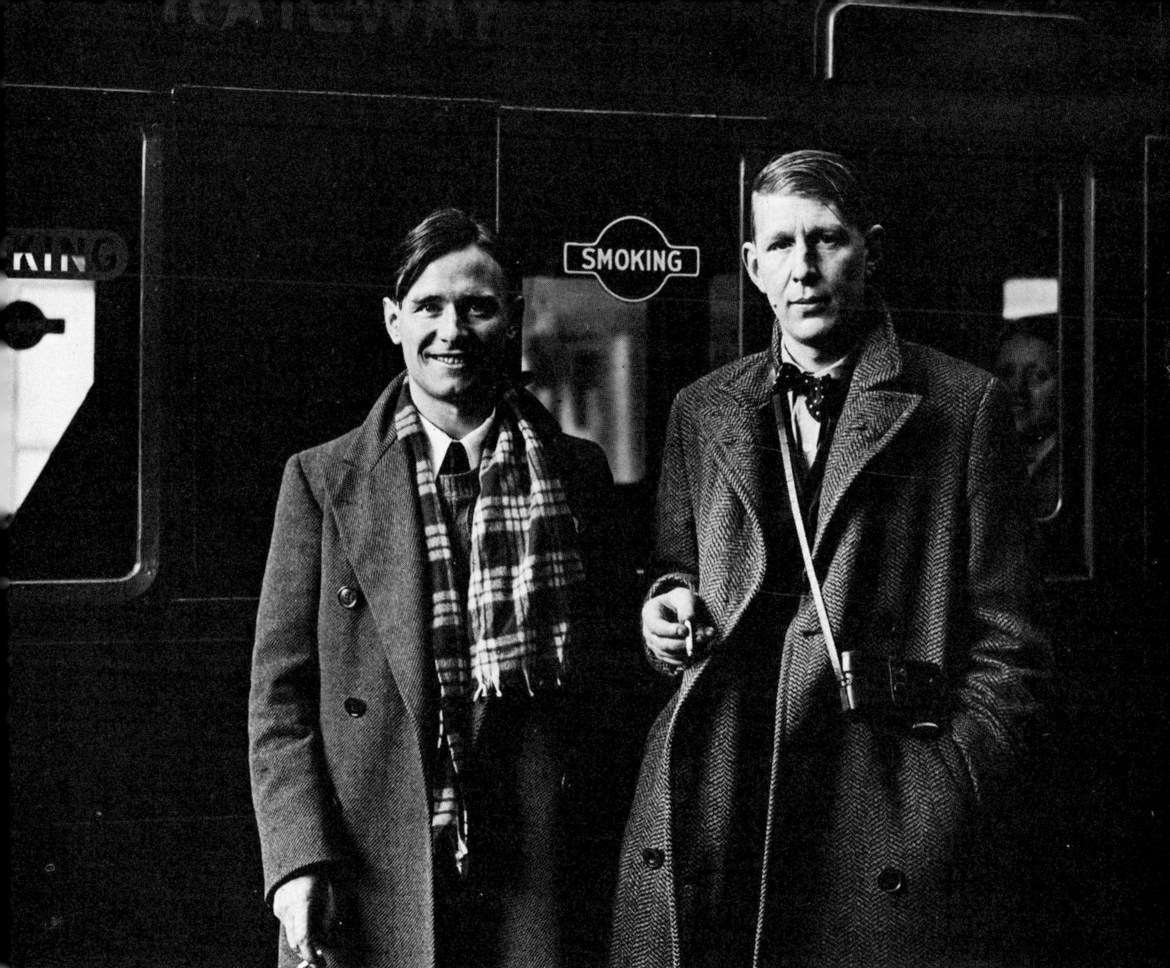

Christopher Isherwood (left) and W. H. Auden leaving for China (1938) and ultimately America.

Auden is our best poet, Isherwood our most promising novelist. They did not suffer from lack of recognition in England, where they received a publicity that they did everything to encourage, nor have they gone to America to animate the masses, for Auden has been teaching in a New England school and Isherwood writing dialogue in Hollywood. They are far-sighted and ambitious young men with a strong instinct of self-preservation, and an eye for the main chance, who have abandoned what they think to be the sinking ship of European democracy, and by implication the aesthetic doctrine of social realism that has been prevailing there. Are they right? It would certainly seem so. Whatever happens in the war, America will be the gainer. It will gain enormously in wealth, and enormously (through the refugees) in culture. England will be poverty-stricken, even in victory, and will have to be either a poor, reactionary state, a little Victorian museum-piece, like Hungary or Austria, or a poor though progressive country, like Denmark. The only alternative which would prove the English refugees to be wrong would be the union of England and France into a single state in which not only the military and financial resources are pooled, as at present, but the raw materials, the exports, the countryside and the climate, so that English workers would commute from sunny dormitories in the Cevennes, and the Anglo-Saxon spirit, humid with sentimental evasion and the South-West wind, be clarified by marriage to the Latin intellect.

All this was before any real danger appeared in Britain. The emigration of Auden and Isherwood and the feeble morale of Cyril Connolly and his fellows in the world of the arts antedated Germany's bombing of Britain. For years people like these had nearly burst their blood vessels shouting that Hitler should be stopped; they had been virulently bitter in condemning the appeasement policy of Neville Chamberlain. But suddenly their belligerency vanished.

In the theatre, with the solitary exception of one American dramatist, they gave no help, sustenance, or guidance. They set the country an example of fear. Put up at the side of the theatre of entertainment theirs was an exceptionally poor performance. In contrast the commercial theatre seemed quite undaunted. Priestley's *Music at Night* continued to play–music at night; there was even a little play, a gallant small romance, called *Pigeon Post*, revived from the previous war, brave, but as pathetic as its title was outmoded; Joyce Grenfell went on undauntedly with her acid little songs and stories, and John Gielgud and Edith Evans were brilliant in *The Importance of Being Earnest*.

It was in these circumstances that Emlyn Williams wrote the first popular success of the war. This was *The Light of Heart*, produced in the first three months of 1940. Other new plays, like *Punch without Judy*, *The Bare Idea*, *Follow My Leader*, *Believe It or Not*, and *You, of all People*, had preceded it, but were quickly forgotten. *The Light of Heart* was not one of the best of Williams's plays, but theatrically it was very effective, and it had one scene which was quite memorable, played by Angela Baddeley and Anthony Ireland with sincerity and love.

The play showed the regeneration of a once-great actor, a man for whom Irving himself had forecast a future, but who was now living in rags in a Covent Garden attic, tended only by his crippled daughter. Out of this decline he had risen again to fame; but at the height of his resumed success, he was toppled from his triumph when, on the eve of playing Lear, he learnt of his daughter's impending marriage. The portrait that Godfrey Tearle drew of the actor was greatly admired, but, except in its moments of subdued declamation, it hardly moved me at all. But there was one deeply touching scene between the girl and her lover, remarkable in the extraordinary rhetoric of the young man's proposal of marriage. In this, with the accuracy of an inventory and the passion of a Spenser, he summarized her charms – charms which, because of her infirmity, she herself could not believe in. This hovered perpetually on the edge of the ridiculous, which is only a step from the sublime.

Theoretically, *The Light of Heart*, *The Importance of Being Earnest*, and *Music at Night* had no social relevance. They were plays of entertainment. But in practice their social relevance was considerable. Audiences left the theatre feeling braver and happier than when they went in. When they thought of the work of those progressives whose work *was* socially relevant, their emotions were quite different.

Connolly, who was the best of these artists, had no *élan*, no spirit. His mind was filled with dark imaginings and alarming comparisons. 'One word more,' he wrote in *Horizon* in March 1940, 'we owe an explanation to those who have commented on our courage in appearing at the present time. This is undeserved, for no courage is required to perform with greater intensity in a crisis a series of actions which would be pleasurable on any occasion, and we betray no more fortitude in bringing out this magazine than does a condemned criminal on his last morning, who, after enjoying a large breakfast, falls asleep, and dreams of a reprieve.' After these words, which are scarcely like the blast of a trumpet, he goes on to say that '*Horizon* receives between two hundred and three hundred contributions a month. By now a thousand have been submitted of which nine hundred have no bearing on the war, while the remaining hundred are either Communist, Pacifist, or Defeatist. No contributor has yet expressed a wish to defeat the Germans. . . . These generalisations apply only to our contributors, and have no bearing on the feelings of the country as a whole. . . . The intelligentsia are confused and muddled.'

Even so, these lukewarm and frightened progressives were thought by some of their fellows actually to be too British in outlook. In March 1940, one Howard Evans wrote after the Soviet invasion of Finland: 'If what I have said is anything like a correct description of the political outlook of a large section of the intellectuals, their righteous fury over Finland is not surprising. They have always refused to accept the fundamentally reactionary role and calculated war-mongering policy of British Imperialism. . . .' That influential section of progressives whom Howard Evans represented, after clamouring for years for active resistance to Hitler, now proclaimed the war to be yet another example of British aggression. Some of them, many years later, were revealed to be spies. But even those who could not be suspected of treachery said and did little to help the fight against Nazism which they had hitherto consistently demanded. When Hitler's ally invaded Finland, they were indignant that the action was condemned by British public opinion and Government alike. 'People screamed,' said Evans in *Horizon*, 'when Stalin, in order to prevent the war of Chamberlain's dreams (and plans), signed the non-aggression pact with Germany. Therefore they scream when, in order to frustrate the new Imperialist plans for switching the war, the Red Army advances against the government of Ryti and Mannerheim, which they have suddenly discovered to be democratic and supported by the entire Finnish people – as if any democratic government would have refused the Soviet terms.'

But elsewhere protests against the disappearance of Auden, whose importance in this connection is that he was the most socially relevant of living dramatists, continued to be heard. They came, however, from ordinary people and ordinary play-goers, not, except with a few exceptions, from intellectuals. The poet Louis

Macneice condemned all the fuss that was being made. 'Why bother?' he asked in *Horizon* in July 1940. 'The explanation [Auden] gave me seems reasonable enough – that an artist ought either to live where he has live roots or where he has no roots at all; that in England today the artist feels essentially lonely, twisted in dying roots, always in opposition to a group; that in America he is just as lonely, but so, says Auden, is everybody else; and with 140 million lonelies milling round him he need not waste his time either in conforming or rebelling . . . he can work better (in America) than in Europe, and that is all there is to it.'

Not all intellectuals, however, shared Macneice's view. Connolly, unlike Auden and Macneice, was troubled in conscience, and in July 1940, published an impassioned *Letter from a Soldier*, who was in fact Goronwy Rees. Rees, forty years later, died in mysterious circumstances. On hearing that Sir Anthony Blunt had been revealed as a Soviet spy, he fell into a coma, which lasted for six weeks. He died without coming out of it. But in 1940 he wrote in *Horizon*, 'Do not be surprised if the artist is without honour. For God's sake, never complain, as I have seen *Horizon* complain, that the artist does not receive his due from society. Why should he? For on his part he acknowledges none.'

Auden's work did not mean a lot to ordinary people. But it meant a great deal to serious students of the drama who were his contemporaries, and it became of extreme and widespread interest when the whole theatre took a turn to the Left in the 1950s. It was then that the demand began to be heard that drama should have immediate social relevance. It was then too that the revisionist school of history came into existence. Questions presented themselves which, in the instant excitement and peril of war, could get no popular hearing. Perhaps it was not until the 1980s, when a generation was in authority that had not been born at the time of Auden's departure, that the attitude to it generally showed signs of changing. Was it, after all, right for Auden to leave Britain? Was our entry into the war against Hitler a mistake? Was Chamberlain right, and Churchill wrong? Is patriotism an evil thing? Is anarchy or authoritarianism more laudable than parliamentary democracy? The answers offered to these questions became less and less certain as the years went by.

In 1940, when Britain was hourly expecting invasion, the vast majority of the nation had no doubt about them at all. It was afraid, and it wanted its fear either to be removed, or to be exorcised. Actually, at that time, there was only one thing powerful and courageous enough to stand between ourselves and surrender. That was the voice of Winston Churchill. No one who did not hear Churchill's speech about fighting on the beaches and the landing grounds can imagine the tremendous effect which it had on the morale of the British people. The spirit of the nation was transformed in the space of ten minutes by a couple of hundred words coming out of the radio. But, though inevitably on a much smaller scale, one night in June 1940, simultaneously with the collapse of France, inspiration of the same quality was to be found in the tiny Neighbourhood Theatre in Notting Hill Gate. It came from a play written by an American, and played by British actors. Its name was *Thunder Rock*.

I remember vividly that at the first performance the few people that the theatre would hold filed into it in a mood of utter despondency. No one smiled, nor did they talk to each other. For once in my life I found nothing to say even to my wife. The news of the day, news of defeat and flight, made many of us think that *Thunder Rock* would be one of the last plays we should ever see, for invasion was expected at any moment, and Churchill's magnificent rhetoric, though it had heartened us to the thought of resistance, did not really give much hope of victory. It was like the sound of a trumpet, but its keynote was 'We will never surrender', not 'We shall win'. When Ivor Novello, the infinitely handsome Novello, sat down in the middle of the hall, as one of the audience, his face was like a death-mask. Neither he nor anyone else in the handful of people that the Neighbourhood Theatre could pack into the small space at its disposal could guess, when the curtain rose, that they were going to experience one of the greatest evenings of their theatrical life, one of the greatest evenings, I should say, in the entire history of the theatre. It clothed a frightened audience with courage; and with hope, too.

One of the remarkable things about this heroic achievement is that the play had no obvious relevance to the events that were alarming us. It made no reference to the war, and it made no mention of England. The action was not only set in the middle of the Continent of North America, which seemed idyllically remote from the turmoil of Europe, but it took place on a small rock in the middle of a lake in the middle of America, so that it seemed remote even from America itself; and, to increase the sense of remoteness almost to the limit, the action chiefly never takes place at all, since it happens only in the thought of a newspaper correspondent who is well on the way to becoming a novelist.

Thunder Rock was thus a fantasy; but it was, on that alarming June evening, a fantasy that, supported by the brooding and at first desolate performance of Michael Redgrave, set up a feeling of extraordinary tension. The resolution of this tension lifted the hearts of the audience as we are told Montgomery's address to the troops before the battle of El Alamein lifted the hearts of the Eighth Army. We were, after all, troops ourselves; and we expected the battle to begin at any moment. We were untrained, unprepared, and disorientated by the prospect of something the like of which had not occurred in Britain since the days of William the Conqueror. Nor did the fact that Conqueror had been the title that William's invasion had won him do much to cheer us up.

There was no change of scene in *Thunder Rock* to divert the eye. The appeal was purely to the intellect and the imagination. Charleston, the lighthouse keeper on Thunder Rock, where a wreck, with the loss of all hands, had occurred ninety years before, is a young American journalist who has lost faith in life and the universe as a result of the events of the last ten years, and has sought refuge from the world in this place of isolation. He was played by Redgrave. His friend Streeter reproaches him for his lack of faith; Streeter himself, equally disillusioned, is determined to get into, not out of, the tumult of the world's chaos, and is on the point of joining the Chinese air force.

Michael Redgrave in Robert Ardrey's Thunder Rock *(1940) at the Neighbourhood Theatre, Notting Hill, London*

Charleston refuses all consolations, resists all urges. The impregnability of his pessimism is not to be broken. He will read no newspapers, listen to no radio bulletins. He can find a semblance of peace only in the pretence that he has surrounded himself with a barrier of silence. He cannot attain to ignorance of the world, but he does his best to ignore it. The great merit of this part of the play, dominated by Redgrave's imposing presence and handsome melancholy, set off by the lighter spirit of Robert Sansom's Streeter, is that it establishes Charleston as a man who cares profoundly for the things he talks about.

The second act repeats a technical experiment that J. B. Priestley effected in *Dangerous Corner* (1932). Roughly ten minutes of that piece was a repetition with very slight differences of an incident that had already been presented in an earlier act. Anthony Armstrong, in *Ten Minute Alibi* (1933) emulated Priestley's accomplishment, and so does Ardrey in *Thunder Rock*. He peoples his stage with half a dozen characters, living only in the imagination, who had perished in the wreck that had occurred nearly a hundred years before; then, when Charleston realises that he has interpreted their characters wrongly, the scene is repeated so that justice may be done. Charleston finds them all honest, sincere people, yearning for progress and improvement. The feminist longs for the rights of women, the doctor for the success of his experiments, and the poor emigrant for the education of his children.

Every one of them has lost heart, and is convinced that his cause can never triumph. It is Charleston's difficult task to convince them that their pessimism is unfounded, because today all those things of which they despaired have been accomplished. And it is then that he realises the corollary to his own situation, and hope for the world's future is renewed in his heart. Redgrave made of this renewal of confidence an inspiring and magnificent thing, and tremendously did the audience respond to it. I looked again at Ivor Novello, who was sitting just behind me. The haunted look had departed from his face, and his dark, splendid profile, which turned so many thousands of female hearts, was once again serene and Italianate of the great age. Our own faces, too, though without Novello's surpassing beauty, were released from anxiety, and our hearts were made light.

So great was the dramatic power of this part of the play that its lack of logic was easily overlooked. For it was a flaw in Ardrey's argument that even the accomplishment of the ship's passengers' desires has still left the earth only in the state described in the first act of Charleston's distress, so that he establishes the reality of progress only in the process of explaining that to him it does not mean anything. But this did not occur to us as at the end we walked out into the summer night. All we were conscious of was that a hopeless cause might nevertheless still be won. It was not till long afterwards that the theatre, and the sections of society who then dominated it, began to wonder whether it had been worth winning.

CHAPTER FIVE
The Serious Theatre Challenged
1939–1947

After the middle of the century entertainment in the theatre came to be despised by Auden's ardent followers. Yet in the hour of great need the brave and mighty voice of Auden encouraging us in authoritative fashion to fight Fascism to the point of death had been strangely silent in the land. Neither had he been present with us to share the danger of bombing raids, incineration of cathedrals and destruction of cities, and almost every night for several months the raging of great flames; nor had he uttered words of fire from abroad. On the other hand the providers of light relief, whose work, once physical danger was over, was to be scornfully treated, remained with us through all peril, and at the heart of explosions and ruin, continuously provided diversions from anxiety and forgetfulness of fear. Auden had prophesied that they would go on fiddling whilst Rome burned. In this he was right. This is what they honourably did.

From the point of view of the sociological historian the most interesting thing about the theatre during the war is this contrast between the courage of the frivolous and the cowardice of the serious theatre. Auden was not the only intellectual to leave London. Tyrone Guthrie transferred the Old Vic to the comparative safety of Burnley.

Thus it happened that, with the shining exception of Ardrey's *Thunder Rock*, and the performances given in it by Michael Redgrave and Robert Sansom, and until Ralph Richardson's and Laurence Olivier's brilliant Old Vic season in 1944/5, the most memorable theatrical achievements of the war years were productions which those who do not know the circumstances of the time now write off contemptuously as trivial and escapist. But those who do know those circumstances take a different view. There was, for example, the comedian Stanley Lupino. In the revue *Funny Side Up*, in the early months of 1940, Lupino was doing all the things he had done when there was no war. He sang an absurd little composition of his own, in which, without any difficulty – remember it was during the days when London was blacked out after nightfall – he persuaded the entire audience (ladies, children, and torchbearers, he called

---

Tyrone Guthrie

them) to join. He delivered an apt disquisition on the ridiculous indignity of being a baby. He presented his celebrated fantastic sketch of a French duel. But the most memorable thing in the revue was an impersonation.

In the cast was Florence Desmond, who had a notable reputation as an impersonator. In *Funny Side Up* her powers flew on a strong wing. She brought Marlene Dietrich and Lionel Barrymore from across the Atlantic as easily as Alice Delysia from the adjoining Criterion. Yet her most effective turn was a straight song called 'Lady in Waiting', in which a girl left out at a dance began by praying for a Tyrone Power or a Charles Boyer, but ended up by being ready to make do with the less romantic figure of an Air Raid Warden. The impersonation which I so vividly remember was not hers, though she had a part in it: it was Lupino's impression of George Robey singing 'If You Were the Only Girl in the World' from the *The Byng Boys* twenty-four years before. Florence Desmond joined him in the part then taken by Violet Loraine. Lupino made up astonishingly like Robey – he had the same tiny clerical hat, the same arched eyebrows, the same juvenile costume almost bursting at the seams, the same air of being a cross between an overgrown schoolboy and a moonstruck yokel.

Whether he had the same voice we did not discover, for he did not sing. He left that to Desmond. Whilst she propelled over the footlights the full-throated sentimentality of the familiar song, Lupino just stared out of the lime-pierced darkness of the stage over the heads of the stalls at a point somewhere between the dress circle and the gallery. He did not blink an eyelid, nor move a muscle. He was like a man transformed into ludicrously coloured stone, or fantastically bewitched. If he had taken his cue with the full intention of singing, and then, as the waves of music washed round him he had caught a sudden vision of the years of folly and crime, cruelty and indecision which had bridged the two renderings of the same song, from one war to another war, in this way, and no other, his lips would have been abashed. A mere trifle, no doubt: but a trifle which showed that we were at the beginning of no mean struggle.

Funny Side Up was produced in January 1940. That was while the phoney war was still on. We were expecting bombs to fall, but they had not yet actually done so. When, however, in the spring of that year the Germans captured the Channel ports, the temper of the London stage was modified for some time. Many old plays came off, and few new plays were put on. 'By nights', I wrote at the time, 'there is heard another noise than the noise of theatrical applause. We may come to know it better, and at closer quarters, before long.'

We did come to know it better and at much closer quarters; London was set alight by things other than fine performances and memorable plays. In that great danger, in that supreme testing of the steadiness of nerves and courage, the theatre of entertainment continued to outshine the theatre of high intellect which despised it. In July 1940, I went to the hundredth performance of a revue called *New Faces*. This was at a time when there were nightly air raids. I was no fonder of bombs than anyone else, and I never afterwards forgot how for a couple of hours in this frivolous entertainment a young actress called Judy Campbell, new to London, lifted the fear out of my heart and out of the hearts of the four or five hundred other people in the audience. So enormous was its effect that it produced in me a state of exaltation that I could express only in prose that bordered on hysteria. 'The orchestra broke into that nostalgic tune just as I slipped into my seat; and, almost before I had settled down, the young actress swept across the stage in the white cloud of her familiar ball dress, followed by the puzzled gaze of an astonished taxi-driver. This actor had, of couse, seen it a hundred times before; he knew as well as I did [I had been present on the first night] the exact moment at which she would clasp her hands together in an ecstasy of excitement; how she would start and turn and pause to the beat of the sentimental music; how the white gleam of her dancing dress as it swirled and swung and flashed before our eyes would light up the gloom of the stage-set London square; and what amazing pressure of recollected happiness she would put into her agreeable, husky voice, as she sang, with puckered face, the words now so familiar to all three of us, taxi-driver, singer and me:

I may be right, I may be wrong,
But I'm perfectly willing to swear,
That when you turned and smiled at me,
A nightingale sang in Berkeley Square.

Admirable actor that he was, the taxi driver showed no awareness of having seen and heard all this before. To a taxi driver, a young girl in evening dress, dancing and wearing a long white scarf in a London public street in the dusky twilight, simply must be a surprising sight: and on that hundredth evening he was as surprised as on the first night. Was this all acting? Perhaps not; for I am no actor, and the small enchantment of that song entranced me as surely as the first time I heard it.'

I have copied out almost word for word what I wrote about Judy Campbell and the nightingale in the spring and early summer of 1940, when the bombs were falling all round us almost every night. It was very bad writing, overwrought and excessively emotional. But this very badness, this hysteria, is in itself a tribute to what light entertainment accomplished for London in the days when London was afraid. What we did not get from Auden, we got from Judy Campbell.

A time came near the end of the war when for a brief period the terror of London grew even greater than it had been in the days when we feared invasion. My feeling at the time of the buzz-bombs is that the nerve of London's population came very near to breaking. These bombs looked like small aeroplanes, but they had no pilot. They were automatic, and when they reached the London area their engine cut out, the aeroplane dived to the earth, and when it reached it the bomb that it contained exploded. The momentary silence between the cut-out and the explosion was very alarming indeed, and the relief caused by the explosion showing that the bomb had not hit you was tempered by shame that you were actually glad that it had probably hit someone else.

Many people who had taken the ordinary bombs of 1940 and 1941 fairly calmly were desperately frightened by this new form of automatic warfare. They fled from London in considerable numbers. Once again the intellectual theatre failed the test imposed on it. The most serious modern play in London when the unfamiliar form of attack began was Robert Sherwood's *There Shall Be No Night*, and it closed down very quickly. The frivolous theatre on the other hand continued unperturbed. Ralph Lynn furnished a remarkable instance of this. He not only took the risk of appearing at a time when buzz-bombs were always a potential danger, but on one memorable occasion he continued his performance impeccably as a bomb was heard approaching the theatre. Now in such circumstances his own particular kind of performance was one which it was very difficult to give, for he was Britain's best 'silly ass' type of comedian, continually flustered, his eye-glass perpetually falling out, constantly flummoxed by life, but always at the last moment extricating himself from some outrageous situation with a cheerful smile and optimististically protruding teeth.

The difficulty was, of course, that eye-glass. It apparently fell at random. But in reality, amidst his nods, his glassy smile, his jerky movements, his nervous restlessness, his amiable mental vacuity, and a self-satisfaction that easily degenerated into terror-stricken apprehension – all these things, of course, being carefully calculated parts of his acting, and not in the least real – amidst all this complicated structure of apparent disorganization, the eye-glass had to fall exactly at a premeditated moment, on precisely the right syllable of the right word chosen by his author, the great Ben Travers, or the comic effect would have been lost. Everything depended on the most exact timing in what appeared to be utter disorder. This was difficult to ensure even in the most normal conditions. But with a bomb approaching it verged on the heroic. One night in 1944 he leaned nonchalantly against a mantelpiece in the farce *Is Your Honeymoon Really Necessary?* A buzz-bomb could be heard in the distance, the noise of its approach grew louder and louder, and the audience sat petrified in its seats, till the bomb passed right over the theatre and then exploded some distance away. All that time, whilst our hearts were beating faster and faster, Lynn continued his customary performance as though nothing outside the theatre could be heard, as though bombs were mere figments of the imagination, and at the precise and proper moment the eyeglass fell, not a moment too soon, not a moment too late. A trivial incident, no doubt; but encouraging to a people in danger, all the same.

The audible approach of an automatic bomb and the uncertainty of where it would fall were undoubtedly disturbing phenomena in a theatre whilst a performance was in progress. Nevertheless 1944 and the first part of 1945 when London ran this danger was in some ways a curiously carefree period. There was

---

Judy Campbell singing 'A Nightingale Sang in Berkeley Square' from New Faces *(1940) at the Comedy Theatre, London.*

Is Your Honeymoon Really Necessary? *(1944) at the Duke of York's Theatre, London, with (left to right) Vernon Kelso, Enid Stamp-Taylor, Judith Rogers and Ralph Lynn.*

no anxiety about the future, simply because there might be no future. Twice a week throughout the buzz-bomb period I drove from my home in the eastern part of London, through blacked-out streets, to broadcast to the United States at two o'clock in the morning. Occasionally the sound of a bursting bomb would find its way on to the transmission, which in those days was always live. This would make that particular transmission more than usually successful. To sit in New York or Chicago and hear a bomb explode in London at the very moment you were listening was an exciting experience. It was an experience even more exciting to be within a few hundred yards of the explosion. At no time in my life have I felt so free from apprehensions of such things as normally plague one's existence – illness, financial insecurity and so on – as I was then.

It is obvious that, since the ablest intellectuals became disorientated, and actors and authors like Rattigan, Olivier, Richardson and Guinness were in the armed forces, the theatre of 1939–46 could hardly expect to be one of the great periods of dramatic history. Yet it provided two of those especial moments which, in speaking of Cardinal Newman, I have suggested are the principal rewards of theatre-going, those moments which throughout the whole course of one's life one never forgets. The first was that impersonation of George Robey by Stanley Lupino to which I have already referred. The second came in 1943 in a play called *The Young and Lovely*. It was by Hugh Burden, and was put on at the Arts Theatre with Catherine Lacey and himself in the chief parts.

Burden's great merit in this play was in a matter in which Charles Morgan, the author of *The Flashing Stream*, had for several years considered himself a master. To show men and women on the stage who are said to be in love with each other is a common enough procedure. It is something out of which the greater part of drama had up till then been made. But to make the audience actually feel the presence of love is a very different thing from merely saying it is there. It is said to have been achieved – but between men only – in the American homosexual musical *La Cage aux folles* (1983). I am not sure that Shakespeare himself, with all his divine eloquence, really makes one realize the veritable presence of passion between Romeo and Juliet. Morgan himself repeatedly drew attention to the failure of dramatists adequately to convey this emotion. He spoke of the lyric cry, but he never attained it. It was Burden's great feat to achieve it, in a play which was otherwise far from perfect.

The hero of *The Young and Lovely*, Mark Winters, has been nursed in hospital by a girl, Lucy (Catherine Lacey), who is his senior by ten years. He marries her and they settle down in a house on the borders of Essex and Suffolk. The question that Burden discussed in this play was whether their disparity in years need spoil the happiness of these people. It was a question well worth considering, for it is one that has affected the lives of millions of people since the world began, and will go on affecting them until it ends.

But the play had a weakness, which lay in the woman that Burden chose to test the strength of the Winters' marriage. Mark had previously been engaged to a young, pleasure-loving girl, Cherry, who had thrown him over because of his physical ill-health. She came down to spend a few days with the Winters, and from the outset was determined to take Mark away from Lucy. She does this because it is in her character to do so, not because – as should be the case if Burden is to stick to his theme – the difference in age between Mark and Lucy makes their marriage particularly vulnerable.

Having stated this theme, Burden then ran away from it. The question of age, which was fundamental to his subject, he made irrelevant, and yet, by repeatedly mentioning Lucy's seniority, he insisted on this irrelevance as though his treatment of it did in fact make it the bedrock of his work. And in the end in spite of this defect of technique *The Young and Lovely* uttered the lyric cry of which Morgan had spoken. In fact this happened twice, both times in the third act – plays were written in three acts in those days – once when Mark explained to the jeering Cherry the reasons for his marriage, and again, and most shatteringly, in the last words of the play, when he spoke directly to his wife. Burden uttered this magnificent cry, in a single sentence, in words of the utmost simplicity, that so long ago, though it seems like yesterday, they carried the heart by storm. Lucy asked her husband if he ever remembered that she was ten years older than he. I expected some banal denial of her fears, some few words of ineffective reassurance. But Burden made no denial at all. He replied: 'I remember it constantly, for you might die before me, and how could I live without you?' My own wife was five years older than I, and these words affected me more than any others I have ever heard in a theatre.

Meanwhile, though we did not know it at the time, Armand Salacrou in France was writing a play, *Les Nuits de la colère*, which dealt with the very question of failure of nerve that was so important to British intellectuals at the beginning of the war. The British public did not see this play until 1951, when Jean-Louis Barrault brought it to London. But its relevance to the problems that had disquieted Connolly and Rees was immediately apparent. Salacrou, with humour, sympathy, and a splendid passion, examined the differences that war reveals in men whose moral qualities seem equal in time of peace. In it Jean Desailly gave a most moving performance. Desailly was the ordinary man who is found wanting. He was badgered and reproached by the friends whose trust he had betrayed, and there was a magnificent moment when he rose out of his cringing self-contempt to make his pitiful defence. With that admirable fearlessness of rhetoric which distinguishes the French theatre from the British he said that he had wished to live like the cathedral of Chartres, serene, untroubled. 'And now', he cried bitterly, 'the cathedral is still standing. And I am wiped out – assassinated.' Here, when for a moment fear was expelled by a sudden realization of life's irony, Desailly was fine indeed. Barrault himself was admirable as the betrayed hero, and he spoke the concluding words of the play, concerning the life of honour in a time of evil, with a heart-rending quietness and simplicity. Madeleine Renaud, as the wife who loved her children more than she hated treachery, was superb.

In August 1944, the honour of the Old Vic, if not of the pre-war avant-garde, was restored. Laurence Olivier and Ralph Richardson were recalled from the Forces, and asked to become joint directors of the Old Vic, operating in the New (later the Albery) Theatre. Whilst the automatic bombs were still falling, Richardson and Olivier began a series of seasons which were the most magnificent within living memory, and whose splendour has not been rivalled since then. They both gave performances of an unrivalled panache, and in the grand manner. Richardson played Peer Gynt, Bluntschli, Uncle Vanya, Falstaff, Cyrano de Bergerac, and the mysterious Inspector Goole in J. B. Priestley's *An Inspector Calls*. Olivier appeared in parts not less illustrious – Lear, Richard III, Astrov in *Uncle Vanya*, and, most famous of all, Oedipus.

It would be wrong to suggest that these great actors, even when they were at the height of their achievement, were always on top form. Olivier appeared in a weak *School for Scandal*, in which he allowed all attention to be concentrated on

---

Ralph Richardson and Sybil Thorndike in Ibsen's Peer Gynt *(1944/5 season) with the Old Vic Company at the New (Albery) Theatre, London.*

Laurence Olivier as Shakespeare's Richard III *(above), and in Sophocles'* Oedipus *(opposite), at the Old Vic, London (1944–5 season).*

the exquisitely fragile beauty of Vivien Leigh's Lady Teazle. He himself was content to make his Sir Peter as crusted as old port, and whenever he said a good thing he smiled enchantingly. But he did not seem much interested in his part, and had little style. This Sir Peter, in his youth, could never have made a leg, nor quizzed a beauty; even had the years permitted, it is hard to imagine his ever having been witty with Rochester, or gambling with Fox. Olivier stood aside, to let the big effects be made by others, especially Vivien Leigh.

But when either Richardson or Olivier really tried, the result was stupendous. To give some, even inadequate, notion of what their great performances were like at this period, Olivier's Richard III may stand as an example. From the moment when Olivier's malign hunchback first entered through a door whose lock he avariciously examined, as if to see that decency and generosity had been shut out, his performance amused, delighted, and astonished. One marked how, in that opening soliloquy, by a waving of his arms, and a swaying of his crooked body, by a mad nodding of his monstrously-nosed head, and a rapid acceleration of his speech, he created a choking, snaring forest; and further, the effect at once pitiful and revolting which he made when, in dropping on to one knee to court the Lady Anne, he fell to one side in his deformity. Yet these were merely preparations for still greater things to come.

Perhaps there is no part in English drama in which great actors have achieved such great effects by mime and gesture as that of Richard III. Booth's amusing entrance, and his kicking sword; Kemble's nerveless arm before the battle; Kean, fighting like one drunk with wounds and leaning against the side of the stage in a very miracle of grace are even now remembered; and Sir Laurence created two stage pictures worthy to be set beside them.

The first was after he had accepted the invitation of Buckingham and half a dozen seedy citizens to be king. He had been reading a prayer book in a window, and Buckingham thought him a man easy to control. But when the last citizen had departed, Richard flung the book of devotion aside, leapt from the window, gained the centre of the stage, and extended his hand for Buckingham to kiss in a gesture of royalty horribly evil, twisted and grotesque, but sickeningly powerful. The relationship between the two men changed on the instant, without a word being spoken. With one astounded look Buckingham realized that what he had thought to be a lizard was in fact a rattlesnake.

This came at the end of the first act, and Olivier finished the play on a note just as striking. There was nothing remarkable in his fighting; he left that to Kean. But after Richmond with his foot planted on his chest had spiked him on his sword, Olivier was tremendous. Convulsively freeing himself from his enemy, but still lying on his back, he performed what, in its shooting out of the legs, like the darting tongue of a viper, could only be described as a horizontal dance. It was an amazing end to a memorable evening. For nearly five years Olivier and Richardson provided us with performances as astounding as this. In the way of spectacular acting they went further than anyone had seen in the present century. And then, inexplicably, they were sacked.

No one has ever clearly understood this extraordinary action, the men chiefly concerned, Olivier and Richardson, least of all. They had intended to devote their whole careers, and their immense talents to a National Theatre formed out of the Old Vic Company. The nation itself had come to expect that the long-discussed formation of a National Theatre, originating with the Old Vic Company, would be successfully achieved by these pre-eminent actors. Not only was the work they were doing the best in London, perhaps in the world, but it was also the most popular. It was breeding new actors like the young Alec Guinness. There were long queues at the box-office. There was at the end of each performance a wild applause from younger play–goers in the gallery which anticipated the hysteria that soon afterwards greeted music hall entertainers like Danny Kaye and Frank Sinatra. Possibly this is what the Governors thought to be an unwise development. Olivier and Richardson were perhaps becoming cult figures, and the Old Vic a two-man show. The animosity to élitism was beginning, and it finally ended the hope that the Old Vic Company would evolve into a National Theatre. When the National Theatre was at last created in the early 1960s it did indeed play at the Old Vic, which had now recovered from the bomb-damage it had suffered during the war. And it was led by one of the two men here so grievously insulted: Sir Laurence Olivier. But it was not an Old Vic Company that he took with him to the Old Vic to form a National Theatre.

The fall of Richardson and Olivier formed part of a regular pattern in the unrest that followed the end of the war. Roosevelt had already gone; Churchill had been dismissed by those he had saved; Hitler had killed himself, and Mussolini had been hanged. Stalin alone remained, a figure we had during the war been taught to love and worship, a miseducation for which we have been paying ever since. There was no confidence in the country, even though the Labour Prime Minister, Clement Attlee, was admired by many of his opponents. When the war ended Britain's position was weak. The delicate balance of power had been upset; the USSR and the United States were both militarily stronger; our economic resources, which had been the foundation of our influence in the past, had been recklessly sacrificed in the effort to win an apparently unavoidable but certainly ruinous war; the British people were weak, dispirited, totally unlike their ancestors, and without ambition, ready to surrender anything to anybody who asked for it and looked sufficiently threatening. The only bellicosity they showed was towards their employers, attempting by ruthless strikes to destroy the enterprises by which they earned their living. One man, a former Trade Union leader, Ernest Bevin, now Foreign Secretary in the Labour Government, made valiant efforts to stay the decline, but failed.

The British theatre at this time had two main difficulties to contend with. One of them – the problem of money – it always has with it, never more than when the drama is subsidized. There was great anxiety among both managers and public about the lack of new plays and authors in London. The costs of production seemed for that time cripplingly high. Before the war a play like *French without Tears* could be put on for £1,000. It now required £3,000 a week for a play to make a handsome profit. Probably the highest receipts ever as yet taken at a London theatre were those of the American musical, *Oklahoma!* at Drury Lane. But such an event is rare, and in any case they are much below New York levels, where Tennessee Williams's *A Streetcar Named Desire* (1947) (a straight play) was drawing £6,000 a week.

In 1948 three new plays by new authors – and remember that it is new authors who were supposed to be wanted – were presented in London, all dealing with new subjects. Travers Otway's *The Hidden Years* dealt with emotional stresses in a boarding school, anticipating by thirty years Julian Mitchell's study of the same subject in *Another Country*. Peter Watling's *Rain on the Just* was about the incidence of taxation on landed estates; and Bridget Boland's *Cockpit* concerned itself with racial animosities between displaced people in Europe. *The Hidden*

Years was not well acted, but in *Rain on the Just* the young Michael Denison showed very delicately the transition from spiritual loneliness to cynicism. Almost unbelievably handsome, he gave a sensitive portrait of a man who knew when the moment had come to haul down the flag. Moreover, the play was witty.

Yet *Rain on the Just* lost £6,000, *Cockpit* £4,000 and *The Hidden Years* £3,500. An American musical, *High Button Shoes*, which some people thought better than *Oklahoma!*, was heartily booed. In these circumstances producers found it safer to present new work in small private theatres like the Neighbourhood, the Boltons, the New Lindsay and the Arts. It was at the New Boltons in 1947 that the first new wave play was produced, the first play, that is, which ran contrary to the principles and morality of the bourgeoisie. This was William Douglas Home's *Now Barabbas*, and it showed the murder of a policeman in which the author's sympathies lay with the murderer. This was in exact line with all the avant-garde drama that was to come after it; the Royal Court, the English Stage Company and their progeny all derive from it. It is to many of them an exasperating reflection.

After *High Button Shoes* the practice of booing continued, and at one time became so mindless and widespread that a light satirist against the Left – Alan Melville – whose *Top Secret* had been loudly booed, actually protested, but with very little effect. The most distinguished did not escape. Even such popular players as Ralph Richardson and Lilian Braithwaite were once booed; so was William Douglas Home's *Ambassador Extraordinary*, a plea for tolerance. But Home was subversive in days when it needed courage to be subversive; not like today, when to be subversive is merely to be self-protective. There was some talk of making booing illegal, for it was rapidly making going to a first night as disagreeable an experience as attending a football match. But booing is a perfectly legal proceeding. This had been demonstrated in 1913 when a music hall artist in the Cardiff Empire was booed by a spectator at the end of every chorus. He was thrown out of the theatre, but brought a case against the management, won it, and was awarded £50 damages.

Salacrou had recalled that Beaumarchais declined to let anyone read *The Marriage of Figaro* before it was played, on the grounds that 'A comedy is not really finished till after the first performance'. The audience, as well as the author and director, has responsibilities; and among these is that of listening to a play sympathetically until it is proved beyond all possible doubt that the sympathy is not deserved.

British audiences of the late 1940s did not show either Salacrou's generosity or his good sense. But they had a considerable influence upon me. The change of attitude which later led me to welcome Beckett and Osborne and Pinter and Duras was brought about by my reaction to the reception given to a play by an unknown author, Neville Croft. His play, *All the Year Round*, had weaknesses, yet it was beautifully acted, and also had real sensibility. It was plain both from the performance and the setting that much hard and even loving work had been put into the production. Yet from the beginning of the first performance there were cat-calls from the gallery, and at the end it was loudly and viciously booed. A dance, a warm night in spring (charming New Yorker stories are to this day frequently set on warm nights in spring), stars shining and music thrumming, an excited girl, a forceful and successful young man to be had for the taking, and another who sweeps the girl off her feet by his stammering realization of the world's wonder and promise – that was Neville Croft's best scene; and it came in the first ten minutes. After that, all admittedly was decline. There were too many Chekhovian farewells and the dialogue was so natural as sometimes to be absurd. There was no suggestion of the disturbed social conscience, the deliberate protest against the Establishment which Home had taught to the Royal Court in *Now Barabbas*. But Yvonne Mitchell was poignant and shining as the girl, and Denis Cannan, in the rapt stillness of his performance of the youth who for one evening in his life was visited by a stuttering poetry was, in the author's best scene, very fine. Booed by a mean-spirited audience *All the Year Round* was withdrawn the next evening, leaving the gallery to congratulate itself on having caused bitter pain to some admirable artists, and the rest of us to regret the blow in the face given to a new writer of potential achievement.

There was however one man who kept up his natural spirits, and refused to alter by one jot or tittle anything of his supreme satisfaction with life and with himself. In 1949, when all around him was wailing and gnashing of teeth, Shaw produced a play called *Buoyant Billions*. Critics complained that it told us where we were going wrong but failed to tell us how we might go right. In fact the only specific remedies for our present ills that I could find in it were to go to Oxford (and leave without taking a degree), and to marry for money. During the course of the evening one learnt that the Church of England was an absurd institution kept going only by its music; that Beethoven was a composer of bagatelles, which he called symphonies; that religion in England had nothing to do with marriage; that the upper classes were useless, and the lower unpleasant; and to marry for love was an ancient superstitition.

Shaw, it will be seen, hits out in all directions in *Buoyant Billions*, but he does very little apparent reconstruction. Yet his play was the most constructive thing that play–goers of the time had seen for years. For Shaw had what the world needed to make it a better place. He had good humour. He had kindliness. The London stage has often been made dreary by people who think they know exactly what it wants to be put right. Signing a pact for world peace or expropriating the exploiters are two of their most popular measures. And why not? The trouble is that the authors of the plays in question seem to have written them not out of liking for the human race, but out of a curious detestation of everyone who does not agree with them.

Now Shaw was not in the least like that. He jeered at the Church of England; he libelled Oxford; he satirized the English gentleman; he laughed at the Labour Government. But – and this is the point – he really liked all these institutions. He did not want to exterminate them, he wanted to make them better. And if he cannot make them better, if they are so incredibly stupid (and the odds are overwhelming that this is what they are) he still goes on liking them. Shaw is the least sentimental of dramatists. He does not preach brotherly love; he manifests it. This was not the specific doctrine of his play so much as the very bone and sinew of it.

The country too was in hardly better shape than the financial aspect of the London theatre. The wild enthusiasm that had greeted the election of a Labour Government after the war, and the fall of Churchill (largely due to the folly of a series of speeches he made representing the Labour Party as a sort of Gestapo, an exaggeration that lost him millions of votes) had by 1950 given way to a feeling of discontent. Rationing still continued. The brotherhood of the Labour Government had itself been broken. The austere and upright Sir Stafford Cripps turned out surprisingly to be plotting to have Bevin replace Attlee. This plot was broken by the loyalty of Bevin himself, who responded, 'What has the little man done to me?' Hugh Dalton, the Chancellor of the Exchequer, had in 1947 been forced to resign as the result of a trifling journalistic indiscretion which in later days would have aroused no comment at all. In the same year fuel supplies broke down in savage weather. There were two and a half million unemployed, and the pound had to be devalued. Nevertheless, Attlee (a man who was never ruffled) remained both calm and confident.

There were two reasons why the theatre should have remained the same. It had assets of high value. It quickly proved to be rich in actors and actresses of the first rank, and the ending of the war also finished its isolation from the theatre of other countries. Thus it was brought into creative contact with both New York and Paris.

At first even dramatists as sensible and level-headed as J. B. Priestley misjudged the situation. Since the time of Maugham the dominating force in the drama had been the author. Priestley saw the high dignity of the author being threatened by the heights of fame reached by Olivier and Richardson. It is true that both these players had appeared several times in plays of his without putting his position in danger. But the Richardson and Olivier who had played in *Bees on the Boatdeck*, *Cornelius*, and *Johnson over Jordan* were not the towering figures they had become when playing for the Old Vic. Curiously enough, Priestley does not seem to have seen where the true peril for the author was to be found. This was in the person of the director, who, after the discovery of Brecht, and the appearance of Peter Brook and Peter Hall, became the theatre's real governing force.

Meanwhile whatever touch of reality there might have been in Priestley's fears was intensified by the vast increase in the powers of Peggy Ashcroft, who appeared in *The Heiress* in 1949. In this play, adapted by Ruth and Augustus Goetz from the novel *Washington Square*, by Henry James, Peggy Ashcroft partnered Richardson and proved to be the equal of the master himself. This play was of great importance because it marked the fact that Britain now had an actress worthy of comparison with the great feminine figures of the Continental stage, Edwige Feuillère and Madeleine Renaud. In it Peggy Ashcroft showed

(Left to right) Gillian Lind, Ralph Richardson and Peggy Ashcroft in The Heiress *(1949) at the Haymarket, London.*

herself to be complete mistress of that moment of supreme emotion which had so struck Froude in the preaching of Newman.

Superficially *The Heiress* was the story of a plain girl who was jilted by a fortune-hunter, and who scornfully rejected him when he returned to her years afterwards. On that level it was no better than a hundred others. But it had a subtler interest. For the intensity of Catherine's disappointment lay in the loss, not of a lover, but of her self-respect and reasonable pride. She would have recovered from her discovery that Morris Townsend did not love her; the irreparable disaster, made so clear to her both by Morris, and still more clearly, more cruelly, more coldly by her father was that she was too plain, too dull, too stupid to be loved by any man at all. That is what withered her heart; that is what, at the end, enabled her to win her pitiful victory.

The victory was indeed pitiful, even though one could not help rejoicing at it. For *The Heiress* had yet a third aspect. At the finish Catherine does indeed re-establish her self-respect, but only because the love that might have grown full and straight in her had become a barren and fruitless thing. We longed to see Catherine triumph. But that triumph, legitimate, deserved though it was, showed all the finer parts of Catherine to be dead, and that was what lifted the play to the level of tragedy.

It was Dr Sloper, ever comparing his daughter with his brilliant lost wife, who first made Catherine see: as bitter a cure of blindness that the stage had known. Sir Ralph Richardson played Sloper very finely; he had a stiff, sarcastic deliberation that was most effective. But was the stiffness that of a ramrod or of a waxwork? Richardson most cleverly raised this question, for, when his absurd, pathetic daughter at last awakened he was no match for her at all. His intelligence, his brains, his wit were a helpless whimpering down the wind. In *The Heiress* we felt the first breath of that theatrical feminist movement which was later to become a tornado.

For Peggy Ashcroft's performance superlatives seem pale and feeble things. In her hands the tragedy of this unloved girl became one of the theatre's most moving experiences. I doubt whether any single line ever spoken on the stage drove deeper than the future Dame Peggy's when, her match-making aunt accusing her of cruelty for her determination to send the young man to the right about, she replied, 'Cruel? Of course I am cruel. I have been taught by masters.' This was the real thing, the knock-out blow; the opposition, as was said of a larger matter, was at all points defeated, and the tragedy was that the victor was defeated, too.

But though in this case women came out top, Richardson, for the men, had also his moment. In the battle of the sexes for dominance he put up a good fight. Here was a man whose wife's death in childbirth had hit him terribly hard. The main quality of Richardson's performance was wariness. This actor balanced each word carefully, as though on some invisible scales; he walked across the stage full of consciousness of the significance of each footfall, as if a wrong step might set off a land–mine. He watched every expression on the faces of those who spoke to him, quizzically, humorously, suspiciously, as though at any moment he might penetrate some concealed secret. He was not a man who had lost confidence in himself; but one who, by some terrible disaster, had lost confidence in the world, and was ever arming himself against the disaster's being repeated.

With all the capacities that might have made everyone loyal to him, he was preparing against a second betrayal. When at the end of the first scene Aunt Pennyman reminded him that his wife's death, which he could not forget, had taken place a long time ago, he replied in a voice that rang round the theatre like a silver trumpet, with the heart-rending cry, 'That is no consolation.' In that cry there echoed the sorrow of a whole world and of a whole existence, and for it there was no cure.

But besides Richardson, Olivier, and Ashcroft there was another actor who had a different but even larger public than theirs. This was Ivor Novello.

Ivor Novello in his musical King's Rhapsody *(1949) at the Palace Theatre, London.*

Novello was the last of the stage's great idols, the Rudolf Valentino of post-war London, the last promoter of impossible romantic dreams. No film star had a greater or more constant charm. He was incomparably the most popular figure in the London theatre. His unexpected death in 1951 brought sorrow to hundreds of thousands of hearts.

In the eyes of intellectuals he was anachronistic. Arthur Miller, fresh from the successes of *All My Sons* (1947) and *Death of a Salesman* (1948), remarked that since America has no kings she must write her tragedies about the lives of common men. No one in Britain really disagreed with him. The divinity of royalty was a superstition long since laid aside for new superstitions, less absurd and often more harmful. But even so the splendour and pageantry of courts, the solemn wisdom of white-bearded senators, the beauty and glamour of young princesses add notably to the scenic attractiveness of stage entertainment; and no one knew this so well, and exploited it so thoroughly or with such skill as Ivor Novello. He also, conspicuously handsome himself, saw to it that his leading ladies were not only able to act and sing, but were extremely beautiful. This was especially true of Vanessa Lee, who appeared with him in his last play, *King's Rhapsody* (1949).

King's Rhapsody gives some idea of what the great public really liked. Written and composed as well as acted by Novello, this play concerns a monarch who is involved in conflict both with his people and with his Parliament, and finishes up by abdicating in favour of his young son. In *The Apple Cart* Shaw had dealt with a theme not dissimilar to this. He too had a king who was in grave difficulties. But whereas Shaw delighted in intellect, Novello was steeped in beauty and romance. A lonely exile, the king stole unrecognized and unfriended into the vast cathedral where his son had just been crowned, and when the surging music had subsided, and the brilliantly dressed courtiers had departed, he fell in solitude upon his knees, clutching a white rose to his breast.

During the run of *King's Rhapsody* Alec Clunes, then manager of the Arts Theatre Club, offered a prize of £500 for a new play. This play was to be everything that *King's Rhapsody* was not. Clunes set out two conditions only. The winning play must be by a British writer, and – these are the vital words – it must have contemporary significance. This was the first formal introduction into the British theatre of the idea of social relevance. The English Stage Company, the Royal Court Theatre, and George Devine are usually credited with first equating the theatre with social relevance, but this does Clunes a great wrong. Clunes's idea did not germinate at the time, though it might easily have done so, for one of the entries was John Whiting's play, *Saint's Day*. Had not *Saint's Day* been butchered by the critics (myself included) it is possible that the era of modern drama would have been anticipated by six or seven years. Actually, however, it had been anticipated already in William Douglas Home's *Now Barabbas*, as I have already mentioned.

There is one glory of the sun and another glory of the moon; and one can see at a glance that the sort of play which Clunes wanted and Douglas Home had already written was quite different from the glory of Novello and of *King's Rhapsody*. The final scene of *King's Rhapsody* gives some idea of what 'relevant' drama has released the public from; or, as many would prefer to put it, what it has deprived the public of. It was one of those one hundred per cent, uninhibited romantic extravaganzas which Novello loved. Novello was no more afraid of overdoing things than Shakespeare was, and his zest had its reward. For what seems ridiculous in description – it seemed ridiculous in cold blood even in 1949 – was quite magnificent on stage, when it was presented with Novello's dark, romantic looks and the fervour of his belief in his own creations, offset by the presence in the cast of an actress of high loveliness and talent. A friend who went with Harry Jacobsen (the accompanist of the wayward, flaxen-haired Frances Day) remarked that in the white rose scene Novello perhaps exaggerated things a little. But Jacobsen would have none of this. 'I don't care if he boils an egg in the font', he declared. The odd thing is that, Novello's magnetism being what it was, Jacobsen was right. If he really had boiled an egg in the font he would have made you think, with romantic flair and panache, that that is precisely what fonts are for.

Novello's death at the age of 58 marked the ending of the tradition of romantic flamboyance in the British theatre. The general impression of the intelligentsia was, if they thought of Novello at all, that he succeeded by giving the public what it wanted. This idea still persists, in spite of the fact that theatrical history is littered with the bankruptcies of those who have tried to find out what the public taste is, and then to satisfy it. The real reason for a career of theatrical triumph unrivalled in modern times in popular theatre (it lasted almost unbroken from his first play, *The Rat*, written in collaboration with Constance Collier in 1924, through *Downhill*, *A Symphony in Two Flats*, *Party*, *Proscenium*, and his great Drury Lane spectacles, *Glamorous Night*, *Crest of the Wave*, and *The Dancing Years*, to *King's Rhapsody* itself) was something quite different.

Though Novello acted at times (more and more rarely in his later years) in other dramatists' plays, like Max Beerbohm's *The Happy Hypocrite*, and even in *Henry V*, he preferred appearing in his own. 'I understand them better', he said when he was on tour in Sheffield. He not only understood them better, he felt them more deeply. These plays, with their lush romanticism, their susceptibility to the charm of picturesque uniforms and grandiose palaces, their lilting, swooning, sentimental tunes, combined with an unexpected licence of language in dialogue deliberately shocking to conventional feelings (Novello could do more with the word 'cow' than the Alternative Theatre can with 'cunt'), sprang from something that Novello genuinely felt in his heart. He had something to say, and he said it, which after all is what Samuel Beckett does. It may not be what Shakespeare or Racine would have said; they had never heard of Ruritania, but Novello was born there and never left it. Instead of telling the public what it wanted to hear, he found the public enormously eager to hear what he wanted to tell it. Novello may not have been the greatest of artists; but his way of working was the way of working of all great artists. Peter Graves records that Caroline

Lejeune, one of the most eclectic of film critics, saw Novello only once in her life. It was a performance of *King's Rhapsody* which he gave only a few nights before he died; and she marvelled and despaired at all that she had missed.

Many things helped of course; his leading ladies; his famous profile, his dark, Italianate complexion; his technique; his easy, confident stage presence; his unswerving attention to detail; even the fact that he never married, leaving him always a delightful possibility to feminine hearts; his kindness, too, won him everywhere goodwill and liking. He was frank, he was friendly, he was godlike, and with his death the stage lost the last ornament of the world of *The Prisoner of Zenda* and *The New Arabian Nights*.

There could have hardly been a greater contrast than that between the flamboyance and romantic exuberance of Ivor Novello, and the reticence, the control, the deliberately flat language of what many people consider to be the masterpiece of English playwriting of the middle of the century. This was Terence Rattigan's *The Browning Version* (1948), with Eric Portman and Mary Ellis. Like *King's Rhapsody* in this, if in nothing else, it dealt with a downfall, the downfall of a schoolmaster, not a king. As well as wonder and delight, it also raised grave doubts in the audience. For some time we had been listening wearily to the banal, clipped, naturalistic dialogue of modern drama with impatience, and we thought that our hearts cried out for writing of courage and colour, for the evocative word, and the bannered phrase. It was one of the elements in the popularity of Novello that he gave us something approximating to, or at least thematically and scenically, suggesting these. But *The Browning Version* made us momentarily doubt (for *Look Back in Anger* was not far in the future) the necessity for this cry.

There was not in it a single sentence that would in itself surpass the emotional level of a railway time-table. There was hardly a word that would be out of place in giving an order for a pound of vegetables. Yet such was Rattigan's craftsmanship, and so fine was the quality of his feeling for an unloved, middle-aged schoolmaster compelled by heart weakness to abandon an already failing career, that when Eric Portman asked the solitary schoolboy who had thought fit to give him a parting gift to pour out a dose of medicine to cover his emotion, the audience could not restrain its tears; and when his wife cruelly remarked that the gift was not a sign of affection or respect but merely a piece of astute policy to get a higher mark in an examination, a visible thrill ran through it. At that moment Portman hesitated whilst polishing his glasses. The action was barely perceptible, but Portman made it show how the whole pride of a man's life can be killed by one blow. It is significant of the richness of the play that in the National Theatre's revival more than thirty years later Geraldine McEwan showed what on the first night in 1948 we would never have thought possible; that the schoolmaster's wife, whom Mary Ellis had represented as being so hateful could, in fact, be played as a figure deserving pity and sympathy. For was not she too entitled to the bitterness of disappointment at finding that the husband whom she had expected to be splendid and impressive should turn out to be drab, undistinguished and professionally despised?

After *The Browning Version* Rattigan, so skilful in dealing with the educated and prosperous middle classes, seems himself to have felt that even his type of drama, so consummate in its way, needed lifting to a more exalted plane. Therefore, like Shakespeare and Novello, he turned to royalty: and in a sense to the failure of royalty. Both Novello and Shakespeare were chiefly concerned with royalty's collapse; not so much in the reasons why this collapse came about as in how their kings and princes behaved after they had fallen. All the great speeches in *Richard II* are lamentations for glory departed, not an explanation of the method of that departure; nor was Novello anything like as interested in the causes of his king's downfall as in the opportunity it gave him to listen to the pealing organ and clutch that white rose to his breast.

Rattigan, however, in *Adventure Story* (1949), drove more deeply into the causes of failure, and asked a question, prophetically, we have ourselves become sadly familiar with as the century has worn on. As British football followers in the 1970s and 1980s became hooligans; as the Empire disintegrated, and countries that had formerly admired now began openly to despise us; as unemployment, greed, and social envy and hatred increased; as the suppression of excellence became the declared aim of potential governments the question was asked over and over again, 'Where did it all go wrong?' And that same question troubled Rattigan's Alexander more than two thousand years ago.

In *Britannicus* Racine marked the exact moment when Nero changed from good to evil. Rattigan's *Adventure Story* attempted no such precision. Alexander, when we meet him first as the young, impetuous, cheerful boy storming the oracle at Delphi, was a Malcolm, unmoved by women and indifferent to wine; but the conqueror plunging into India is a Macbeth, luxurious in the Shakespearean sense, and a drunkard. Yet the moment when Alexander passes from one phase into the other is nowhere indicated.

Perhaps in this want of precision Rattigan was right, and Racine wrong. Perhaps there never is a single crisis of change. The process of transformation from good to evil, or from evil to good is more gradual. The theme that underlies the murders, poisons, and intrigues, as well as the lovely interludes of affection and friendship, in *Adventure Story* struck us even at the time of its first presentation as coming nearer to our own distresses (small as they were then in comparison with what they were to become later) than any mere tale about a successful conqueror. Across the gulf of twenty-two hundred years it breathed a message as poetically beautiful as it is politically sad.

Great is truth and shall prevail when no one cares if it prevails or not, said Patmore bitterly. *Adventure Story* is not at all a bitter play, but the upshot of it is that when truth prevails it has already become a lie. Alexander, as most people in some measure do, desired peace. But peace cannot be maintained without power, even without absolute power. But all power corrupts, and absolute power corrupts absolutely. The fact that the hero of this play changed from a frank and open boy into a crafty lecher had no particular importance in itself. The tragedy is that the very means by which an ideal triumphs distorts its nature. At the beginning of the war of 1939–46 the British destruction of Dresden by saturation bombing and the American atom-bombing of Hiroshima would both have seemed crimes of which neither nation was capable.

Unfortunately *Adventure Story* was not an outstanding success. It did not entirely convince audiences of its reality. The theatre is more exacting than history, and the fact that something has actually happened (most of *Adventure Story* is to be found in Plutarch) does not necessarily make us believe it when we see it on the stage. When urged to surprise the Persians by a night attack Alexander's 'I will not steal a victory' no doubt greatly moved his hearers, gathered together in the midst of enemies, many hundreds of miles from home. But as Paul Scofield spoke it, it seemed a piece of cheap rhetoric. If Rattigan had invented the incident he would have made it, by proper building up, much more effective. Were it not true, he would have made it truer.

His invented scenes were in fact very fine. The play had some splendid things in it. The last interview between Alexander and the suspected traitor Philotas owed nothing to Plutarch or to history, and it was extraordinarily moving, Robert Flemyng's Philotas, which at this moment of supreme trial united sensuality with a rough and uncompromising honesty, deeply stirred the audience. Again, the episodes of Alexander's beautiful courtesy to the Queen Mother of Persia were exquisitely done, a great deal in them being due to Gwen Ffrangcon-Davies's sadly serene performance. But Paul Scofield's Alexander, which had been eagerly awaited, though controlled, intense and tragic, was without magic.

That was a great pity, and in its consequences momentous both to Rattigan and to British drama. There was then a race of critics in possession, men of keen appreciation of theatre, and integrity of character, who rejected Rattigan's serious plays and rejoiced in his lighter work, in *French without Tears* (1936), *While the Sun Shines* (1943), and *Flare Path* (1942), which had already come, and *Separate Tables*, which was to be seen in 1954. But in the course of time these critics one by one disappeared, and Rattigan in his lighter mood was left with few or no supporters. A new set of people, demanding a sense of social obligation which Rattigan's comedies lacked, occupied the chairs of authority. They were unaware of his serious work, and they despised him with a scorn almost incredible in its ferocity. This broke his spirit and deprived the British theatre of much gaiety and happiness.

But a few years were still to elapse before the social impact of plays became the primary concern of critics, and theatrically speaking they were years of great splendour. Arthur Miller, about the time of *King's Rhapsody*, had said that America, having no royalty, must find its tragic heroes amongst common men. That this could be done he proved conclusively in *Death of a Salesman*, which was presented in London in 1948. It had in London a very different presentation from that which it had in the United States, a difference which, though no one guessed it at the time, had some bearing on Alexander's question of 'Where did it all go wrong?' America was the most powerful nation in the world. She had a force, a strength, an energy that Britain lacked; and this was sharply illustrated by the different interpretations of the principal part given by Lee J. Cobb in New York and by Paul Muni in London.

Willy Loman, 63 years old, is a travelling salesman who has always believed that success comes to the biggest talker, the loudest laugher, the most aggressive personality. In the last twenty-four hours of his life, weary, discouraged, sacked, he wildly, feverishly, in bursts equally of rage and frustrated affection, tried to preserve the shams and illusions with which he had attempted to comfort himself from the attacks of his elder son, who was impelled half by maddened love and half by a deep-seated resentment to tear them away. Before the final suicide there flitted through Loman's brain many scenes from the past; his skylarking with his son in the garden; his quarrels with his neighbour, his only friend; his disappointment when one of his sons failed in his examinations; and his bitter humiliation when that same son discovered him committing adultery in a hotel in Boston.

In the show-off side to Loman's character Cobb was not rivalled by Muni. Muni had a pathos, a resignation to defeat, a want of confidence that were not to be found in Cobb. Cobb carried inside him a dynamo of energy that made him spring across the stage like an athlete, while Muni either shuffled or staggered like a drunken man. Cobb slapped men on the back and women on the bottom as if he were going to propel them over the top of the Empire State Building, while Muni was half-hearted and shamefaced about it. When Cobb says that the secret of success is to be not liked, but well-liked, the zest of a man who has penetrated the ultimate mysteries rang in his voice, whereas Muni hesitated and stammered. Now both Muni and Cobb were Americans. What is significant is that the one kind of performance was accepted in London and the other in New York.

The American energy of Lee J. Cobb's acting was also shown in the enterprise of an American dramatist, Tennessee Williams, who, until 1949, was unknown in London. In *A Streetcar Named Desire* Williams explored areas of psychological pathology – hitherto virgin (if that is the right word) territory to British dramatists. The spirit of daring which he thus introduced into the London drama was in many quarters received with a venomous opposition unparalleled since Clement Scott's denunciation of Ibsen. Like *Ghosts* it was widely spoken of as 'a nasty and vulgar play', and many theatre–goers walked out of the performance in noisy disgust. Not many years later they were to walk out of *Waiting for Godot* also, but that was merely because of boredom and intellectual limitation. The reaction against *A Streetcar Named Desire* on the other hand, was sheer, half-witted, moral horror. Its leading player was Vivien Leigh, and her husband, Laurence Olivier, was driven to passionate distress by some of the epithets hurled at her by unintelligent and self-righteous commentators. Nevertheless, this play, which London saw, was as challenging in a stimulating sense, as Cobb's Willy Loman, which it had not seen.

It was the story of a woman, otherwise irreproachable whose sexual nature was, against the strivings of better things in her, rendered so uncontrollable by circumstances that she ended in madness. Far from being morally repugnant, it was strictly moral. There were some people who recognized (and said so at the time) that *A Streetcar Named Desire* adhered rigidly to the proposition that the wages of sin is spiritual death. But their voices were drowned by the unctuous screams of the excessively virtuous. In vain it was pointed out that it is no good saying that characters in many ways resembling Blanche du Bois are never suggested upon the stage. It was Tennessee Williams's frank and honest way of looking at Blanche, of admitting and stressing her abnormality, of setting forth its consequences that was new. In musical comedies and farces girls like Blanche were common enough; only they ended, not in an asylum, but in sables and Park Lane.

The play had moments of great tenderness. Williams, it is true, looked at Blanche with inflexible judgement, but also with human pity, and he legitimately found in her story, despite the opprobrium with which it was widely received, many things to look upon with happiness and a mind at peace. Driven out of her home town in poverty, Blanche came to her sister's slum tenement in New Orleans, and met with suspicion and hostility. At the close of the third scene of the opening act Harold Mitchell, the best of her blustering, filthy-tempered brother-in-law's poker-playing friends, offered to light her cigarette. It was the tiniest thing in the world, the commonest courtesy; it was also the first kindness shown to Blanche since the curtain rose, and she almost broke down. Anyone who could watch this scene unmoved (and many, I suppose, did) must have been as insensitive as he was prejudiced. Vivien Leigh's performance had a score of details of great pathos. Particularly heart-rending was her timid, nervous brightening at the merest suggestion of a compliment. Pale, worn-out with passion and misfortune, she drifted down her terrible path of degradation and nymphomania, except for a few moments of distracted hope, with a frightening, quiet inevitability that made her performance one of the great things in post-war London theatrical achievement. That she could give such a performance night after night in the face of ignorant and unmeasured contempt and abuse was evidence of outstanding courage.

But if America brought energy, boldness, and courage to the London stage, it also brought something else: repose. And it brought repose to a most unexpected place, the music hall. At the Palladium in 1949 Danny Kaye in vaudeville had as sensational a triumph as London has known. The brutality shown towards Vivien Leigh and Tennessee Williams became adoration where Danny Kaye was concerned, though he did not win all hearts at first sight. I was not the only person baffled by much of his performance in *New Faces*. This consisted, in a

---

Tennessee Williams's A Streetcar Named Desire *at the Aldwych Theatre, London (1949), with Vivien Leigh (top left), Renee Asherson (top right), Bonar Colleano, Lyn Evans and Theodore Bikel (bottom). (Reproduced from* The Sketch, *1949.)*

ENTER BLANCHE DU BOIS : Vivien Leigh plays the tragic ex-schoolmistress who has gone to the bad and who comes to visit her sister in New Orleans

"OH, IF HE WAS JUST ORDINARY! JUST—PLAIN—BUT GOOD AND WHOLESOME. BUT—NO—THERE'S SOMETHING DOWNRIGHT—BESTIAL—ABOUT HIM!" : Blanche complains to her sister, Stella (Renee Asherson), about Stella's husband. A scene from the first act of Tennessee Williams' play *A Streetcar Named Desire*, at the Aldwych Theatre

SENSATION of the THEATRE YEAR

Tennessee Williams' *A Streetcar Named Desire* at the Aldwych Theatre

A Streetcar Named Desire has been running for three years on Broadway, where Jessica Tandy scored a great personal success in the leading role of Blanche Du Bois, played here by Vivien Leigh. The story is sordid and violent in the extreme. Blanche Du Bois married when she was very young a youth whom she soon discovered to be a degenerate. She had been deeply in love with him and the shock started her on the downhill path. When the play opens, Blanche, past her first youth and with her looks beginning to deteriorate, comes to visit her younger sister in New Orleans. She is shocked at first by the poor tenement in which the Kowalskis live; and she is disgusted by the brutality of her brother-in-law, a Pole whom she terms a "Polack." Stanley, who resents her, soon discovers that her life has been that of a prostitute and tells his friend Mitch, who has fallen in love with her experienced although fading charms. Mitch leaves Blanche but returns to demand favours which she refuses him. Blanche's sister, Stella, is taken to hospital to have a baby. While she is there Stanley returns, drunk, to find Blanche, wearing an old ball dress and indulging in the make-believe that she is the belle of the ball. He assaults her. When Stella returns from hospital, Blanche has become insane. The authorities are summoned and a doctor and nurse come to take her to the asylum. The play ends with them leading her away, while Stanley tries to comfort his wife.

"WHY DON'T YOU WOMEN GO UP TO EUNICE'S?" : Stanley makes it plain that his wife and sister-in-law are not wanted at the poker table. Left to right are Renee Asherson as Stella; Bonar Colleano as her tough Polish husband, Stanley Kowalski; Lyn Evans as Steve Hubbel; Vivien Leigh as Blanche Du Bois; and Theodore Bikel as Pablo Gonzales large measure, of Kaye's singing in a strange gibberish in which there occasionally occurred, as if by mistake, an intelligible word or so. The hysterical exploration of the madness of sound was accompanied by appropriate gestures. Danny Kaye wildly ruffled his long, untidy hair; he jerked about the stage as if in a paralytic spasm: all the time making those queer, disturbing noises, as though he were a rabbit in agony, or – now and again, for his voice had a surprising range – a bull with the toothache. Yet right from the beginning of his act my own astonishment and incomprehension were mingled with admiration.

The enormous house was justly laid under a spell, even if it did not know what the spell was. The analysis of magic is a tricky thing, for if it can be explained it is not magic. But from the beginning it was evident that Kaye had great technical expertise. He did not sing, dance, or speak like Caruso, Astaire, or Ainley. But he did all three well. His appearance also was greatly in his favour, tall, slim, and reasonably good-looking; he was pleasant to the eye without being aggressively handsome. Thirdly, he not only had a range of voice, but of subject-matter. His scope of reference, for a music hall player, was remarkable. He satirized Stanislavsky, and had heard of Ben Jonson.

But these things were only the props and crutches of Danny Kaye as an artist. They were part of the means by which he propelled himself; but they were not what was propelled. That precisely was the unexpected thing, considering the febrile energy which he displayed. It was this sense of repose. Somewhere, in that whirling, fantastic commotion, there was a centre; and the centre was absolutely still. That it was there all the time Danny Kaye proved repeatedly when, in the flash of an eyelid, he made its influence felt right to the circumference. There were moments of utter quietness in his performance, and he could apparently induce them at will. He could pass, with a transition as sensationally swift as the vanishing of Rashleigh Osbaldistone's smile in Scott's *Rob Roy*, from a bout of frantic disturbance to so simple and true a declaration as that any artist who has once been a success is always anxious whether the success will last. 'There should not be anxiety,' he remarked, 'but there is; and there is sadness at the heart of this happiness.' For a moment the vast house was held in complete silence. For Kaye was expressing exactly its own position. It was part of a nation which had won a great victory. But already it had begun to wonder whether that victory would continue.

Then, after a moment, tensions relaxed, and there was peace. That, oddly enough for a music-hall artist, is what Danny Kaye brought. He possessed a repose so unchallengeable that he could scatter it to the winds, and yet not lose an ounce of it. He could whirl round the stage like a Dervish, uttering wild, unintelligible cries, and then, standing absolutely still, almost unbelievably relaxed, a moment later, without elaboration, almost in a whisper, he could sing some common little song like 'Cockles and mussels' that wrapped two thousand

---

Danny Kaye

people in the protective cloak of memories of times when there were no bombs, and no one sought to be better than his neighbour.

There is only one more thing to be said about Danny Kaye. Like all actors and actresses, he read all the reviews that were written about him. But unlike most of them, he forgot those that derided him, and remembered only those that were good and kind.

CHAPTER SIX
The Foreign Revelation
1947–1955

The American contribution to London theatre coincided with the stage in Britain entering into one of the brightest periods of its history. Our great actors – Gielgud, Richardson, Olivier, Ashcroft – remained at the peak of their achievement; a new author of scintillating promise, Christopher Fry, was discovered, and Eliot came back to creative drama with potentially tremendous force. In 1947 the Edinburgh Festival was founded, and for several years the Shakespeare company at Stratford (later to become the Royal Shakespeare Company, and of world-wide renown) accomplished great things. The deep emotionalism and phenomenal theatrical skill of Jean Anouilh were progressively revealed; the Renaud–Barrault company blazed a great light over our path, the Comédie-Française taught us lessons in grandeur and dignity, and after Danny Kaye, another music hall comedian and film player, Maurice Chevalier, illuminated us with the zest and joy of life.

Chevalier came to what was then the Hippodrome (the scene of some of the triumphs of Jack Buchanan, who was still with us, but alas, except in films, not dancing any more) in 1948. We had of course all heard of Chevalier's famous gaiety. But what one had never guessed from his films was something that cried and shouted itself in the theatre during every moment of his performance. There was an exuberance in Chevalier that prevented his being still even for a single second: there were springs in all his joints. Danny Kaye was equally mobile, but in his almost incessant activity there was a touch of hysteria that was lost only in his moments of repose. The activity of Chevalier was quite a different thing. In his every movement there was the sheer joy of physical action. He would suddenly stretch out his leg, with a slow, delighted deliberation, as of a man to whom the extension of a muscle is a miracle to be prolonged to the last possible moment, to be savoured to the last delicious taste; in the great swift circles in which he endlessly promenaded the stage, he would, without for an instant disturbing the rhythm of his progression, lift up his knee with the pleasure and pride of a high-stepping horse in its first run of the season. Better than the superb athletes, better than the great screen lovers did Chevalier, with apparently entire unconsciousness, express the splendour and harmless joy of the body. With his boater and his happy smile he lived in a world that knew not arthritis.

Nor perhaps grief. That perhaps was a worrying question. The joy of the body: yes, there was no doubt about that. But what about the joy of the spirit? What of the wistfulness of Danny Kaye when he wondered whether fame and success would endure? In spite of rationing (which still continued), in spite of fog, in spite of defective car batteries, life was a great, even a glorious thing, not to be surrendered without bitter struggle. But can it possibly be, to a sensitive spirit: was it even then quite as gay as Chevalier made out? 'But at my back I always hear/Time's wingéd chariot hurrying near.' The passing of time, the fading of roses have fascinated poets as they fascinated Chevalier. But whereas to Shakespeare or Landor or Marvell they caused a not unpleasing pathos, to Chevalier they were only a tremendous lark. Everything in life provoked from Chevalier the same response, a highly agreeable response. That pretty girls should one day be forty, and have double chins; that wives should deceive their husbands and not be found out; that dogs should grow old and still try to bark as they did when they were lusty young puppies: all these things brought to Chevalier's face the same bubbling smile, the smile that embraced every created thing, every imaginable incident, the smile of which we never tired.

It was a perfectly genuine smile. The proof of this is that even the fact that Chevalier was himself not so young as he had once been was to Chevalier an enormous joke. In his entire universe there seemed to be no room for tears, nothing to wail or knock the breast about. Chevalier understood women (had he not been educated by Mìstinguett?) but he would not have understood Mme de Cintre, for whom there were things she couldn't ask about – that she was afraid, for her life, to know. When Chevalier was there we stepped out of the Charing Cross Road, from amongst those thousands of hurrying, ill-dressed, unromantic figures on the pavement, and we found in the Hippodrome a world of sunshine and wine and laughter brought into being and held in shimmering existence for the space of two hours by a single gay and effervescent being, assisted only by a piano, an accompanist, and a unique talent. Eat, drink, and be merry, says Chevalier, especially be merry. He had forgotten, or so it seemed to me – he did not believe – that tomorrow we die. In private life I accepted that he was a good Catholic. But on the stage he was the happy pagan, whom the shadows had never touched.

I say that this is how Chevalier seemed to me. I am sure that that is how he appeared to his audiences, and that is why he spread around him so much joy, and healed so many sorrows. But he was deeply wounded by such a view: not of course, by statements that he added to the world's gaiety. Of that he was proud enough. But he was hurt by the suggestion that he had never known grief, and was unacquainted with sadness. He did not think of himself as pagan at all; he was, on the contrary, he said to me with emotion, deeply religious, and saturated with the Catholic faith. It was not long afterwards that Jean-Louis Barrault also said to me, '*Je suis croyant.*'

Barrault first appeared in Britain at the second Edinburgh Festival, in 1948, a Festival that was distinguished by Tyrone Guthrie's triumphant demonstration, in his thrust-stage production at the Assembly Hall of Sir David Lindsay's *The Three Estates*, that Scottish drama had had an illustrious history even before Barrie and Bridie came on the scene. At that Festival, some considerable time before the Renaud–Barrault company enchanted London first under the management of Laurence Olivier and then in Sir Peter Daubeny's illustrious World-Theatre seasons, Barrault played *Hamlet*. Now, according to what were then West End standards (which he himself did much to change by his example) Barrault was a highly incorrect actor. He used every aspect of himself instead of confining himself merely to the voice, as British actors then largely did. Like a good cricketer he played with every part of his body. Over his white, bony, Gielgudish countenance, there passed at the Lyceum, in Edinburgh, a constant succession of the major emotions – anger, terror, ecstasy, hatred, and despair; his face could be read as easily as an elementary spelling-book with letters an inch deep. His long upper lip seemed to audiences that still remembered the war to be as mobile as a flight of fighter aircraft. His wrists wreathed and writhed like the Jam Sahib's. His arms rippled like an Egyptian dancer's, and his very knee-caps were eloquent. This may sound ridiculous, but it looked sublime.

At that time (when the British theatre knew an elegance which was soon to vanish) it seemed that Barrault's style of acting would in Shaftesbury Avenue have been exquisitely painful. There some of the most admired actors, in their beautiful lounge suits or dinner jackets, used to treat the body as if *rigor mortis* had set in, and acted only with the voice, which they took care often enough to make inaudible. But in Edinburgh, where everybody, from the police busy sticking labels on cars left for a moment unattended to the crowds eating the excellent cakes of the Festival Club, was full of energy, it seemed rather refreshing, though it hardly prepared us for the revelation that the Renaud–Barrault company was to bring to London.

Yet even in Edinburgh Barrault had the defects of his qualities. Like Sir Walter Scott it was evident that he could do the 'big bow-wow' stuff yelpingly, but in execution, and also in conception, he exaggerated. Or at least so we thought. In his entertaining mime *Baptiste*, a mime in which he fell in love with a statue, and murdered an old-clothes man, he stretched his face till it nearly cracked, he leapt and cavorted, every feeling was blown up almost to caricature. We saw at once that Barrault could splash manfully at a full-size canvas, but we doubted whether he could write the Lord's Prayer on a threepenny bit. In our blindness we did not foresee the glory of his production of *Partage de midi* nor the delicacy of his *La Vie Parisienne*; we did not guess that we were in the presence of the greatest theatrical *animateur* of the age.

Indeed, as we left the theatre, we reflected that it is only a single bound from exactness into exaggeration, and that to Barrault, whom we rather patronizingly called 'a charmingly acrobatic actor', that bound was the easiest thing in the world. Exuberance was the note of all his work in Edinburgh, an exuberance devoted to subtler things than those on which Kaye and Chevalier worked, but less under control. When he said '*Mourir . . . dormir*' he breathed out such a sigh as would break the heart of a world. He clasped his friends to his bosom as if he were afraid that they would dissolve into air unless he grappled them to him. Every dramatic situation in which Hamlet found himself he rolled upon his tongue with succulent relish. It was all magnificently emphatic, and it made Barrault's visit rival Guthrie's *Three Estates* as the Festival's most successful achievement. But it left us questioning whether Barrault was a great actor, and very conscious that he was a small man. We said in a superior sort of way that Garrick was a small man, too, but guessed that his audiences forgot it. In a word, though we appreciated Barrault, we misjudged him. We thought of him only as an actor, whereas (though he is a very considerable actor) his greatness is as a *metteur en scène*. And we made the enormous, the unbelievable error of failing to recognize in his wife, Madeleine Renaud, a very great actress indeed.

But then it slowly began to dawn on the British theatre that exuberance, far from being a thing to be avoided, was one of the lessons that the French theatre had to teach us. For the classical, staid Comédie Française came to London in the same year as Barrault and Chevalier appeared in Britain. They brought *Le Misanthrope*, and lo and behold they were almost as bursting with energy as Barrault. Pierre Dux, a magnificent figure in the velvet breeches and feathered hat of a Dumas musketeer, entered with all his guns roaring. If the devil had pinched his soul while he wasn't looking, his Alceste could not have made a greater fuss than he did over a mere abstract consideration of mankind's perfidy. The sinfulness of men in general gave this Alceste a brow of thunder, and as Dux swashed and railed about the stage in only a general indignation one wondered how he could possibly work up to a climax when he should discover the particular betrayal of Célimène. But it was churlish to be afraid. The solution, when it came, was beautiful in its simplicity; and the lucid French intellect, so different from the muddier English brains, no doubt saw it from the beginning.

The first suggestion of it appeared when Philinte upbraided Alceste for his love for the frivolous and inconstant Célimène. The whirlwind of Alceste's passion dropped immediately to a calm; and it was with singular gentleness that he breathed out

> L'amour que je sens pour cette jeune veuve
> Ne ferme point mes yeux aux défauts qu'on lui treuve;
> Et je suis, pour quelque ardeur, qu'elle m'ait pu donner,
> Le premier à les voir, comme à les condamner.

And at the end, when it was found that Célimène's love for Alceste had boundaries which were very sharply defined, Dux's rage actually died away; he subsided into a broken peace; here was a disappointment too deep for jeers. If you are on top of a mountain, you cannot go higher. What you can do is to come down lower. This is what Dux beautifully did; he worked up to a diminuendo.

Annie Ducaux's Célimène, rippling high in speech that was more like the song of a bird than the ordinary locutions of society, made out of the flashing lines of Molière sounds not to be heard in any British drawing room. This accomplished and witty player made one realize that most English actresses, in their flat, realistic speech, deprive themselves of half their vocal wealth.

When the French players left us it seemed as if a light had gone out. The Old Vic failed badly with a production of Congreve's *Way of the World*. The only people in it who had music and style were Edith Evans as Lady Wishfort and Robert Eddison as Witwoud. The truth is that the temper of the age was against an adequate performance of Congreve. The stage cannot be separated from life. At a reception at the French Embassy Mlle Ducaux carried herself like one who, even in private life, was conscious of belonging to an institution of royal lineage. In great ballooned skirts she descended a wide staircase, cutting a corridor of lofty solitude as she swept by. It is of such stuff as this that the entrances of Millamant are made. 'Here she comes, i'faith, full sail, with her fan spread and her streamers out.' The only British actress I have seen walk with such regality is Judi Dench, at the royal opening of the Barbican. And even she had not the advantage of a Dior skirt, whereas Madeleine Renaud was dressed by Dior in private life, and Edwige Feuillère by Balmain.

Paris saw nothing strange in such luxury. The full-skirted style of Dior, each dress using many yards of material, led to the revival of the French textile industry, which had collapsed during the war. The success of Dior provided jobs for workers in their thousands in many parts of the world. His death in 1957 was a severe blow to the industry. The abandonment of the extravagances of *haute couture*, which revived in France after the war, despite the influence of Chanel, satisfied the consciences of egalitarians, but had to be paid for in unemployment in the textile industry.

Oddly enough, there had been one thing in the Comédie's repertoire in 1948 which I had found displeasing. Perhaps Alec Clunes saw it, and shared my sentiments, thus leading to his demand for plays of social relevance. Racine has since become my favourite French classical dramatist, but at that time his *Andromaque* roused me to unusual indignation. 'It is broadly true to say', I pontificated, 'that the average popular film assumes that the most powerful of emotions is romantic love. It is held to excuse all faults and all disloyalties. I constantly see on the screen husky young fellows practising the most disreputable tricks in order to secure the girl of his choice. This is Racine vulgarized. It is Racine without his poetry, Racine without his music, Racine without his distinction of mind, Racine without his impeccable taste. But it is Racine.

'In *Andromaque*', I went on, 'which is very typical of its author, the characters seem, in the main, to know no feeling apart from the highest intensity of human passion. Pyrrhus, the king who is in love with Andromaque, widow of Hector; Hermione, who is in love with Pyrrhus; Oreste, ambassador to Pyrrhus, who is in love with Hermione, are aware of only one emotion, dwell upon it, shout about it, argue about it, sing about it, plot about it, commit murder for it, even go mad, but never for a single instant forget it.

'Without the slightest troubling of conscience, they sacrifice to it all other obligations, all other ties, all other duties, all other loyalties. In fact, they seem to me unaware that other loyalties, other obligations, duties, or ties exist.

'The Comédie Française approached Racine's great, throbbing speeches as if they were arias. Jean Yonnel, as Oreste, pealed nobly like an organ; there were notes in his voice that made the ground shake. At the other end of the scale was Annie Ducaux's Andromaque: her voice was like the shiver of violins in a chorus of Handel's. As drama this performance may have lacked acceptable doctrine; as opera it was magnificent.'

We were soon to get doctrine in plenty to satisfy those who found Racine unacceptable.

Meanwhile, the Comédie Française and the Renaud–Barrault company between them had wakened the British theatre to a realization that a contemporary drama, as well as contemporary players, existed in France. One author in particular, Jean Anouilh, perhaps the finest theatrical writer of his time, for the space of a few splendid years figured large upon the British stage. He, too, like Racine, was absorbed by the subject of love, but with a romantic, passionate conviction, a perception of its terrors and dangers, as well as of its marvels which conquered all prejudices. His *Ardèle* was presented in Birmingham by the Birmingham Repertory Company in 1950. It seemed to me that this extraordinarily fine play had been misunderstood when produced in France itself. Unlike Chekhov, Anouilh deals much, as he did in this play, with violent melodrama. In *Ardèle* a couple of hideous hunchbacks fell in love and killed themselves, for all the world as if they had been Antony and Cleopatra, which is not at all the sort of thing that Chekhov went in for. But he is like Chekhov in that his plays call for the most subtle direction; if the balance is disturbed by so much as the push of a finger, the piece tumbles to the ground. Whether this, or something else, was the reason, French critics, whilst admitting, even enthusing over, the wit, theatrical adroitness, and poetry of *Ardèle*, were distressed by what they took to be its black pessimism, its rejection of the vital principle of life itself.

The great merit of Douglas Seale's production at Birmingham was its awareness that this pessimism and this rejection were not final. Anouilh's characters are here soaked in a stew of passion; and it makes some of them sick, or mad. Upstairs is the woman crazed for love screaming in tones that the peacock mocks; darting from bedroom to bedroom is the debased and pitiful and ridiculous old general who, by attempting a greater kindness than his nature can support, has fallen below even what it might have been; in the foreground are the flippant count and ageing countess and her absurd, embarrassed lover. In these people Anouilh dissects love, or lust, with a wit and a cruelty beyond the capacity or the desire of English dramatists.

His bewitched horror culminates in the last terrible scene – terrible in the sense in which Clytemnestra's throwing open the doors of her palace after she has murdered Agamemnon is terrible. The madwoman appears, and whimpers, shrieks, and gabbles her dreadful curse on the world's concupiscence, which makes even the flowers foul to her. If this were the summary of Anouilh's intention (as Jean-Jacques Gautier took it to be) then *Ardèle* would be a frightening, yet still memorable, experience. But it is not. Though even the young people who move through the play are tainted, there are the hunchbacks, one of whom is seen for a second only, and the other not at all. Whilst everyone else thinks, talks, dreams about and sullies love, these mis-shapen beings, whose behaviour shocks all but the count, actually feel it; and the answer to the madwoman's blasphemies, wonderfully satisfying, is the pistol shot that shows that two people, if everyone is determined to stop them from living for love, can at least die for it.

There is a long scene in the second act in which, after her relatives have abused and ridiculed the deformed Ardèle, the count talks to her more kindly through her bedroom door. For delicacy and humanity of feeling, for dramatic justness, for lightness of touch and certainty of aim this scene ranked high in the modern theatre, and Eric Porter as the count played it exquisitely. Such was the production of *Ardèle* as it was seen in Birmingham. Unhappily when it came to London with a better-known cast it was worse acted; and a fatal effort, by lengthening the intervals, to disguise the fact that it is very short for a full-length play ruined its rhythm.

The effect of Anouilh's *Eurydice* (played here as *Point of Departure*) – it came about two months after Birmingham's *Ardèle* – was equally powerful. The spirit of *Eurydice* was and is as strange as it is terrible. The play struck audiences as being as beautiful as Webster's *The White Devil*, and as frightening. (*The White Devil* by the way had recently been given the West End in a production that was both ludicrous and chaotic. A lunatic incomprehensibility pervaded the entire performance until, near the end, a young and at that time unknown actor, Patrick Macnee, brought order and beauty into the theatre by the simple enunciation and perfect timing of five short words, 'That is not true, madam.' These have remained fresh in my memory since they were uttered thirty years ago.)

Eurydice was magical; it revealed Anouilh at his highest pitch of inspiration. First, it showed Anouilh's unfailing eye for a romantic situation. A railway station, with the scream of engine whistles and the flash of carriage windows past an empty waiting room was as irresistible in Anouilh as it had been in the 1920s in Arnold Ridley's *Ghost Train*. In the first and third acts of the play the long-drawn out whine of a distant train was as heart-bursting as the wail of a violin, or, in a masterly production, the sound of a broken string can be, but rarely is, in *The Cherry Orchard*. Second, Anouilh wrote in *Eurydice* some of his finest speeches, such as that exuberant outburst of Orpheus when, in the tide of young and triumphant love, his eyes are suddenly opened to the astonishing qualities, the essential chairfulness, so to speak, of chairs; and that other in which the old and sensual and battered and defeated but very far from downhearted wandering harpist rolls his tongue over the consolations of life, the succulence of a good meal or an exciting glance from a pair of pretty eyes. (In Paris this speech always failed, but in London Hugh Griffith delivered it with such relish, with such a rich savouring of pleasure, the apotheosis of apéritifs and cheap cigars, that it was one of the evening's great successes.) As Harold Pinter wrote of Dalston Junction and Tom Stoppard of cricket bats, so did Anouilh of the French equivalent of Parker Knoll.

Anouilh (like Macnee) is also a master of the simple phrase, as when he made the mysterious M Henri look out of a window over Marseilles and say meditatively, 'It is a fine town. There aren't as many suicides in the Old Port as they say, but it is a fine town', charging a great half of his author's philosophy into a single unexpected word. That evening we were impressed by Anouilh's creative richness in character, which extended even to the presentation of two waiters, one with a suspicious moustache and the other as distinguished as a *Sociétaire* of the *Comędie Française*, who were as different from each other as Falstaff and Hamlet. And, on top of everything, there was the skill in narrative that enabled him to make altogether poignant the sad and poetic tale of a soiled, modern Eurydice, grimed by the life of a touring player, and her strolling musician Orpheus, who nearly brought her back from death, and died himself.

The tale is beautifully told, and it was beautifully acted by Dirk Bogarde and (but for her broken accent) by Mai Zetterling; Peter Ashmore modulated its production like a piece of heart-breaking music. It was the music, too, of a broken spirit. The meaning of Anouilh's play is that young, physical love is the only thing that matters, and that it is better that lovers should die than that love should become degraded. For to Anouilh life degrades inevitably; men grow foul, belching, and dirty; women become coy and floppy-chested.

With a cruelty that would be horrifying if it were not patently the manifestation of a revolted heart (as Dr Sloper's cruelty to his daughter in *The Heiress* is a reaction caused by his sorrow for his dead wife) Anouilh matched each of the three scenes of lyrical affection with one of love coarsened and defiled. The middle-aged lovers, played with bravura by Brenda de Banzie and George Hayes, and the reprehensible old father had at any rate courage and vitality; and, for this reason only, Anouilh, in love with surrender and collapse, shrank from them in a refined disgust.

The upshot of *Eurydice*, despite its beauty and its magic, was, as Gautier put it, just this: 'A la question, "Est-il possible à vivre?", il semble donc qu'Anouilh réponde, après examen, par la négative; et, convaincu de l'inefficacité de l'amour, n'aperçoive d'autre issue, pour l'homme qui se veut fidèle à ses premières exigences, que la mort.' It is easy to understand why some theatre–goers thought the play a blasphemy against life; but it was lovely just the same.

It was not altogether possible to draw the same consolation from Peter Brook's production of *Colombe*. The play, not quite so relentlessly presented in London as it had been in Paris, was as impressive as any of Anouilh's work, but in it Anouilh seemed to give way to a pessimism so black as to justify some of the criticisms usually levelled against him. It is odd also to reflect that the theatre in which audiences first encountered the work of Anouilh soon afterwards came to be dismissed as a theatre devoted to frivolity. This was a total misconception. It was in many ways a tragic theatre.

In the authoritative Paris production of *Colombe*, admirably acted by Danièle Delorme and Yves Robert, the effect of the play was of such unrelieved pessimism and bitterness that even Anouilh's most fervent admirers were disquieted. In *Colombe* Anouilh seemed to have reached the same point that Thomas Hardy got to in *Jude the Obscure*. In some episodes of *Jude the Obscure* Hardy showed an absolute determination to exclude happiness at every point, to condemn all his characters to unqualified misery. This is what Anouilh did in *Colombe*. Nothing satisfied him but the rendering of human nature in terms of contempt and dislike and bitterness. Despite the surface gaiety of the play – it was set in the backstage of a theatre, and every other line was a jest – audiences guessed from it that its author had come to hate and despise humanity.

Colombe was a shy and gentle girl whose husband, Julien, called away on his military service, tried to entrust her to the care of his mother, a prosperous and ridiculous actress, who was greatly resented as a gross caricature on Sarah Bernhardt. Julien was a stern and puritanical young man, and he solemnly warned Colombe against the temptations and wickedness of the theatre.

To the wide-eyed and shrinking girl, played in London by Claire Bloom, these warnings conveyed no meaning at all; and she opened herself to the dangers and moral obliquities that horrified her husband. Julien upbraided and reviled her in a scene of extreme emotional violence, which was made all the more remarkable in that Colombe could hardly understand a word that he was saying: his morality made no contact with her mind or conscience at any point at all.

The end of the play showed Julien and Colombe vowing to love each other for ever. This was a touch as adroit as Ayckbourn ever invented, for it turned out to be a flashback to their first meeting two years before. Its flavour, after the main part of the play had shown what eventually Julien and Colombe had come to, was bitter in the extreme. Anouilh's skill remained as great as ever, but it made many people long for the days when he had been able to write of young love without poisoning it, and to find something in human nature to like and admire.

They soon returned, for in 1953 he wrote *L'Alouette*, which was directed in London two years later by Peter Brook, with Dorothy Tutin playing Joan of Arc. Anouilh's sleight-of-hand in *L'Alouette* was miraculous, and used for purposes of joy. For he altered the ending. He finished the play, not with her burning at the stake (which he brought into an earlier scene) but with the coronation of the Dauphin, with bells pealing in triumph, for, he declared, the story of Joan is a story that has a happy ending, and all his people jumped for joy in the streets. Somehow the performance in Paris had more éclat than it had in London, and Suzanne Flon had a resounding success in the part of Joan. It seemed to me a finer and more exciting play than Shaw's *Saint Joan*, more triumphant and ecstatic.

In Paris Anouilh conducted a more or less continuous war with critics, who never came to love him as they in time learned to love Barrault. But in the early fifties even Barrault spoke of them with some lack of enthusiasm. They called his production of Albert Camus's *L'État de siège* (1948) at the Théâtre Marigny

'Existentialist'. This did not altogether please him. When I asked him why Sartre's philosophy had so great an appeal for France, he looked at me in mild astonishment. 'Has it such an appeal?' he inquired with a gentle smile.

'Well, the critics this morning all say that your own production, *L'État de siège* is existentialist', I replied.

'Ah,' exclaimed Barrault, his expression now vehemently changing, 'this play is not existentialist at all. It is full of zest for living.'

'But the critics?'

'The critics are all bourgeois,' said Barrault, dismissing them with not unfriendly contempt.

'And you? Vous êtes révolutionnaire?'

'Je suis homme libre,' said Barrault, not without pride.

It was soon after this that he achieved his great fame in Britain. In 1951 his company was presented at the St James's Theatre by Sir Laurence Olivier. It was one of the greatest services that Olivier has rendered to the British stage, though even in 1951 Barrault the actor did not immediately conquer. In *Les Fausses Confidences* he played Harlequin, and fantasticated the character so that it ceased to harmonize with the realism imposed on the other players. Nevertheless, the first two nights of his season at the St James's were memorable in the history of the British theatre. They opened our eyes to glories not yet dreamed of, and showed us the desperate power of a kind of drama which, in T. S. Eliot and Christopher Fry, we were just then trying to inaugurate in Britain.

The first revelation was Madeleine Renaud, Barrault's wife and leading lady. They had first met whilst making the film *Hélène* in the late 1930s; it was the *coup de foudre*, and they were married in 1940, when she was 40 and he 30. They have been together ever since, in triumph and in disasters that their courage has turned into more triumphs. That Monday evening in *Les Fausses Confidences* Madeleine Renaud's performance was exquisite. I have never seen the dawn of love so beautifully, so delicately portrayed as in her Araminte. The gaiety that bubbled out of her was founded on an inner radiance that illuminated the heart, and her moments of seriousness, which did not for a moment break this radiance, were enchanting. Jean Desailly's shy Dorante, too, was charming, and his startled jump backwards when he discovered that Araminte loved him, was perfectly in character with his engaging self-depreciation.

But it was the next night, the Tuesday, that the great shock, the moment on the road to Damascus, came. That night Barrault presented his consummate production of Paul Claudel's *Partage de midi*, which was partly autobiographical and had been written forty years earlier. Claudel had never before permitted it to be performed, and no one but Barrault, the irresistible and impulsive, inspired Barrault, could have persuaded him to do so then.

The case against Claudel was strong and easy to make. Here was a man who, in Gide's sneer, 'thinks he can get to heaven by Pullman,' a man who wrote interminable speeches apparently on the principle that if you never stop talking you are bound in the end to be lucky enough to say something worth hearing;

Edwige Feuillère and Jean-Louis Barrault in Paul Claudel's Partage de midi *(1951) at the Aldwych Theatre, London.*

who, when chance worked in his favour, and he came upon a burst of fine poetry, invariably followed it up with a line as flat as stale soda-water; whose sense of spiritual values was so erratic that he could permit the hero of *Partage de midi* without compunction to murder a friend as a casual step towards salvation; whose writing and construction were in fact so cloudy that we in the audience on that first night often did not know what was happening, nor why, nor even where, whether in this world or the next, or somewhere in between.

Nevertheless, the audience felt immediately that in twenty or forty years' time or so, when we came to consider the theatre since 1920, *Partage de midi* would be reckoned, along with John Gielgud's *Richard of Bordeaux*, Laurence Olivier's *Richard III*, and Ralph Richardson's *Johnson over Jordan* as one of the greatest, most exciting experiences the stage had given us.

We certainly could not deny Claudel some of the credit for this (indeed a great deal). His hero, Mesa, was called by God, and then, when he offered himself to the divine service, he was inexplicably rejected. He found himself, on the hot deck of a boat in the Indian Ocean, tempted to adultery with an attractive woman, Ysé. Few things could be more banal than Mesa's attainment of salvation by resistance to this temptation.

It was Claudel's brilliant theatrical achievement in this play, and we at once recognized that it outweighed all his shortcomings, that he sprang on us the surprise, which he made absolutely convincing, of saving Mesa, not by resisting temptation, but by falling into it. For by the agony he then suffered, the heart of Mesa, which till then had remained hard and cold, was burst open to a full realization of what love really means, the love of Christ as well as the love of men and women. About Claudel's handling of this theme in the play's later stages there was an unqualified magnificence.

The part of Ysé brought Edwige Feuillère to London. She showed herself that evening to be an actress so resplendent in her own right that she could not be fobbed off on us as some mere reincarnation of a star of the past. Her voice was miraculously soft and comforting and caressing. She wore her Edwardian costumes with the most supple grace; she apparently had the gift of being able to make her eyes swim with tears at will; at every moment she was in complete command of her performance; she could utter words as simple as 'Qu'il fait chaud' with such languor, with such a sense of voluptuous suffocation, that the air of the theatre seemed heavy with heat; and she had a gaiety which it was interesting to compare with that of Madame Renaud. It struck me that night as being less youthful than Renaud's (possibly because of the maturity of her part, for she is in fact the younger woman). Into the laughter of both actresses pain can enter. But whereas with Renaud one knew that the pain would soon pass, and the sunshine return, with Feuillère the pain was always there, though the rippling laughter hid it.

Barrault's Mesa was found puzzling by those who were convinced that God speaks only to men six feet tall and moony-eyed. Barrault did at times look very young; but to the great moments of the play, to the love scene in the second act (when his hands flickered around the body of Feuillère without ever touching it, as he poured out Claudel's great litany of passion); to his description of his divine rejection; to his final transfiguration beneath the canopy of the glittering stars of a tropic night, he rose with splendour.

It was a tremendous moment when he came to the front of the stage, backed only by the shining constellations in the black sky, and pronounced with unshakeable conviction Claudel's resounding assertion of salvation gained:

> Adieu! je t'ai vue pour la dernière fois!
> Par quelles routes longues, pénibles,
> Distants encore que ne cessant de peser
> L'un sur l'autre, allons-nous
> Mener nos âmes en travail?
> Souviens-toi, souviens-toi du signe!
> Et le mien, ce n'est pas de vains cheveux dans la tempête,

et le petit mouchoir un moment.
Mais, tous voiles dissipés, moi-même, la forte flamme fulminante,
le grand mâle dans la gloire de Dieu
L'homme dans la splendeur de l'août, l'Esprit vainquer
dans la transfiguration de Midi!

It was with this same enormous, transforming spirit of triumph and joy that *L'Alouette* had ended when it was performed in Paris. The stake set up was torn down and replaced by an altar. Everyone knelt down, Charles the about-to-be crowned king, and then the other members of the royal family. Only Joan stood erect, leaning upon her standard and smiling as she does in the paintings on church windows. The Archbishop placed the crown on Charles's head.

Triumphant organs, clamouring bells, cannon-shots, doves released, and the play of lights which threw into relief the stained glass of the windows of the cathedral – all were there as the curtain slowly fell on a picture that might have come from a Book of Hours, whilst Charles, bursting with excitement and happiness, cried out: 'La vrai fin de l'histoire de Jeanne, la vrai fin qui n'en finira plus, celle que l'on se redira toujours, quand on aura oublié ou confondu tous nos noms, ce n'est pas dans sa misère de bête traquée à Rouen, c'est l'alouette en plein ciel, c'est Jeanne à Reims dans toute sa gloire . . . La vraie fin de l'histoire de Jeanne est joyeuse. Jeanne d'Arc, c'est une histoire qui finit bien!' It was like Beethoven's Hymn of Joy.

It was not echoed in Peter Brook's London production of *L'Alouette* (1955). Brook took the play in a more serious, not to say sombre, spirit than Anouilh had done, and gave the final speech to Cauchon, the equivocal bishop of Beauvais, rather than to the mercurial Dauphin, to whom, in Anouilh's text and in the Paris performance, it was rightly given. Two things followed from this. Since Cauchon's character was doubtful, the speech took on an irony which was different from any that Anouilh might (if he intended irony at all) have wished to suggest. Cauchon, being a prince of the Church and accustomed to brooding over grave matters, spoke Anouilh's words with a somewhat depressing solemnity; whereas Michel Bouquet, playing the impressionable Dauphin, legitimately gave to them a high excitement outside the province of an exalted spiritual dignitary.

After the dismissal of Olivier and Richardson from their leadership of the Old Vic, however, the British stage might be excused some momentary lack of resilience such as Brook's in *The Lark*. For great things had been expected to flow from the united work of these actors, had it been allowed to continue. One of these was the speedy establishment of a National Theatre, which Richardson and Olivier were ready to set up. All immediate hope of that naturally vanished when they were told that their services were no longer required, and the actual establishment of a National Theatre was in consequence delayed for many years, until 1963 in fact, when Olivier directed Peter O'Toole as Hamlet at the Old Vic in its inaugural production. With Richardson and Olivier, there disappeared too, for the time being, the immediate expectation of thrilling performances of Shakespeare.

This is where the work of Anthony Quayle became of such great importance in the history of modern British theatre. Anthony Quayle is a man to whom sufficient justice has never been done. Peter Hall and Trevor Nunn have rightly become famous in the development of the Royal Shakespeare Company. It was Hall who brought that Company to the Aldwych in 1960, thus giving it a permanent London home where it could play both Shakespeare and contemporary plays; and it was Nunn who continued Hall's work at a very high standard both at the Aldwych, and when it later moved into the Barbican. What, however, is too rarely remembered is the part that Quayle, himself an excellent actor, played in this development. When Peter Hall took over the Stratford Shakespeare Company in 1956 (when it was not yet Royal), it was already a going concern, and it was entirely due to Quayle that this was so. For at the time when Shakespearean theatre was dying in London, Quayle took over the Directorship of the Stratford Memorial Theatre.

This theatre, entirely devoted to Shakespeare, had been in existence for a very long time, and it had done admirable work. But it was with Quayle's appointment in 1948 that it took on international stature. He presented or acted in (sometimes both) *Othello*, *Macbeth*, *A Midsummer Night's Dream*, *Hamlet*, *Much Ado About Nothing*, *Hamlet*, *As You Like It*, *The Taming of the Shrew*, *Titus Andronicus*, *Troilus and Cressida*, and *Richard II*. Moreover he persuaded several of Britain's most famous actors to appear in these productions. This is what gave the productions such high stature, so that when London lost Olivier and Richardson from the Old Vic, the country retained a high proportion of their Shakespearean glory at Stratford. None of this could have happened without the work of Anthony Quayle.

Quayle was not only the cause of great Shakespearean performances being given at Stratford. Inspired by a singularly questing mind he saw to it that not only was Shakespeare played memorably, but also freshly and with a new outlook. Thus, in 1951, Stratford presented Michael Redgrave in *Richard II*. Both Gielgud and Alec Guinness had played Richard in London, and it was astonishing that after both these actors had reaped the field before him, Redgrave found it possible to come home with his arms filled with sheaves that they had overlooked. It was questioned at the time whether Redgrave discovered anything so moving as Gielgud's luxuriant self-pity or Guinness's beautiful exercises in spontaneous poetry. What was striking about the performance and the production was the power of its credibility. It was more credible than any that had been seen before, and was quite new and original.

The briefest way of expressing the original quality of Redgrave's Richard is to

---

Anthony Quayle in Shakespeare's Henry VIII *(1949) at the Shakespeare Memorial Theatre, Stratford-upon-Avon.*

say that his was the only Richard Britain had seen who could conceivably have suppressed Wat Tyler's rebellion. We know that Richard as a boy did suppress this rebellion. We know also that Shakespeare did not stress this fact, which perhaps means that the actor playing Richard should also forget it. Gielgud and Guinness did forget it, but Redgrave and Quayle did not, and this is what made the production of such great importance in the development of modern theatre. It was an early example of a principle which the Royal Shakespeare Company later developed to an enormous degree, and which subsequently became a dominating factor in nearly a hundred per cent of revivals of classic plays, namely, the principle of reading beyond the text. That, in this play, meant showing the audience how the chief character could have performed feats (which we in fact know that he had performed) that so far as the surface text (the so marvellous surface text) suggests, or more than suggests, he could never have performed at all. Gielgud had offered us a Richard who would have met the rebellion with adolescent tears, Guinness a Richard who would have met it with adolescent verses. Neither of them would conceivably have been able to defeat it. But Redgrave's Richard, on the other hand, would have met and overcome it with strong adolescent nerves. And this he did most subtly.

He gave a Richard who, when the play opens, could only just dominate Bolingbroke and Mowbray, because he could only just dominate his own nerves. The subtlety was that, as the performance progressed, Richard's nerves got visibly worse, which implied that when he was younger, as at the time of Tyler's rebellion, they had been better. This actor of enormous stature, handsome and fair, lent to Richard a magnificent appearance, but the twitching fingers, the overcharged breast, the restless movements, the sudden shifting of the eye revealed at what tremendous cost of inner tension the magnificence was kept up. It was a performance intelligently keyed to a coming breakdown, and it gained in consistency and striking originality what it forfeited, no doubt deliberately, in emotional sympathy.

Quayle showed another aspect of his originality in casting against type. This again is a principle that the contemporary theatre has taken up with enthusiasm, without giving Quayle the credit for first notably showing what could be achieved with it. He first displayed it in presenting Ralph Richardson as Macbeth in the 1952 Stratford season, and in this particular instance he aroused considerable opposition. If in fact one looked in it for the obvious qualities of Macbeth, the qualities of a bold and wicked soldier miraculously endowed with poetry, one was bound to be disappointed, even though Richardson spoke much of the verse finely enough. But it is not in Sir Ralph's nature to show heroic evil, and this probably accounts for the chorus of censure that the production received from critics who did not allow sufficiently for its originality and

---

Searle cartoon of the Royal Shakespeare Company's 1951 season, reproduced from the 1952 programme of the Shakespeare Memorial Theatre, Stratford-upon-Avon.

The 1951 Season as seen by Ronald Searle in Punch

Michael Redgrave as Richard II
Harry Andrews as Bolingbroke
Hugh Griffith as John of Gaunt

Richard Burton as Henry V
Hugh Griffith as the Archbishop of Canterbury
Alan Badel as the Dauphin
Michael Gwynn as the mad King Charles of France
Richard Wordsworth as Pistol
Michael Bates as Bardolph

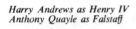

Harry Andrews as Henry IV
Anthony Quayle as Falstaff

enterprise. (Even Richardson himself does not realize the excellence of his performance.) The great actor, the *monstre sacré*, is often bad because inspiration is the foundation of his work, and inspiration is something not to be commanded. But often he is bad, or appears to be bad, because the thing that gives him his value as a creative artist, his individual view of life, is at odds with the play in which he exhibits it. This was the difficulty with Richardson's Macbeth, a difficulty which could not have arisen had not Richardson been a great artist.

Richardson, in a quiet, English way, looks at life, and like Kafka in his wilder, madder fashion, finds it incomprehensible. Behold, I show you a mystery; in Richardson's best performances there is always the note of puzzled perplexity. He knows not where we come from, nor where we are going, nor why we are here. As Bottom he had a moonstruck wonder; as Johnson, his incomprehension, till the final resolution after death, hammered on his brain agonizingly; as the bank clerk accused of murder in a play by R. C. Sherriff called *Home at Seven*, it broke against the impregnable simplicity of his character; as Dr Sloper in *The Heiress* his recoil from the senselessness of his wife's death was transmuted into a cruelty of clinical exactitude; in *Peer Gynt* in the great seasons with Olivier he circumnavigated the globe in bewilderment. In all these performances, so widely different, the Richardson universe was surrounded with a mystery which, despite the actor's prosaic appearance and his fondness for motorbikes, had the real, the rare, the rich poetic excitement.

Now between this temperament and Macbeth there is a natural discrepancy. Macbeth knew why he wanted to kill Duncan. He had met the witches; he wanted to be king; he had a very persistent wife. But Richardson's Macbeth was caught up in a murder which he did not understand; he walked about with eyes glazed, driven by unrealized forces. This is good Richardson, though it is hardly convincing Macbeth. But in the middle of the play author and actor met on common ground. There was a baffled pathos in Macbeth's wonder that it was Duncan, and not himself, who had attained to peace, and all the violent inexplicabilities of the banquet scene were superbly done. The play got better and better as it went on, a thing that rarely happens; until at the end one was bound to admit that Quayle's courage in casting against type had led to Sir Ralph's performance, though it began unsatisfactorily, giving stronger and deeper delight than the Macbeths of Michael Redgrave, Gielgud, or Alec Clunes.

In London a new star, Christopher Fry, rose brilliantly above the horizon, with his famous discovery of a kind of poetry which he permitted to be called 'sliced prose', one of those technical developments whose originality Daniel Rops said are essential to the creation of new forms of art. In *The Lady's Not for Burning* (1949) his accused witch, Jennet, spoke thus of her alleged powers:

> I burn a sprig
> Of thyme, and time returns, a little crazy,
> The worse for burial, hazily re-enacting
> The palatial past: for instance, Helen comes,

And brushing the maggots from her eyes,
Clearing her throat of several thousand years,
She says 'I loved — '; but cannot any longer
Remember names. Or Alexander, wearing
His imperial cobwebs and breastplate of shining worms,
Wakens and looks for his glasses, to find the empire
Which he knows he put beside his bed.

'Reality?' as Fry exclaimed in his preface, 'We don't perhaps, bark our shins against solid furniture as it is possible to do in many plays of our time, but even furniture has an atomic dance of its own, as true, in its way, as the solidity.'

It is no wonder that we were dazzled and delighted and excited by language such as Fry's. Listening to his play one could imagine that the aurora borealis had turned humorist. Fry jested with stardust, and was witty in blank verse. For a flashing phrase he ransacked history, literature, the natural sciences, the calendar of Christian saints, and the digestive processes; he leapt startlingly, to use his own words, from Alexander's breastplate to the backside of immortality. Yet, though he dazzled like Sir Thomas Browne, he had as many laughs in him as Ben Travers.

He was already well-known as a writer of short religious plays, and *The Lady's Not for Burning* was immersed in theology. It was fascinating, not only for itself, but because it aroused strong hopes at the time that it would eventually turn out to be the precursor of a revival in Britain both of religious and of poetic plays. Was it possible that, after all the theatre's desperate searching for survival and salvation during the twenties and thirties, now that war was over it had found an answer? Many people confidently hoped that it would be so.

Fry's tale was of a medieval village that set up a hue and cry after a witch, whom one Thomas Mendip, a discharged soldier of fortune, weary of life, tried to save by diverting the chase after himself as a supposed murderer. Many scenes in it proved to be very actable. There was a charming old chaplain, for example, to whom an old actor, Eliot Makeham, gave a nutcracker face perpetually on the grin. Always fingering his violin, with the universe just Greek to him – except that, of course he understood Greek – the breath of fifteenth-century piety and humanism blew gently through this kind old man. There was a sharp pathos in Pamela Brown's 'I am a creature of habit, and have got into the way of living', when she came to the stake, for all that the simplicity of the phrase is highly mannered.

And Gielgud's Mendip, a character in search of the gallows, dirty-gartered, half-shaved, with stubbly hair and not yet cleansed from the mud of Flanders, had many a resounding gale of rhetoric with which to make the echoes ring and sing and thunder. Too often the throat of the nightingale is allied to the brain of a baboon, but in Gielgud's performance we did not know which to admire the more – his alert, understanding mind or his superb physical endowments. Both were needed in this play, both were used, and at the end, when he walked out into the night, a free man with the unburned lady, and prayed to God to have mercy on their souls, one almost believed that these two characters, which had sometimes been only a mist of words, did have souls indeed.

A new planet had certainly swung into our ken, but somehow perhaps we wondered whether it could be inhabited. The only doubt that dampened our hopes was that Fry seemed more concerned with his amazing powers of displaying than with the nature of the goods displayed. In spite of, or even because of, the glitter of the words, one had not been greatly troubled for Jennet Jourdemayne and Thomas Mendip. Pamela Brown's curious, haunting, high-pitched voice, and her fascinating sloping face suggested something not of this world, but the play nowhere had the horrible, surging emotion of a frightened village thirsting for a cruel cure: there was no smell of faggots, and Thomas Mendip gave us rhetoric instead of love. But it was generally recognized that for those whose wit was alive and their learning not quite dead, *The Lady's Not for Burning* had provided a rare, to-be-remembered joy.

In Fry's next play, *Venus Observed*, which Laurence Olivier presented at the old St James's in 1950, the brilliance remained, and so did the questions. Olivier, with a neat, somewhat greying moustache, drew with accomplishment the portrait of a duke who, in yet another mist of shimmering words, lightly waved aside the advance of age; Denholm Elliott, with no less poise, presented the Marquis whose summer was yet to come; and Heather Stannard provoked and satisfied as the lady of their common but distinguished choice.

Then in 1951 came Fry's best play, *A Sleep of Prisoners*, a play that set doubts at rest. In *A Sleep of Prisoners* Fry asked himself a question: Must humanity go on for ever slaughtering itself, must there always be wars of independence, wars of revolution, wars of aggression, wars of defence, bloodshed and carnage to the end of time? For once the matter became of more importance than the words. The proposition, said Burke at the time of the American War of Independence, is peace. And Fry, like others but with more certainty, repeats it in *A Sleep of Prisoners*. And when Fry says peace, he means, not peace after victory, not peace next year, not peace with honour, but peace without conditions, peace now, peace absolute.

The proposition is greatly debatable; a Figure whom Fry would not reject, came to give, not peace, but a sword. But Fry does not debate, he asserts. He asserts as one having authority, not as the scribes and Pharisees. One may or may not agree with Fry's convictions. But Fry holds them with a stirring faith; and in *A Sleep of Prisoners* he made the holding of them a moving and noble experience.

The story is of four soldiers, prisoners in a bombed church in enemy territory. One of them, unable to take anything seriously, plays 'Pop goes the weasel' on the organ, and irritates the others; there is a scuffle, and the man of unseemly gaiety is nearly killed. The four men dream themselves back into the stories of the Old Testament, and Cain kills Abel before our eyes. He kills him also before the eyes of Adam, who vainly tries to intervene, but is held back by invisible hands; and his straining body, with arms outstretched, and head bent forwards,

The design by Roger Furse for Act I and Act II scene 2 of Christopher Fry's Venus Observed, *performed at the St James's Theatre, London, in 1950.*

with a harsh light blazing on him, suddenly becomes the figure of a man crucified. Not a word is spoken, but one realizes with a shock, which momentarily unseats the values by which one has judged men's strife down the ages, that every time man's blood is shed, for Fry Our Lord is crucified again. For Fry the shedding of blood is the supreme crime; there is nothing that can excuse it, not war, not even sacrifice, and when Abraham in one of the dreams lifts his knife to offer Isaac to God, his hand is seen to be bright red. In yet another of the dreams Joab staggers with the slain body of Absalom slung across his shoulders. David asks him what he is carrying, and Joab bitterly replies, 'The victory'.

The long misery of war, the repeated failures to bring about good by it, the pathetic enduring belief of men that somehow, this time if never before, its results will be what we desire, could hardly have been set forth with sharper irony than in *A Sleep of Prisoners*.

This resurgence of religion in drama, this return, as Dilys Powell had remarked in her review of *The Waste Land*, to the old values and certainties by which we once lived, was evident also in the work of other dramatists besides Fry. In 1949 T. S. Eliot had offered *The Cocktail Party* at the Edinburgh

The Very Revd Sir George MacLeod, Bart., Lord MacLeod of Fuinary addressing the Iona community just after the Second World War.

Festival, where Alec Guinness played the Unidentified Guest, and Robert Flemyng was a memorable Edward.

Sir Alec's was a major achievement in the modern British theatre. On the cold and lonely heights of Eliot's searching intellect his foot never faltered; his great triumph was the certainty with which he suggested that on the ultimate peaks there is a mystery which cannot be pierced by the keenest gaze, nor stated by the most exact definition. Euclid may contribute to, he may even preponderate in, the making of a saint; but he cannot explain how he did it.

Eliot used the utmost precision to establish the inexplicable, and in words apparently devoid of emotional overtones he asserted the transcendent merits of a useless martyrdom, involving the remotest reaches of human and divine experience in the trivial chatter induced by a dry Martini or a gin and water. No other dramatist so successfully as Eliot made the commonplace create a vision that is beyond the reach of rhetoric.

Then there came, but more questionably, Graham Greene, with *The Living Room* in 1953. What was striking about this play was that Greene, as a religious man, treated divorce seriously, with a sense of rapture and deadly peril. Yet though one admired it, there was also a feeling of regret. Its denials were a thunderous roar, its affirmations only a distant echo. Its Noes were insisted on, its Yeses scarcely heard. One could not deny that, even at its height, religion in British drama was far from the joyous certainty of the last speech in Claudel's *Partage de midi*. The admirable and inventive plays in which it found expression were written in a temper too restrained and elegant to give the conviction that they came out of their authors' guts, as the heroine of Tom Stoppard's *The Real Thing* (1982) insisted that real plays should. Whether her views on drama were sound or not, whether her theory of playwriting was or was not mistaken, Stoppard made them the subject of debate. But there is no doubt that they were, at the time of *The Cocktail Party*, beginning seriously to be considered. These English religious plays lacked the gusto which Martin Dodsworth says Hazlitt detected in Raphael and Michelangelo as the 'validating sign of genius' (*Times Literary Supplement*, December 1982). I have found the full consciousness of religious faith expressed – triumphantly – in the French theatre, and in the preaching of the Very Reverend George MacLeod, one of the few great orators of our time: but in the work of modern British dramatists, never.

CHAPTER SEVEN
The Great Uprising
1955–1968

In 1960 Anthony Quayle and Celia Johnson appeared in a play called *Chin-Chin.* Its curious title was due to the fact that its author, a Frenchman, François Billetdoux, believed that this phrase was uttered by the British every time they drank a glass of sherry. It was a religious play of a kind so rigorous that few of its few spectators realized that it was religious at all. It was a play that had ripped out the author's guts, and it had in abundance that gusto desiderated by Hazlitt. But it failed, and was derided by such theatre–goers as happened to see it. It had the same quality as Claudel, a fierce persuasion of faith, – the same quality which Fry and Eliot, to say nothing of Greene, were said, despite the best of intentions and very high talent, to be unable to convey to an audience. Why then, if it had that element whose absence was thought to have caused the rapid decline of influence in English religious drama, did it nevertheless resoundingly collapse?

The answer is that in the years between *The Cocktail Party* and *Chin-Chin* four plays had been written which so totally changed the climate of opinion that the possibilities of success for a religious play, for a play founded on the doctrines of Christianity, were slimmed down to almost nothing, even though, as in the case of William Douglas Home's *The Lord's Lieutenant*, they continued to be written with charm, wit, and theatrical finesse.

One first began clearly to realize what had happened when in 1968 the Renaud–Barrault company brought Billetdoux's *Il faut passer par les nuages* to the World Theatre season at the Aldwych. Because of then fairly recent experiences theatre–goers in Britain had become more or less expert judges of plays that affect the regeneration and salvation of society. But this very experience had made us regard plays that deal with the salvation of the individual soul as trivial, obscure, and, theatrically speaking, even downright indecent (such had been the general attitude towards *Chin-Chin*). We had got to know the people better than we knew people.

What was unfamiliar to us in *Il faut passer par les nuages* was simply the same thing as had shocked many people in *Partage de midi*, namely, that the play was

Madeleine Renaud in François Billetdoux's Il Faut passer par les nuages *(1968) at the Aldwych Theatre, London.*

involved exclusively with questions of individual behaviour, rectitude and spiritual destination. Both Billetdoux and Claudel regarded the fate of the human soul as of supreme importance. Now it is too often forgotten that what matters is never the subject discussed, but the passion, theatrical skill and grasp of mind with which the discussion is carried on. For this reason audiences were as much thrown by *Il faut passer par les nuages* as they had been by *Chin-Chin*. It required an equally drastic revision of the common point of view, and Madeleine Renaud and Jean-Louis Barrault found it as difficult to bring about this revision as had Celia Johnson and Anthony Quayle before them.

The censorship of the stage by the Lord Chamberlain was at that time on the point of being abolished, so that audiences were able to take Billetdoux's remarkably uninhibited language easily enough. With an effort we could accept that a woman who had renounced all worldly splendour should continue to be dressed by Yves St. Laurent. After all, one of the things that made Madeleine Renaud so enchanting to look at was that both on stage and off she was gowned by that eminent couturier, a fitting complement to her exquisite figure and serene smile. What was harder to believe was that the salvation of the soul of a rich woman is of such cardinal importance that it justifies the disintegration of nearly everyone around her; and hardest of all that the condition of absolute beatitude is attained only when we achieve total desertion by all our friends, and the world's reviling, cursing, persecution and scorn. That was the doctrine that Billetdoux preached in *Il faut passer par les nuages*, as he had preached it earlier in *Chin-Chin*. It is what he called optimism – *l'optimisme chrétien*.

The decisive moment in the life of the inordinately rich Claire Verduret-Balade came when to the dismay of her family, she resolved to walk, a small, resigned, unshakeably obstinate figure, in the funeral procession of her first lover, Clos-Martin, who had once been wealthy, but who had died poor and despised – that is, blessed. From time to time his spirit appeared to her, urging her to further and further renunciation. The results on the children she enriched were disastrous. Indeed, they could not be anything else, since Billetdoux believed that the possession of wealth is the beginning of damnation, and he is a strict logician. One son became a confirmed thief; another, obsessed with sex and remorse, sought a mother-figure in a middle-aged wife; a third committed suicide. Claire was stripped of all her friends, all her consolations, until at the end, surrounded by mocking and derisive figures, she stood alone but for a small child – but, we were left to understand, saved.

It was, and it still is, a hard doctrine, but Madeleine Renaud played Claire with an implacable and unsentimental sweetness, with a resolution all the stronger because it was so quiet and undemonstrative. She asked, on the part of Claire, for neither pity nor blame, because she had passed beyond these things into another universe with different values. In its immoveable peace this was a great performance.

Barrault directed the play with smooth control of all its many factors, visual and philosophical, and was himself the perfect embodiment of the haunting

Clos-Martin. Jean Desailly's Jeannet, the sex-ridden son, wiping the sweat from overheated hands even at the confessional box, was a performance that sympathized with all and extenuated nothing. It was a portrait at once piteous and pitiable. But it was all no use. Billetdoux could not convince us. We had lately been schooled to believe, or to convince ourselves and others that we believed, that a society based on the acquisition of wealth was evil; but a play that demanded the renunciation of wealth was still more than we could take.

As I say, four plays had so changed the national outlook that concern for the spiritual welfare of an individual seemed a new blasphemy. The plays in question were Bertolt Brecht's *Mother Courage* (1955), Samuel Beckett's *Waiting for Godot* (1955), John Osborne's *Look Back in Anger* (1956), and Harold Pinter's *The Birthday Party* (1958). They mark the most brilliant years of modern British drama. They transformed its nature, and made it for a time the most celebrated in the world. They set the course of the British theatre for the next quarter of a century, begat a host of inferior imitators, almost destroyed the commercial theatre, stimulated the move towards the establishment of a National Theatre, encouraged the proliferation of fringe theatres, and, though they were all extremely entertaining themselves, enabled their less talented followers to propagate the theory that entertainment in a play is a mark of mindless frivolity.

They were the watershed of modern British drama. From them all the great rivers flowed.

Their history began unpromisingly. It was started by the first production in Britain of a Brecht play. This was not unpromising in itself, for Brecht has been one of the most potent influences in drama throughout the western world. The unfortunate part is that, though *Mother Courage* was directed by Joan Littlewood for Theatre Workshop, it was not a good production. Joan Littlewood gave a colourless, indecisive, and often inaudible performance of the play in the Queen's Hall, Barnstaple. (The Queen's Hall was a most enterprising place. Barnstaple is not a large town; it is far from London; yet one week the Queen's Hall would have Joan Littlewood, and another the exuberant Billy Danvers, fresh from the race-course, in grey topper and morning coat, and beaming with happiness at audiences contented but sadly small.)

Nevertheless, even in the lamentable proceedings of that only half rehearsed first night it was evident that *Mother Courage* was a work of quality. Brutally, lewdly, heroically and humorously it showed the degraded fascination of battle, and its perverted, pervading creativeness. Brecht's famous character, who has attracted more admiration than he intended, pulls round with her through mud, blood, filth and lechery, a cart in which she sells drink to soldiers. Here of course was Brecht's famous lesson that it is the profits of war, and the dangers and miseries of others, that keep her old rags together. She has no conscience about this, but she has in its place an indomitable spirit, for, though her sons are killed, and her dumb daughter is shot, she never dreams of giving in. She fights the battle rat-like to the end. Even that disastrous night she was impressive in her excellent theatrical speech on the theme that defeat for princes does not necessarily mean disaster for their subjects; the fleas can live even if the dog dies.

It was on that June night in north Devon that audiences first made acquaintance with the celebrated doctrine of alienation. It penetrated even through the chaos of the Theatre Workshop production that Brecht wanted Mother Courage to appeal, not to our emotions, but to our understanding. This is why the actress must put us at a distance. She must never raise the question, 'Do we like Mother Courage, or do we despise her?', but only the questions, 'How did Mother Courage come to happen? What were the social conditions that produced her?' We must comprehend the social process, not pity or condemn the individual. With this theory in their hands young producers were able to undermine the supremacy of the outstanding actor or actress, and to develop to the full their own potentialities of interpretation or domination. It left no place for such characters as Celia Coplestone, or Mesa or Ysé, or Claire Verduret-Balade. It threatened the whole theatre that Fry and Eliot had set out to rejuvenate, and at the same time it made the passion and gusto of a Billetdoux seem, with its insistence on the importance of the individual, positively anti-social. An animosity sprang up against the theatre as London had known it in the late 1940s. Albert Hunt spoke with contempt of critics who 'measured the drama against a yardstick of Christopher Fry and T. S. Eliot.' 'The individual, unable to come to terms with society, unable or unwilling to place his ideals at its service, is crushed by society. And society, drained of its life-blood, slowly dies.' (*Encore*, January/February, 1960).

After Joan Littlewood, there have been innumerable Brecht productions all over Britain. Brecht has helped to mould every theatre worker, and yet no British company, not even the National Theatre with its acclaimed *Galileo*, has succeeded in giving a performance that does him justice. That is because his disciples have found it easier to assimilate some sort of comprehension of his doctrine than to display his theatrical flair. The poverty of British productions of Brecht, heavy, sententious, and void of life, was exposed by the Berliner Ensemble when it came to one of Peter Daubeny's World Theatre seasons, and played *The Resistible Rise of Arturo Ui* with verve, melodramatic vigour, and regard for theatrical effect as well as doctrinal orthodoxy. To the Berliner Ensemble had been revealed a truth hidden from their British rivals, namely, that Brecht and entertainment are synonymous.

Mother Courage was most respectfully received, even when produced by Joan Littlewood at her most confused. Brecht never had any opposition to overcome in Britain. It was different with a dramatist who invaded the British scene with a play called *Waiting for Godot* less than two months after Barnstaple and the ciritics had taken *Mother Courage* without flinching. Collie Knox, a notable and engaging columnist, a man of great charm and kindness, described *Waiting for Godot* as 'a conglomeration of tripe' and a 'glorification of the gutless'. Nearly all the first-night audience, only two critics excepted, were bored and outraged by it. Beckett and Brecht are the two greatest influences on the modern drama. It is curious that one of them, the one who was supposed to foment revolution, was

The Nottingham Playhouse production of Bertolt Brecht's Mother Courage *(1968).*

accepted with calm even by the conservatively-minded, whilst the other, who showed no overt political motive or interest, was reviled and abused.

It was not altogether difficult, on that memorable first night at the Arts Theatre Club, to see why those whom it so offended were disorientated and disgusted. The miraculous production by the young Peter Hall had nothing in it to seduce the senses. *Mother Courage* had been set on a battlefield, a place of horrors; but audiences were accustomed to battlefields on the stage. They aroused no repulsion. But the unattractive setting of *Waiting for Godot* was new, and for that reason more repellent. Audiences had never before seen anything like the spectacle provided by *Waiting for Godot*. Its drab, bare scene was dominated by a withered tree and a garbage can, and for a large part of the evening this lugubrious setting, which made the worst of both town and country, was inhabited only by a couple of tramps, verminous, decayed, their hats broken and their clothes soiled, with sweaty feet, inconstant bladders, and boils on their backsides.

Nor was this all. Mother Courage too was verminous, but she was active. She was always on the move. Audiences and critics alike of the old school who had

The first production at the Arts Theatre Club of Samuel Beckett's Waiting for Godot *(1955), which later transferred to the Criterion Theatre, London.*

watched *Mother Courage* undisturbed could not abide *Waiting for Godot*. In contrast to Brecht, Beckett was a writer in whose plays nothing happened. There was no action in *Waiting for Godot*, and such dramatic progress as it made was not towards a climax, but towards a perpetual postponement. Vladimir and Estragon were waiting for Godot, but this gentleman's appearance was not prepared with any recognizable tension, for the audience knew well enough from the beginning that Godot would never come. The dialogue was studded with words that had no meaning for normal ears; the play repeatedly announced that it had come to a end, and would have to start again, a piece of information that the audience received with dismay. It never reconciled itself with reason.

Certain early lines in the play, such as 'I have had better entertainment elsewhere' were received with ironical laughter and applause; and when one of the characters yawned, the yawn was echoed and amplified by a humorist in the stalls. Yet at the end the play was quite warmly applauded. There were even a few calls for 'Author'. But these were rather shame-faced cries, as if those who uttered them doubted whether it were seemly to make too much noise whilst turning their coats. The next morning the play was butchered by the press.

But here and there a solitary spectator realized that Vladimir and Estragon wore their rags with a difference. They had a sort of universality. Vladimir was eternally hopeful; if Godot did not come that evening, then he would certainly arrive tomorrow, or at the very latest the day afterwards. Estragon, much troubled by his feet, was less confident. He thought the game was not worth playing, and was ready to hang himself. Or so he said. But, to the audience's profound exasperation, he did nothing. Like Vladimir, he just went on talking. They were both spinning away the great top of their lives in vain expectation that some master whip would one day give it eternal vitality. Meanwhile, their conversation had the delusive simplicity of music-hall cross-talk, now and again

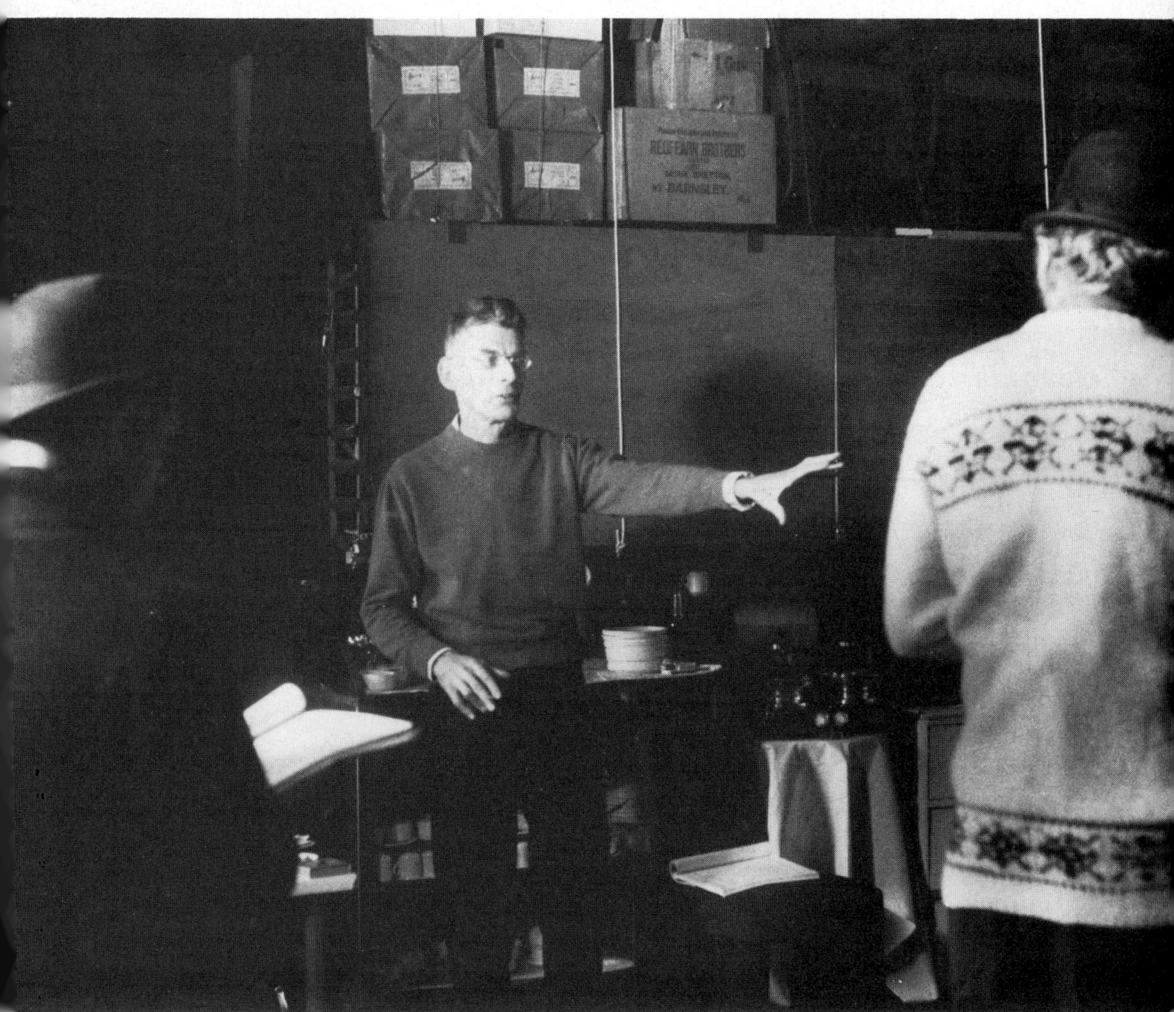

Samuel Beckett directing the Royal Court Theatre production of Waiting for Godot *(1964).*

pierced by a shaft which seemed for a second or so to touch the edge of truth's garment. It was bewildering; it was insidiously exciting. But that night few people thought so.

Then there was Pozzo, the big, brutal bully, and the terrible white-faced slave he leads about on the end of a rope. The audience found Pozzo and Lucky particularly irritating. Sir Ralph Richardson had been offered the part of Pozzo, but refused it. Sir John Gielgud refused Vladimir, and Sir Alec Guinness also declined to appear in the play. One sometimes wonders mischievously how many of the university professors who now write books on the works of Beckett, and the Ph.D. candidates who prepare theses on him would have recognized his greatness as a writer if Ken Tynan and I had not been in the audience that first night to recognize instantly his greatness and to proclaim it far and wide; and how many of them, if they had come to it without instruction, would have been on the side of the Philistines. After all, there were no academic treatises on Beckett until *Waiting for Godot* had been acclaimed in London.

It was in fact no wonder that Beckett had first written *Waiting for Godot* in a foreign language; and when many people showed themselves determined that, if they had any influence at all, it was in a foreign language that he should continue to write, no voice was raised in his defence in any British or American university. In the groves of Academe no learned commentator perceived that here was one of the most moving plays of our generation, a threnody of hope deferred and deceived, but never extinguished; a play suffused with tenderness for the whole human perplexity; with phrases that come like a sharp stab of beauty and pain; with strophes and antistrophes as musical as any imagined in the Book of Common Prayer. In the sixties, seventies and eighties the philosophers and the seats of higher learning poured forth their volumes of analysis and praise; but they had no praise for Beckett in 1955. The professors of English literature kept silent, and even the sociologists were dumb.

With John Osborne's *Look Back in Anger* (1956) the case was rather different. *Look Back in Anger* was not so much ignored or abused as misunderstood. It was taken by those who liked it to be the protest of an Angry Young Man against his elders and the whole edifice of soceity. It was praised as a call to something like revolution, and the overthrow of all accepted values. It was in fact nothing of the kind. Really there were two plays in *Look Back in Anger*. One of them was ordinary enough, and Osborne wrote it with some wit but more prolixity; the other was sketched into the margin of the first, and consisted of hardly any words at all, but was controlled by a fine and sympathetic imagination, and was superbly played, in long passages of pain and silence, by Mary Ure. This was the play that showed Osborne's real talent, but in the opinion of critics, public, and the Royal Court Theatre itself (where the play was performed by George Devine's newly formed English Stage Company) its importance was subordinated to that of the other.

The play to which importance was attached was yet another of youth's accusations against the world. Jimmy Porter is a young intellectual who, with his

Kenneth Haigh and Mary Ure in the first production of John Osborne's Look Back in Anger *(1956) at the Royal Court Theatre, London.*

less-bright-witted partner, Cliff Lewis, keeps a sweets stall somewhere in the Midlands. He has been to a red-brick university, has married Alison Redfern, a girl out of the upper-middle-classes, has been despised and spied on by her relatives, lives in a one-room flat, and reads, at enormous length, what he calls, in a sort of admiring hatred, the 'posh' Sunday papers.

His part is a long, sustained scream at society, literary critics, and his wife. She stands, for what seem whole days, at the ironing board, smoothing trousers, shirts, ties, while he insults her in phrases of a passionate bitterness edged with a frustrated love. His complaints against her are endless; she has tried to keep up some of her friends; she still clutches round her the rags of her old social smartness; she still writes letters to her mother; she cannot be goaded into speech; she is fighting a long delaying battle against absorption into his way of living as though she had not a tongue in her head. So the endless tirade goes on, while Cliff Lewis tries ineffectively to defend the battered, punched, brow-beaten and trampled-on girl, who says nothing and does nothing, but goes on ironing, ironing, with a look of blanched sorrow on her face, which is white and exhausted after a hundred sleepless nights, tormented by a hundred ceaseless headaches. Now this was the play that mattered, and this was the play that was overlooked. The consequences were enormous.

All this time – and it was the greater part of the evening – Jimmy Porter, with his grievances, his anger, his injustices, and his cruelty held the centre of the stage. Even in this part of the play Osborne showed more than a flash of theatrical talent. His wit was amusing and often penetrating, and the use of a trumpet off-stage excellently suggested an atmosphere of breaking nerves. The opening of the third act, with one vital difference (it is not Porter's wife who is at the ironing board, but her friend) brilliantly repeated the opening of the first. Kenneth Haigh played Jimmy Porter with confidence and strength, but he did so from the outside, as a continual flow of bitter rhetoric, not as the inevitable expression of a tormented spirit, and there were passages of whimsy that might have made Barrie blush. Nevertheless, this was what in the play caught the vociferous admiration of its admirers, who totally missed the play's real virtues. The phrase 'Angry Young Man' was adroitly coined to describe Osborne, and it vividly impressed the minds of younger play–goers, just as it equally enraged the old and the middle-aged. There were many angry young men about at that time, and their elders were afraid of them.

Yet Alison Porter was what gave *Look Back in Anger* its tremendous merit, though not its immediate influence. It is not she, but her husband, who throws back into the past a maleficent gaze. But it is her endurance, her futile effort to escape, and her final breakdown which are the truly moving parts of the play. The dramatist that is in John Osborne comes in the end to feel this himself, and it is to Alison, when at last she makes her heart-broken, grovelling, yet peace-securing submission, to whom the final big speech is given.

Hers was in a way a kind of victory; and because it was a kind of victory, it released instead of depressing the spirit. To know when to give up the struggle, to realize when the battle no longer counts, this also is a sort of triumph. There was a poignant moment during the second act when Alison desperately cried, 'I want a little peace.' And it is peace that she gets at the end, as Raskolnikov did when he ceased to maintain himself innocent.

Yet Osborne's advocates did not see the play so. They took it to be merely a belligerent document of discontent. They thought so then, and they went on thinking so, and when later they found in Osborne's subsequent plays love and regret and admiration instead of only hatred they thought that he had turned reactionary. They led a protest movement, and they have gone on protesting. They remind one of Phyllis Morris's fox-hunters. 'They have always hunted, and they will go on hunting till they die.'

Tom Milne was one of the most vocal of them: 'There aren't any good, brave causes left,' cried Jimmy Porter. This, precisely, is the inner dilemma of a world waiting today for the big bang, in an atmosphere of moral and social disintegration. 'The chain reaction of relief is one of violence,' he exclaimed in *Encore* in 1960. But 'the phrase "There aren't any good, brave causes left" to which critics of *Look Back in Anger* have attributed a central explanatory role,' according to Professor Arthur Marwick in *The Pelican Social History of Britain Since 1945*, Osborne himself declared to be 'merely an expression of ordinary despair. . . . At every performance of any of my plays, there are always some of these deluded pedants, sitting there impatiently, waiting for the plugs to come singing in during natural breaks in the action. . . . There they sit, these fashionable turnips, the death's heads of imagination and feeling, longing for the interval and its over-projected drones of ignorance.'

It is because these plugs were less easy to find in *The Entertainer* (1957), *Inadmissible Evidence* (1964), *The Hotel in Amsterdam* (1968). *West of Suez* (1971) and Osborne's later plays that these have received less praise than they deserve. *The Hotel in Amsterdam*, for example, was the best English contemporary play in London, though it was not critically enrolled as such. It was the richest in wit, the most arresting in mood, the most accomplished in presentation, and (what is still more important) the most far-reaching and haunting in performance.

Osborne in it took a subject of great particularity. A group of workers in a film studio escape from the domination of K.L., their boss, for a weekend of anonymous freedom in Amsterdam. They have left, or think they have left, no address behind them. They congratulate themselves on their complete liberty; they chuckle over the discomfiture of K.L. when he finds that they have vanished. 'Let K.L. crucify himself,' says one of them, Laurie, a writer.

Most of them are well-heeled, but Laurie is actually rich. (They did not seem to be hampered by the £50 travel allowance which was in operation at that time!) Laurie draws ideas, and therefore money, out of the air. He is the creative artist. He is dazzling in words, and barren in deeds. With an amused bitterness he excoriates his poor and dependent relatives. He can and does deliver with panache a speech in Italian. He is an exhibitionist and the permanent centre of attention. He is too delicate and highly wrought even to telephone to the room waiter for drinks. He leaves that to someone else.

He cannot make up his mind which restaurant to go to for the party's first night of liberty in Amsterdam. Nor can anyone else. They toss up suggestions and abandon them. The words trail off, and yet again they picture with reassuring glee the dismay of K.L. when he discovers that they have gone. But they are not reassured; they are afraid. The shadow of K.L. lies across them.

The curtain of the first act fell on a scene of great power. Laurie sat as the lights were turned out, looking across the audience from the stage; and his eyes

Paul Scofield in The Hotel in Amsterdam *(1968) at the Royal Court Theatre, London.*

were glazed with terror. Paul Scofield played Laurie, and gave the performance of his life. There were moments in the play when his face collapsed, and the incredible personal distinction of his movement and bearing sagged: at these times his face was that of ruined genius, unable to forget the memory of the flame that had been, and perhaps, still was, inside him. Again one remembered that Danny Kaye, years before in a music hall act at the Palladium, had asked anxiously, 'Why does it have to get harder?'

But *The Hotel in Amsterdam* was not merely a story about show-business people. It had the mark of a true poet, in that, as F. R. Leavis once demonstrated in discussing a few verses of Wordsworth, such a mark is the capacity to take a simple, concrete case, and to draw from it resonances that echo in the most distant places. Essentially indeed *The Hotel in Amsterdam* was not about show business at all, except insofar as it exposes the quivering nature of the creative artist, his need for encouragement, his sad and inexhaustible capacity for being wounded.

It was about fear: the fear, sometimes well-founded, but more often not, that seizes on people in middle life, when the future no longer seems bright and certain before them. It was about friendship. It was about goodness. No dramatist of our time is more responsive to goodness than Osborne has been since *Look Back in Anger*.

In *The Hotel in Amsterdam* the public-schoolboy, affectionately laughed at (Joss Ackland), the secretary (Susan Engel), the designer who had come up from the working class (Donald Burke), the two wives (Isabel Dean and Judy Parfitt) were all good people. And the writer, Laurie, was he good, too? Well, a soul in torment should not be judged too glibly by the standards of the vestry.

The play was also about the condition of England. For England, by then, had entered show business herself. The country might be going to the dogs, without confidence and without ideals, but it had the best entertainment, the best actors, the best theatre in the world. We were constantly saying this, and most countries agreed with us. But I doubt that it satisfied John Osborne, for he has always been devoted to England with a passion that is almost frightening. He was not one of those patriots who are vocal in praise of our blood and state – but who live in Switzerland. He was tortured by our decline, and angry at our lazy and selfish complacency; in *The Hotel in Amsterdam* they wrung from him cries of true distress.

The fourth of the dominant figures who broke into the British theatre about the same time as Osborne, Beckett, and Brecht was Harold Pinter. His first play to reach London, *The Birthday Party*, is famous not only on its own account, but also for the brutal unanimity of its critical rejection. Yet one would have thought that the power of its atmosphere alone would have made some impression on even the most inert mind (one must remember that the critics who attacked *The Birthday Party* with such virulence and stupidity are not the critics who were writing thirty years later). 'The sense of threat', to use Michael Billington's admirable phrase from the *Guinness Book of Facts and Figures* 1982, is everywhere in this play. It breathes in the air. It cannot be seen, but it enters the room every time the door is opened. There is something in your past – it does not matter what – which will catch up with you. Though you go to the uttermost parts of the earth, and hide yourself in the most obscure lodgings in the least popular of towns, one day there is a possibility that two men will appear. They will be looking for you and you cannot get away. And someone will be looking for *them* too. There is terror everywhere.

After the success of *The Caretaker* in 1960 critics and audiences had begun to attune themselves to the especial temper of a Pinter play. So in 1969, when the Royal Shakespeare Company presented two of his shorter plays – *Silence* and *Landscape* – they were not upset by the similarities – the audacious similarities – between them. But Pinter does not watch cricket for nothing. He knows how to bowl quite different deliveries with the same action of the wrist.

Both were quietist plays. In the first, three people, and in the second, two, sit on chairs and talk, less to each other than to the audience, and less to the

Above: (Left to right) John Stratton, John Slater and Richard Pearson in Harold Pinter's The Birthday Party *(1958) at the Lyric Theatre, Hammersmith.*

Opposite: David Waller and Peggy Ashcroft in Harold Pinter's Landscape *(1969) at the Aldwych, London.*

audience than to themselves. In each play what was talked about was remembered, or only half-remembered, things: brief love-affairs illuminated by fleeting shafts of fading sunlight, or wan and grey in the invading dusk of age and feebleness. Both in *Silence* and in *Landscape* the smooth surface erupted into one of those bravura passages about ordinary matters – the barrelling of beer or the mystery of a bird perched on a tree – for which Pinter had been famous ever since his rhapsody on the bus at Dalston Junction in *The Caretaker*. In either play the audience had to piece together into some sort of shifting coherence the fragmented details of the partly recollected past, and in each case what was important was not the past, but the continuing influence which this past exercised on the present, which was before our eyes on the Aldwych stage. The great difference between the two plays lay in this present.

One got the first impression of it from the masterly settings which John Bury had designed for them. That for *Landscape* was naturalistic; it situated the two characters of the piece – a housekeeper no longer young young and her robust and extrovert ex-cellarman husband – precisely in a particular place: the kitchen of a great house. But where the three characters in *Silence* found themselves is beyond time and space: their chairs are on a polished and reflecting floor, and their large shadows are for a time thrown back on to the sloping surface of an engulfing sea. *Silence* is universal; it was a comment, a verdict rather, on the whole of life: whilst *Landscape* was about a particular marriage, a marriage that, because of an unexpected incident, is an exception to the condemnation implacably embodied, though never stated in any words spoken, in *Silence.*

The age of the three characters in *Silence* – a woman and two men – progressed from youth to the very end – and, perhaps, beyond the end of life, as, in Peter Hall's faultless production, they lived again the chosen events of their interconnected past. One of them, a farmer, was richer than the other two; he might perhaps have married the woman when she was young, but he did not. The second man was a farm-hand; he had tried to persuade the girl to go away with him, and she had refused, neither of them knowing of any reason for such a refusal that they could put into words. Neither man understood how he had missed happiness; the farmer, as he contemplated his life, was puzzled, perplexed, protesting. The farm-hand felt more strongly; he was angry and resentful at what life had done to him, and he did not understand why. Of the three it was the girl who had the greatest capacity for joy. In her youth a radiance intermittently shone about her; and consequently the inexplicable hostility of life wounded her even more grievously than it did the other two. The almost querulous tones of Anthony Bate, the blind rebellion of Norman Rodway, and the swift alternations of Frances Cuka's hopes and despair made Pinter's beautiful and arcane text very poignant. But it would be foolish to deny that the audience, though respectful, found the play difficult.

But there are secret ways of escaping from the disillusionment of everyday existence; and *Landscape* shiningly showed us one of them. Dame Peggy Ashcroft's Beth lived entirely in the transfiguring memory of an encounter she had once had with an unnamed man by the seashore. Against the impregnable armour with which this clothed her the common chatter of her rough but not unkindly husband beat in vain, and the confession of unfaithfulness on which he set regretful store was powerless to darken even by a shade or for a moment the brilliant light of her remembered joy. His cheerful affection for her, his desire, even at the end his surging and good-humoured lust were wonderfully counterpointed and rebuked into irrelevance by her last devoted and ecstatic cry of 'Oh my true love' to a presence not there but which nevertheless filled the house. This was one of the great moments of my theatrical experience.

We were never told who the man on the beach was. In Pinter's plays there are many things which we are never told. One of the principal reasons why the critics of yesteryear were so contemptuous of *The Birthday Party* is that they were not informed where the two men who mysteriously came to fetch Stanley from his seaside boarding house came from, nor who they were, nor where they were taking him. They were accustomed to plays in which everything was cleared up at the end, and every mystery solved. But Pinter does not belong to the orthodox school of thought which demands that an author should know everything about his story and his characters. He has always insisted that he knows nothing but what he sets down in his text.

In this he has a strong affinity with Marguerite Duras, whom he admires. Several of Marguerite Duras's plays have been seen in England, notably *The Square* at New End in 1980, and *L'Amante anglaise* at the Royal Court (1969), where it was played in French and in English. The English production was very poor, and the French magnificent, as we should expect when we learn that the chief part in it was played by Madeleine Renaud. She played it, moreover, only a month after Peggy Ashcroft had appeared in *Landscape*, and this made it all the easier to note the similarities of the techniques of both Duras and of Pinter; and of Madeleine Renaud and Dame Peggy also. Both these authors and both these actresses have a delicacy of nuance; they suggest those things that the eye cannot see, and the ear cannot wholly seize; they are the still, small voice uttering simple yet mysterious words that take us out of thought, and are more vital and more impressive than the loudest of songs. They are what remains when all the theories have been found wanting, and the explanations have failed to explain, and there only remains an ineffable reality, poignant, uncomprehended, never to be forgotten nor ever understood.

Since one spellbound evening in the late 1950s, when I read the few score pages of *Le Square*, I have regarded Marguerite Duras as a novelist without peer or rival. She is by nature attracted (as is Harold Pinter) by two kinds of story; in the one, something, preferably extremely violent and criminal, happens all the time; in the other, nothing happens at all. In Pinter's case *The Dumb Waiter* (1957) and *The Homecoming* (1964) belong to the first class, and *Silence* (1969) and *Landscape* (1969) to the second; corresponding works of Marguerite Duras are *Dix heures et demie du soir en été* and *L'Après-midi de Monsieur Andemas* (1962). Now *L'Amante anglaise* is unique in her work in that it is a story of the first kind considered from the point of view of the second. The basis is the brutal beheading of a deaf and dumb servant by her mistress, and the unruffled surface is that of an almost undisturbed but gradually increasing anguished tranquillity.

The play is severely classical in form. It keeps the unities both of time and place, as well as of action. It consists of two successive interrogations, that of Pierre Lannes, the husband, who can think of no explanation of his wife's crime if she is not mad; and of the murderess herself who – and this is the haunting and indeed heart-rending value of the piece – can think of no explanation, at least no valid explanation, at all. Claire, the wife, is an extraordinary creation, and the Interrogator is scarcely less so. The director, Claude Régy, used them both with genius.

In the questioning of the husband (Jean Servais), the Interrogator was unseen.

Madeleine Renaud and Michael Lonsdale in L'Amante anglaise *(1969) at the Royal Court Theatre, London.*

Only his voice, relentless, throbbing, probing was heard coming from the back of the theatre. The man questioned was seated alone on a raised platform on the stage, brilliantly lit, and surrounded by darkness. When his place was taken by the accused woman we saw that she had a patient, tired beauty; that her hair was aureoled with light, that she was frail but unbreakable, with eyes that pierced the darkness, yet saw nothing, in spirit totally co-operative but in her anxious and unfrightened veracity sane, honest, and quite incapable of truth, for neither she, nor I, nor you, nor Pilate know what truth is.

The tension during the first scene had been fairly slack; but from the moment we saw Madeleine Renaud upon the stage it tightened so as to take the audience by the throat. The Interrogator, who had in questioning the husband been only a disembodied voice, now, in the shadow of the aisle, moved ominously towards the stage, steadily pursuing in his even and resonant tones the grave questions with which he strove to find the motive behind the woman's terrible crime. The relationship between them is what I meant when I implied that this play is without parallel. They were prosecuting counsel and criminal dealing with an admitted crime, but they were not enemies; they were fellow-searchers after an unfindable truth. When in the still but stupendous climax the Interrogator, now having reached the stage, placed his hands on her neck in the full illumination of light, they are less hands of execution than of protection.

Although, unlike the Barraults, Marguerite Duras is no longer a Christian, one understood the dramatic impact of the play best if one remembered the forty-sixth verse of the twenty-seventh chapter of St Matthew. For Madeleine Renaud stretched out her hands to the Interrogator of Michael Lonsdale, so loving and so terrible, and cried 'Écoutez-moi', that is to say, 'Eli, Eli, lama sabachthani?'; and the Interrogator went slowly and sadly away into the impenetrable darkness. In the enormous pathos of Madeleine Renaud's despair and pleading there was a healing beauty that left the audience exalted and serene.

In the second half of the century, especially at the Olivier Theatre, there were many productions of great elaboration; but none of this elaboration had as great an effect as Régy's simple device of making the Interrogator emerge out of the void, and creep nearer and nearer to the stage, his threat and menace gradually increasing with every step he took. In the English production of the same play which followed, the Interrogator (Gordon Jackson) was on stage all the time, fully seen by the audience from the beginning to the end of the performance. His effect was about as striking as that of a cold Christmas pudding.

CHAPTER EIGHT
The Sequel
1968–1982

Brecht, Beckett, Osborne, and Pinter, with the abolition of the Lord Chamberlain's powers of stage censorship in 1968, were the forces that transformed the theatre built up by Galsworthy, Maugham and Shaw, by Eliot and Priestley and Fry, gaining some things and losing others. New poetic drama entirely disappeared; high comedy, except for the work of William Douglas Home, vanished; the characters favoured by dramatists became working people instead of the elegant idle rich; there developed a powerful drama of political propaganda to take the place of Shaw's drama of political discussion; restraint of verbal expression ceased; instead of being a necessity, it became a handicap to a player to have a standard English accent; the commercial theatre, hitherto the mainstay of the drama, wilted because many dramatists first offered their plays to the National Theatre, and much of the middle-class public began to stay away from the playhouse because they missed the old, comfortable, reassuring, nicely spoken, well dressed entertainments they had been accustomed to see; the new dramatists were disturbing, passionate, exhortatory; many people were shocked by the exhibitions of homosexuality and nudity which became common.

The new, democratic, popular theatre brought with it one great surprise. It was natural enough that dukes and marquises should no longer arouse interest. What was astonishing was that the power which creates dukes and marquises, that is, royalty, continued to exert its peculiar fascination over the British theatrical public. What dazzled Shaw seemed, so far as the British theatre was concerned, to have dazzled the revolutionary Brecht. Thus whatever may have been the author's conscious intention, which was sometimes betrayed even by Brecht himself (as in the character of Mother Courage, to whom he gave greater glamour than he had bargained for), the upshot of Frank Dunlop's production of Brecht's *Edward II* for the National Theatre at the Old Vic was that Brecht emerged from it as a man with an admiration for royalty that even the truest blue patriot might have considered excessive. According to the National Theatre's Brecht in 1968 the things that monarchs do may be evil, ruinous, or unnaturally

John Stride in Bertolt Brecht's Edward II *(1968) at the Old Vic, London.*

vicious. Nevertheless, there is in a king an unbreakable resolution, an unshaken defiance that raises him above the level of ordinary men. In *Edward II* Edward twice says so, once when his barons ask him to banish his paramour Gaveston, and again when he is called on to abdicate. These were the critical points of the drama; and Brecht, following Marlowe, conceived them, or so it seemed at the Old Vic, in a mood of loyal hagiolatry obsolete since the Middle Ages.

The play had some fine images, as of the unusual number of birds flocking over the battlefields; it also had scenes of perverse grandeur, as when Edward seated Gaveston beside him on his throne, leaving a humiliated Queen literally standing. John Stride was a rough-hewn Edward and Geraldine McEwan unselfishly provided a harrowing study of the Queen's declension from the condition of affectionate wife to that of blowsy harridan.

Later in the same year Ian McKellen gave us the finest Richard II since John Gielgud's and Michael Redgrave's. From the moment of his entry we saw that this Richard regarded himself not, as we have always thought, as divinely God-protected, but as actually divine himself. McKellen moved on to the stage with a more than human smoothness, and his arms were upraised from the elbows, framing the godhead and the crown, and fixed like the many arms of an Eastern Deity. His Richard was a god, but neither Christian nor Hebrew. He knew neither compassion for his creatures, nor at first revenge. His serenity was celestial and appalling, and when he spoke it was with an astonishing swiftness, sweeping aside commas and full stops as imperiously – no, as omnipotently – as he did the injuries of his angry subjects. And yet this god, this Deity, when he was with his boon companions, his Bushy, Green, and Bagot, was not a god at all, but only an educated pot–boy.

It was between these two poles that his tragedy lay. It was the tragedy of a Deity who is a sham, who discovers that he is a sham, who poignantly sees and misses his moment of possible salvation, and falls into absolute degradation and misery. Such, magnified on an enormous scale, is the penalty of self-deception. This performance became the sensation of London (after its first presentation at an Edinburgh Festival), just as John Gielgud's had as the same unhappy king in Daviot's *Richard of Bordeaux* fifty years before. It raised McKellen immediately to as dangerous a height of reputation as any young British actor has known.

In 1969 there arrived a play in London which was less reverent of pomp and ceremony. It was called *The Ruling Class*, and it represented the new, iconoclastic drama whose origin had been in the Royal Court. In it Peter Barnes, a new author, attacked both State and Church, and especially the House of Lords. But he did so with a verve and humour and a surrealistic fancy lacking in most of the radical drama of the day. *The Ruling Class* presented us with the most outrageous possibilities, and they seemed as inevitable as tomorrow's breakfast. The fourteenth Earl of Gurney thought (going even further than Richard in the intensity of his conviction) that he was God. When asked why, he answered with breath-taking logic, 'When I pray to Him I find I am talking to myself.'

Derek Godfrey and Vivienne Martin in The Ruling Class *(1969) at the Piccadilly Theatre, London.*

Five years later Barnes launched in *The Bewitched* an assault upon monarchy less good-humoured and more powerful than his mockery of religion and the aristocracy in *The Ruling Class*. It was one of the most important plays of the modern generation, though its merits were widely overlooked. A Royal Shakespeare Company production, it was directed by Terry Hands with a vivid sense of plasticity, colour, and shock. It was written by Peter Barnes with a passion, and a mastery of language varying incessantly and vertiginously from the sheerly magnificent and poetic to the deliberately banal and obscene, which cannot be matched in the work of those who, like Howard Brenton in *The Romans in Britain* (1982), put a simple trust in the effectiveness of elementary four-letter words which used to be known only to errand-boys and gentlemen.

It is a sober fact that the most important thing in Europe in the 1690s was the penis of Charles II of Spain. (There had been nothing wrong with that of Charles II of England.) It was baffling to anyone to see this in its full historical and social significance who was not as familiar as Barnes himself with the millions of words in Saint-Simon's Memoirs. It was (and always will remain) difficult to appreciate that behind the copulations and the flagellations, the prancing Velázquez dwarfs, the gorgeous robes gleaming in half-darkness, the diseased, stuttering, tottering idiot-grinning King Carlos II, who was played by Alan Howard, and his patient earnest queen (Rosemary McHale), offering herself to him in desperate hope and purple drawers, there was always the spectre of a terrible war, and the deaths of a million people.

Yet this is what gave the play its pity and its terror.

There are very few historical plays like *The Bewitched*. It is not, like *Henry VI*, a chronicle of events. It is not a moral study, like Anouilh's *Becket*. It is not, like John Drinkwater's *Abraham Lincoln*, designed to exalt, nor, like Hochhuth's *Soldiers*, designed to slander its chief character. It is a poetic, imaginative, uninhibited fantasia upon a theme. That theme is impotence. Barnes presented it to us in a vast variety of ways: blasphemous, indecent, and pathetic; he was obsessed by it, and he was right to be obsessed by it.

The climax to the first act showed Carlos and his wife monstrously aggrandized into golden puppets of enormous size. Carlos was aroused by an *auto da fé* as some men are aroused by a bullfight, and from his magnificent, hieratic robes emerged a huge, golden penis which, across the entire length of the stage, as the fires burn, slowly approached the acquiescent figure of the disheartened queen. This might have seemed revolting or obscene, and certainly it carried pictorial permissiveness to great lengths. But it was a wholly justified, a magnificent climax. It was perhaps the most astonishing feat of historical imagination, strictly founded in poetic truth, that the theatre had yet shown. (It was in any case less offensive than the scenes of cannibalism and accusations of lesbianism against Queen Victoria in Edward Bond's *Early Morning* (1968), which was the last play to be banned by the Lord Chamberlain, and played at its first performance behind locked doors.)

Moreover, Barnes did not treat Carlos altogether without tenderness. There was a moving scene, agonizingly played by Alan Howard, when Charles at last realized that he could have no children. His limbs momentarily straightened, and the shackles fell from his tongue in a great cry of misery as he cursed God as Job was asked to do; and again God answered him out of the whirlwind. There was something heroic as well as grotesque in the efforts made by Barnes's exploited and deformed cripple to defeat the hostility of nature.

At the end of Barnes's *The Bewitched* there was a fascinating example of that superiority of poetic truth over prosaic fact so famously proclaimed by Aristotle. When Carlos, very finely played by the naturally handsome Alan Howard, with wayward legs, shaking knees, and protruding jaw, was dead, the Spanish throne was ascended, literally, by the young Duke of Anjou, who became Philip V. Now at that time the Duke was a most attractive man. Years as King of Spain lengthened and paled his face. But when Saint-Simon in 1721, as the representative of France, made him an official but improvised speech, he was astonished at the king's intellectual eminence. Philip took up every point raised by Saint-Simon, and perfectly answered it, though he had been quite unaware of what Saint-Simon had been going to say. Yet when this remarkable man sat on the throne and faced the audience one realized with a shock that Barnes made him wear the head of an elephant. That elephant's head may have traduced Philip V, but it impressively presaged the warlike stupidity into which Europe was about to enter.

If royalty began to be treated with severity, there was no mercy shown to the lower echelons of society who figured in what came to be known as French window plays. Terence Rattigan, specializing in these, was so virulently and continuously attacked by dramatists emanating from the Royal Court that for several years he gave up writing plays at all. But in the last months of his life his reputation began to revive, and with *In Praise of Love* he enjoyed an unexpected critical triumph. It was particularly dangerous to have family connections with the aristocracy, and the spirited, witty comedies of William Douglas Home, such as *The Secretary Bird* (1968) and *Lloyd George Knew My Father* (1972) were ludicrously underestimated merely because their author was the son of an Earl, though the public, wiser than the critics, flocked to them in droves.

To use the term entertainment in a derogatory sense is clearly a mark of a certain intellectual inferiority. It implies that the user finds no entertainment in *Agamemnon*, *Hamlet*, *Bérénice*, *The Skin Game*, *A Sleep of Prisoners*, Beckett, Pinter, Brecht, Osborne, Wesker, Brenton, Storey, Stoppard and their colleagues, all of whom are writers of entertaining plays. Nevertheless, there is a type of play whose style of entertainment is less strenuous than that of these masters; and it is this type of play which has received particularly rough treatment in recent years. But two of its authors have received a free pardon by the indefinable but vastly important phenomenon known as the temper of the age, the sort of pardon that was for a long time withheld from Coward and Rattigan and has never been issued to William Douglas Home at all. The fortunate men who have pleased all sections of theatre–goers, from the intellectually 'unco guid' to the frivolous are Alan Ayckbourn and Michael Frayn. The reason for their deserved success is not really that they have had the luck not to have been born into the nobility, but that, whilst their plays are uncommonly amusing, they also have a feeling of dissatisfaction and malaise that is in tune with contemporary attitudes.

The British people have never recovered from the war of 1939–45, or again from the fiasco of Suez in 1956. For a brief period the magnetism of Churchill and the burning zeal of his oratory, and the masterly victories first of Wavell and then of Montgomery in North Africa brought into them something of the confident and buoyant spirit which from time to time they had had in the past. But the deep-down, real temper of the people was less that of Churchill than of Chamberlain. The war tried the people beyond their strength, and left them with a conviction that fundamentally there was something wrong with the world and especially with Britain and its rulers. The thought that there might be something wrong with themselves does not seem to have occurred to them. They experienced the 'failure of nerve' which David Pryce-Jones says is the subject of Connolly's *Enemies of Promise*.

Yet the fact is that the prevalent post-war mood of Britain and the West is a repudiation of its customs and achievements, of Homer, of Shakespeare, of

Christianity, of conventional morality, and as such it is vividly represented in the contempt for our traditions and history shown in many contemporary plays.

In times when Britain finds Sherriff's *Journey's End* chauvinistic, it is not surprising that in the realm of comedy those plays of merit which manifest an underlying unease as well as an outward laughter should find most repute. In nearly all his work Ayckbourn shows a distrust of the concept of family: in *Absent Friends* he writes of the death of love; in *Joking Apart* of the pathos of failure; in *Sisterly Feelings* of sisterly jealousy; and in *Way Upstream* (1982) there is one heart-shaking moment, when he has a genuine vision of Hell, and the presence of evil is everywhere in the theatre.

Even his famous bravura exhibitions of theatrical technique are rejections of traditional methods, as when in *Sisterly Feelings* he made two separate versions of the play. In one the characters go to the races; in the other it is a question of a night under canvas; and in theory which one was played (in practice, too, on the first night and at some subsequent performances) depended on the toss of a coin and on the arbitrary choice of one of the actresses.

The dissatisfaction of Michael Frayn is of a different kind from Alan Ayckbourn's. It is more institutional and less personal. But it is equally funny. In the enormously successful *Noises Off* (1982) he jeered at the inadequacies of a touring theatre company, and was hilarious over the progressive decline of their

Selina Cadell, Greg Hicks and Andrew Cruickshank in Alan Ayckbourn's Sisterly Feelings *(1980) at the National Theatre, London.*

(Left to right) Glyn Grain, James Grout, Peter Blythe, Leonard Rossiter and Prunella Scales in Michael Frayn's Make and Break *(1980) at the Lyric Theatre, Hammersmith.*

performances as they wandered hopelessly from one third-rate regional theatre to another. In *Make and Break* (1980), which equally prospered, he exposed the incompetence of big business and the financial obsessions of big business men. The principal character was so infatuated with his business that he accidentally brought about the death of one of his colleagues.

Here Frayn had a moment of mercy. One of the partners in the firm was a light-heartedly atheistic salesman, Frank Prosser, (played by Peter Blythe), whose gaiety was suddenly eclipsed by his colleague's unexpected death. The dead man had been a Roman Catholic, and Prosser, breaking into momentary seriousness and sincerity, half-ashamedly and with great emotional delicacy, brilliantly holding the centre of the stage, almost apologetically said that though everybody knew that what the dead man believed was nonsense, nevertheless, it had given him a kind of rest and peace which, he implied, he and his colleagues had not got. We had not had in the theatre a particular moment like this since the appearance of the salesman in *Rocket to the Moon* by Clifford Odets. There was also another incident of grace in the play, when Prosser sensationally broke out of flat dialogue prose into the ringing song of the Hymn to Joy in

Beethoven's Ninth Symphony. The effect was unexpected and great. But of course Peter Blythe, in his casual, frivolous, young-man-about-town way, is a very fine actor. He has (or at any rate had, and I have no reason to suppose that he has changed) a good tailor; and his tailor had a splendid actor to deal with. There was a similar effect in John Osborne's *A Sense of Detachment* (1972). This play was a protest against pornography, and with its characteristic and obstinate perversity the British public persisted in misunderstanding it, and took Osborne's exposure of pornography as a demonstration of it. Preceding *Make and Break* by nearly ten years, it achieved a similar effect when Ralph Michael, without warning or a note being given him, burst during a pornographic conversation into a full-throated rendering of 'Rock of ages, cleft for me' that lifted up the hearts of the audience and nearly took off the roof of the Royal Court Theatre.

In general the language of British theatre has become frequently objectionable. But we should not overlook the fact that the stage has some finer aspects. Sometimes it happens that, though indisputable, they are not immediately apparent. This was the case with David Mercer's *Flint* (1970). The principal character in Mercer's play was a 70-year-old clergyman, who had been a non-stop lecher, and an agnostic ever since he was ordained. When he found a pregnant, deserted Liverpudlian Roman Catholic teenager collapsed in one of his pews he was as ready to seduce her in the vestry as he was to help, succour and encourage her.

It was a play full of incident. A church was burnt down, and there was a murder, a fatal accident, and a visit to the Pope. The dialogue was outrageous, unexpected, true to character, and extremely funny. Some members of the audience regretted, and some raucously rejoiced that *Flint* was blasphemous. Both were wrong, because one of the play's strengths was that it created a world in which blasphemy was as irrelevant as bows and arrows in Vietnam. Perhaps the knife in the back was melodramatic, but what does a scrap of melodrama matter against the play's outstanding merits? One of them was the tenderness between the girl and the still potent old man. Its special excellence is that it skirts marvellously the edges of undisclosed profundities whose mysteries are left, as mysteries should be, unexplained.

The young doxy was played throughout with a touching simplicity and even innocence. At the end she brokenly sang a heart-rending song about her baby and Flint, whom she believed to be now burning in hell. But one felt that surely in this belief she was wrong. Flint had that essential quality without which to speak with the tongues of men and of angels is vanity and vexation of spirit. His life had been disgraceful, and yet Mercer left us in no doubt that he was in a state of grace.

The importance of *Flint* is that, though the changes of the 1950s had made impossible the further statement of religious belief in the terms employed by Eliot and Fry, the spiritual needs that these playwrights had striven to satisfy continued to trouble the minds of men and women. This disquiet, this feeling

Julia Foster and Michael Hordern in David Mercer's Flint *(1970) at the Criterion Theatre, London.*

that loaves and fishes (though earnestly striven and fought for) are somehow in themselves not enough, went on throughout the quarter-century that followed Osborne's electrifying play. It haunted the imagination even of dramatists who could not honestly find any justification of it. This appeared in more than one play produced during that time, but in none more vividly than in Dennis Potter's *Only Make Believe*, which the Oxford Playhouse Company presented at the Playhouse in Harlow.

Like William Douglas Home's very moving *The Lord's Lieutenant*, which also was a religious play cast in unusual terms, it had moments of great amusement. *Only Make Believe* began with a scene of naturalistic comedy. Christopher, played by John Fraser, called in a temporary typist, to whom he wished to dictate a television script. The indulgent and disconcerting comments of this stony-faced young lady (Brenda Cavendish) on the untidiness of Christopher's room, which to Christopher had always seemed rather chic, were a delightfully gentle, even if, as things turned out, deceptive beginning to a play which before long took on dimensions of considerable ambition.

The script that Christopher wanted to write was about an angel. Now Christopher, who was not a happy man (his wife had deserted him), believed in angels. He believed particularly, because the Epistle to the Hebrews says so, that they can be entertained unawares. And indeed it appears both from Potter's play, and from the play that he makes Christopher write, that in fact this is so. There was no bitterness in Douglas Home's heart. *The Lord's Lieutenant* was about a momentarily doubting character written by a believing author. But in Potter there are both bitterness and disappointment, which, no less than Home's serenity, are valuable dramatic qualities. *Only Make Believe* was a play about a believing character written by an author who is full of doubt, but who in doubt is restless. The virtual eclipse of Fry and Eliot by the secularity of the new movement, which is generally regarded as the regeneration of British drama, had not brought peace.

The angels certainly come, but they go away. What Potter was telling us, especially in his memorable climax, was that what is important is not that you do not recognize them, but that whether you recognize them or not, they refuse to help. Either they fly away, as in Christopher's play, or, as in Potter's, they slam the door. And when the angels have gone, there is nothing to be done but to appeal to God himself. This is in fact just what Christopher did. For, with Fraser's frightened, anxious face lit by a bright light in gathering blackness, Christopher, like an actor panic-stricken at having forgotten his part, lifted up his eyes, and cried, in a phrase that desolatingly echoed the last words in *Ghosts*, 'Give me a prompt.' But no prompt was given. God is a great way off, and will not hear. The new theatre had enthusiastically abandoned the God whom Claudel knew, and yet it was not happy, nor could it forget that it now lacked what had in the past been a stay and a comfort.

Religion even invaded productions of *Hamlet*. Peter Hall himself said that his *Macbeth* (1967) was a Christian *Macbeth*, and Caspar Wrede's *Hamlet* in the 1968 Edinburgh Festival was a Christian *Hamlet*, though it brought with it as much unhappiness in its certainty as Potter's doubt did in *Only Make Believe*. From the beginning the audience was struck by the fact that, whenever Tom Courtenay spoke of anything pertaining to religion, his accent was firm and sincere. His Hamlet was a believing Hamlet, and because of that he was a faithful lover, and would have been a good husband. I do not mean that he was sanctimonious. In a play by James Bridie before the war called *Marriage Is No Joke* Ralph Richardson recited the formidable characteristics of the Calvinist God. A friend asked, 'Does all that comfort you?' 'No', replied Richardson. 'Then why on earth do you believe it?' Richardson's reply was shattering, and I have never forgotten it. 'Because it is true,' he said. I had not heard an accent of such simple conviction until I saw Tom Courtenay's Hamlet. His Hamlet was a man who believed in his religion, and yet was ruined by it. His way was no more prosperous than Christopher's. It was because of his religion that he feared that the ghost might come from the devil; it was because of his religion that he needed the play scene, not to astonish the audience, but to convince *himself*; then again he had new resolution, new spirit, to kill Claudius, and then again his religion defeated him. For he found Claudius at prayer. Few people believe that if a man dies on his knees he will therefore go to heaven. But Courtenay's Hamlet did, and for that reason his spirit died within him. This was the most original Hamlet of the century, the one whose echoes rang through the mind most movingly and disturbingly.

Beckett and Brecht had broken the naturalistic conventions of the theatre. Some companies went further, and spat in the audience's face, stamped on its feet, and shone bright lights into its eyeballs. The Bread and Puppet Theatre did not go as far as this, but they adopted a method of symbolic and apparently anarchic staging which it is unlikely that they would ever have developed but for what had taken place in the 1950s. They too were concerned with religion. Their play, whose title *The Cry of the People for Meat* shows its political commitment, covered the story of mankind, its tribulations, its glories, its splendours and its griefs, from the creation of the world to the death of Christ. In fact it carried the story farther. The series of short scenes in which this great conspectus was taken was only in appearance naive; its simplicity held considerable sophistication. So much so that many people found it baffling.

The company came from America, and visited Paris before venturing into the Royal Court. In Paris the avant-garde critics had either ignored it or disliked it, and from their own point of view they were right to do so, for it had no G-strings, no nakedness, no eroticism, nothing to titillate, horrify, or disgust the senses. The bourgeois critics equally could make nothing of it. They were gloomily estranged by its having no author, practically no text, no actors who could speak clearly, and apparently no knowledge of the rules of preparation, climax and catastrophe. They resented the stage being a confusion of plastic bags, heaps of newspaper cuttings, and gigantic dolls; and they could see no point in what they heard – the banging of drums, the shrill blowing of whistles – being a dissonance and a discord.

There were times also when the Royal Court audience seemed to be completely at sea. In the company's grave and haunting representation of the Last Supper, the players distributed amongst the audience Communion bread (very good bread) which they had baked themselves. There were people in the theatre who so far mistook the nature of what was happening that they began to pelt the stage with this bread in a spirit of happy pantomime derision. Some of the players were visibly grieved at this want of communication, which was no fault of theirs. One of them moaned in a stricken voice, but without anger or insult, 'Please don't do that. Please behave better.' No rage, no violence, only a great sadness, typical of this strange, wandering American company.

Certainly some expansion of vision was at this time necessary to enter into understanding sympathy with the Bread and Puppet Theatre. It gave people much to brood over. That huge Easter Island Christ, towering at least fifteen feet high, with the face of a Red Indian seen through the eyes of an El Greco, raising his vast hands in slow, grotesque and touching benediction; the Magdalen at his feet anointing him; and the relentless fight between the man and the pig-faced beast that becomes a man, and his unwearying, indefatigable perseverence in the face of repeated and contemptuous defeat were only three of the things that did not seem likely to fade from our minds: to which must be added the split-second bombing raid that destroyed the Christ and brought the play to an end.

Peter Schumann's production had the vitality, the noise, and the primeval appeal of the fairground; his players merged and grew into the enormous puppets which from time to time they brought on the stage. Although at the first performance, and indeed now, I did not understand some of the play, including a bewildering procession of patriarchs, nevertheless it had in it things whose transcendental implications the world after the war was still yearning for. The covering of the flight to Bethlehem, for example, with the unemotional words spoken by a Vietnamese woman (quoted from the *New York Times* of 1 June 1967) whose husband had been killed by bombs from aeroplanes flying in the formation of a fish (he had never seen aeroplanes before, and did not know what they were, and so stood up to look, and was hit) was of great poignancy; it made the reception of Mary and the Child by the sad-faced woman in the inn strangely contemporary.

I have said that the Bread and Puppet company spurned preparation in the theatrical sense, but this is not quite true. For this scene was completed at the end when over the grave disciples at the Last Supper the fish-aeroplane appeared, and the bomb fell, and the stage was plunged into darkness, as the table was overturned, and the disciples were scattered, and the Christ crashed to the ground. The message that the Bread and Puppet Company brought with it was that politics in itself is not enough, and yet cannot be done without if the world's injustices are to be righted.

For a time the English Stage Company at the Royal Court, and all those who were following what they thought was the lead given to them by John Osborne, hoped that this was not so. The most constructive of British dramatists who believed that the world could be reformed by political action alone was Arnold Wesker. Wesker was unique amongst radical political writers in that he loved the oppressed more than he hated the oppressors. The driving power behind his work was an idealism not found elsewhere. He expressed it in many notable plays, such as *Chicken Soup with Barley* (1958), *The Kitchen* (1958), *Chips with Everything* (1962), *I'm Talking about Jerusalem* (1960), and above all in *Roots* (1959). The moment when the hitherto tongue-tied and baffled Beattie Bryant breaks into an eloquent paean of rejoicing as she realizes the illumination that may come to the underprivileged in an age of enlightened socialism has justly become one of the most celebrated scenes in modern drama.

Most political and progressive dramatists, however, were more vitally interested in denouncing the evil in society (and in their view there was little in it that was not evil) than in proposing anything better in its place. Edward Bond

Joan Plowright in Arnold Wesker's Roots *(1959) at the Royal Court Theatre, London.*

was particularly forceful in attacking what had been established by the past rather than in giving any hope of a better future; and so was Howard Brenton. The power of Bond's writing was so great, as in a scene in *Saved* in which a baby was stoned to death by a group of hooligan boys, that he shocked many people; yet in this play he did not go beyond the bounds of what may be read in almost any daily newspaper. In his *Early Morning* (1968) he had a savage moral purpose. He wished to expose the horrible débris left in the minds of thousands or millions of people by the education they receive in certain kinds of school and even Sunday school. Yet he did so with a fury that seemed almost to be a variety of enjoyment. It was with an undisciplined rapture that he showed Queen Victoria, Prince Albert, and their children revelling in cannibalism in heaven. The play revealed Florence Nightingale changing sex twice, with Queen Victoria as her lesbian admirer; Gladstone as a sort of trade union leader teaching his people how to kick their opponents; Siamese twins of whom one becomes a skeleton; armies falling over a cliff in a tug-of-war; Disraeli plotting with Prince Albert to kill the queen; heaven as a place from which rises a ludicrous Christ; and the dead gnaw at the bleeding flesh and dismembered limbs of their fellows. So might a child with an overheated brain dream whose head was a jumble of misunderstood fragments of what misguided elders had told him about sex, religion, and the sort of history that is made up exclusively from palace intrigues, plots, murders, and wars where 'ignorant armies clash by night'. Bond demanded nothing less than a complete reform of our system of education.

In the late sixties and early seventies there came a flood of productions, especially on the Fringe, whose hope was to demolish the foundations of society such as it was then known in Britain. The destruction of the nuclear family, peace promoted by riots and attacks on the police, homosexuality, lesbianism, and frequent reminders that colonialism was an evil thing, were the messages most frequently projected from the stage. The most substantial of the new left wing dramatists discovered during this period was Trevor Griffiths. He was given golden chances, since his first play to be seen in London, *The Party*, had for its star Sir Laurence Olivier. It proved well to deserve him, for it contained political discussion of a *gravitas* and quickness of mind which had not been seen in a comparable setting since the heyday of Bernard Shaw. His second play, *The Comedians*, brought to the London stage Bob Peck, a comic actor of great ferocity, who had played Shakespeare in Edward Bond's *Bingo* at its first production in Exeter. A few years later he nearly startled audiences out of their wits with his Petruchio in an RSC *Taming of the Shrew*.

The Establishment showed little perturbation at the increasingly subversive nature of the theatre. Many of the Nottinghamshire clergy had flocked to see Peter Barnes's *The Ruling Class* without expressing disapproval, and Canon Stephen Verney of Coventry Cathedral actually commissioned Edward Bond to write a play. Bond was not a man whose integrity could be shaken by flattering advances from the Establishment, and the Church was by no means disconcerted by plays that dealt powerfully with the problems of people living in big cities,

The first production of Edward Bond's Narrow Road to the Deep North *(1969) at the Belgrade Theatre, Coventry.*

with the violence that breaks out in them, and with the crushing weight of authority, colonial, national, civic, and religious.

The cathedral, which had been rebuilt after destruction by German bombing during the war, was an admired piece of modern architecture. The authorities must have grown sick of the praise that had been lavished on it by learned and laity: on its architecture, its use of unusual material, its modernity, its affirmation of living values integrated into an industrial society. Bond's attitude to their great praise must have come to them like fine rain after a long drought, dampening but refreshing. 'I know the cathedral,' said Bond. 'That it is ugly goes without saying. An insult to the intelligence.'

Not for the first time in its history the Church inspired a fine play. A play not reconcilable with formal Christianity, but a fine play, nevertheless.

In *Narrow Road to the Deep North* Bond continued to be obsessed with horrors. He believed that the noblest actions may produce the most disastrous and criminal effects. He had no confidence that if you resist the devil he will flee from you. He maintained that no religion is any good at all, but if you insist in having one, then Buddhism is preferable to Christianity. None of this doctrine will go comfortably into the Gospels. But the tone, which is what counts, is another matter. Most people left the Belgrade Theatre better than when they went in.

In the process of so becoming we were entertained by the simple freshness of Bond's imagination; by the strong spareness of his deceptively naïve style; by the poetic inspiration that underlies his plainest prose. We were horrified by two scenes of enormous power, in which the ludicrous is mixed with the murderously stifling and frightening; and at the end we were left purged by the spectacle of a glorious but totally useless death; not a Crucifixion, but a ritual suicide by a Buddhist monk, who sits on the stage and faces the audience and slowly, with an unflinching courage and exquisite endurance, superbly rendered by Paul Howes, cuts his stomach open from one end to the other.

One might think this must be horrible, even revolting. But it was not so, any more than is the bloodied Figure on the Cross. It belonged to the same order of grandeur, though not of optimism, for in Bond's faith there is no resurrection, and no sure and certain hope of anything.

The scene of *Narrow Road to the Deep North* was Japan at indeterminate times in the seventeenth, eighteenth, and nineteenth centuries. The Japanese poet Basho seeks enlightenment and does not find it. He refuses to rescue a baby abandoned by its parents on a river bank, and this baby grows up to be the tyrant Shogo who rules despotically over a great city. Basho does, however, though reluctantly, save another baby, the king's son, many years later.

The results both of his courage and his cowardice are equally catastrophic. For when an absurd, tambourine-banging woman missionary boldly refuses to tell Shogo which of five children is the royal heir, he murders them all. This was a very fine scene, and the centre of it was, surprisingly, the distress of Shogo himself. Just as excellent, but in a different spirit, was that in which a monk put a sacred urn over his head and was unable to get it off. Shogo was defeated, and his body dismembered.

But is this victory? Bond's final comment was the monk's suicide. The beautiful and simple settings, – a tree, a bush in front of an unchanging quiet brown frame – were by Hayden Griffin, and the play was directed by Jane Howell with a proper sense of Eastern deliberation.

Bond offered no alternative to the Christianity and colonialism which he derided. But no great dramatist has ever been called on to offer solutions. Shakespeare did not propose a remedy for the misery of Lear, nor John Osborne for that of Bill Maitland in his *Inadmissible Evidence*. There are some problems, said Bond in *Narrow Road to the Deep North*, which are insoluble.

Howard Brenton, one of the most influential political dramatists of the seventies and eighties, whose work is the subject of endless controversy, and in the case of *The Romans in Britain*, of legal prosecution, seems to believe that somehow there was at one time a solution to our problems, and that unfortunately we let it go by. Brenton's terrifying imagination made his *The Churchill Play* a very disturbing experience. It unsettled the foundations of the world on which England unsteadily rested. One of the few matters on which there was general agreement in 1974, when the play was produced at the Nottingham Playhouse, was that in 1940 Britain had need of someone to save her, and that she found him. The haunting and alarming suggestion in Brenton's play is that the man England found was the wrong man; that the war of 1939–45 was less Hitler's war than Churchill's; that the British, and especially the Scottish, people were so demoralized by bombing that they bitterly resented Churchill's keeping them at war; and that this was the cause of our loss of Empire, and the moment when our freedom went.

My own experience of the people's reaction to the bombing of London does not fully support Brenton's argument that the nation was terrified by it; and no one has ever suggested that the Scots are less brave than the English. On the contrary, history would tend to support the contrary belief. Brenton was very young at the time, and his play contained a good deal of evidence that he had listened to, and been unduly impressed, by some very lurid stories: stories no doubt factually true, but not because of that necessarily universally truthful. One cannot therefore accept as valid his attack on Churchill as the man responsible for dragging an unwilling nation into war. When this nation, probably against its real will, got into war it was Churchill who put courage into it. On this count, then, Brenton's play was unjust; but its feeling that the war ruined Britain is another, and altogether more debatable matter. *The Churchill Play* is a work of aesthetic and intellectual power, a play as self-defended and ambiguous as was Sartre's *Les Mains sales* when Sartre was at the height of his creative power. For it is defended, and it is ambiguous. The portrait of Churchill in *The Churchill Play* was drawn in such a manner that Brenton himself could have repudiated it. *The Churchill Play* was set in 1984 (which still seemed a long way off). Brenton supposed that by then England would have become a country of concentration camps. A gentle, bewildered, liberal officer in one of these camps thinks it would be therapeutic for the internees to write and present a play of their own. His commanding officer is doubtful about the wisdom of this, but allows it to go forward. An NCO, Sergeant Baxter, thinks it a sign of contemptible weakness, and makes no secret of his view that the internees should be shot like mad dogs. But they are not shot. They act their play before a Parliamentary delegation, and it is in this play that the attack upon Churchill is made.

It would have been perfectly possible for Brenton to have maintained that the attack was only what one would expect from political prisoners. But there was no such suggestion of a counter-case. The furthest that the play would go in defence of the class from which Churchill came was a passage in which Brenton showed, in speaking of the shining youth of Lord Randolph Churchill before he was stricken with syphilis, that he was not indifferent to the grace of an English aristocrat who had been to a great public school.

There was a moving scene in which Churchill, played by Paul Dawkins, as the internee playing Churchill, suggested that Churchill was haunted by the fear that he might inherit his father's appalling disease: a suggestion which was paralleled in my mind by the thought that Brenton himself is haunted by tales of bombing he had heard in his childhood. He is as compassionate towards his internees as William Douglas Home, a dramatist who belongs to a class the same as Churchill, was to the prisoners in *Now Barabbas*. Is this compassion an implicit approval of what the internees say? One would suppose that it was.

What makes Brenton a significant dramatist is that beneath the politics of his work there lies a mysterious spirit of poetry. In Brenton there is the wild strangeness of the best scenes in *The Woman in White*. This strangeness, in the frantic walk of Captain Thompson (Julian Curry), or the inexplicable tale of an incident on an unidentifiable plain recounted by a Welsh internee (James Warrior) is what makes Brenton's play memorable. In *The Churchill Play* the wind was malign, and the bones ill at ease in their sockets.

In that Brenton has no doubts he differs from his fellow-dramatist, David Hare, with whom he has been often associated. The hero of Hare's *Knuckle* (1974) was a very literate fellow; gun-pocketed and epigrammatic; quick-thinking but out of his mind; passing instantaneously and without visible logic from one baroque image to another, from his father's story of five-pound notes to a girl anally smoking in Vietnam; a theatrical character fascinating, baffling and irresistible; knowing the worlds both of Moore's *Principia Ethica* and of Mickey Spillane; knowing also that he is incapable of living satisfactorily in either without wrenching his character or laying upon himself a burden greater than he can bear.

From this philosophic basis Hare proceeded to a condemnation both of capitalism as manifested in property development in Guildford, and of the ultimate moral weakness of those who seek to destroy it. He pursued this disillusioned theme with a verve and a freshness, a vertiginously varying pictorial imagination rare in political dramatists, though the play was little appreciated by the general theatre–going public.

To those who perceived its value *Knuckle* was both important and enjoyable on several different levels. Curly (Edward Fox), a gun-runner, returns to the home of his father, a merchant banker, to find out what happened to his lost sister. She had last been seen on the Crumbles beach at Eastbourne, leaving behind two return tickets between London and Eastbourne. Had she been murdered, or had she committed suicide? And if she had committed suicide, who was morally guilty, her paranoic self or her father, whose business activities she regarded as evil? This is the problem that Curly seeks to solve.

It led him to grill allusively a superbly secretive night-club hostess. In this part Kate Nelligan made her debut in what was to become a dazzling career. It led

---

David Bradley (left) and Raymond Westwell in Howard Brenton's The Churchill Play *at the Shakespeare Memorial Theatre, Stratford-upon-Avon.*

him also to watch her in a bikini turning somersaults on the Crumbles at night; to find his father's middle-aged housekeeper and mistress sedately undressing; and to fire three pistol shots point blank at the audience, a gesture that many people resented. *Knuckle* in fact was as exciting as an Agatha Christie thriller.

But there was more to it than that, however. In his *The Romantic Rebellion* Lord Clark reminded us that when William Blake thought of the sunrise he asked, 'Do you not see a round disc of fire somewhat like a guinea? – Oh, no, no, no, I see an innumerable company of the heavenly host crying, "Holy, holy, holy is the Lord God Almighty".' Hare's imagination has, either in this play, or in *Plenty* a couple of years later, little to do with any company of angels, but all the same *Knuckle* was impressively apocalyptic. So far as Hare is concerned in *Knuckle* no primrose by a river's brim a yellow primrose is to him: somehow or other he turned it into an appalling symbol of the City of London. Eastbourne and Guildford are no longer pleasant, peaceful towns: out of the darkness they are seen as visions of only too imaginable horror. Kate Nelligan's tremendous apostrophes exulted and exalted and made one shiver. For Hare, the steep High Street of Guildford is trodden exclusively by red-hot stockbrokers, and infirm old men ready to fall down at the sight of a pretty girl so that they might grab at her legs to save them from collapse.

Now and again, as in Alan Bennett's *Forty Years On* (1968), in which Sir John Gielgud made his first entry into the field of contemporary drama, there shone for a moment a gleam of nostalgic admiration and love for England and her people, though even this was expressed in terms of burlesque which some audiences mistook for contemptuous ridicule. At the opposite extreme, there was one powerful and belligerent producer and author, Steve Berkoff, who did not falter in his hatred of all that is in modern Britain. In *Decadence* (1981) Berkoff still managed to express his unqualified loathing for the upper classes without misgiving. Here at any rate was a soul that was unknown to foreboding; which was firm in its convictions, and apparently did not reflect that both in the French and Russian Revolutions those who invoked them were signing their own death warrants. Millions of people of all classes survived these revolutions: the only people whose death they made certain were the people who started them. Marat was slaughtered; Danton was slaughtered; Robespierre was slaughtered; Beria was slaughtered; and though Trotsky fled to one of the most distant parts of the earth, he was slaughtered, too. But the Duke of Orleans survived and flourished. Did not Kruschev say that if he were an Englishman he would vote Tory?

But despite Berkoff's stubbornness, the element of fear was in the 1970s and 1980s entering into progressive British drama. The old panache of *Look Back in Anger* and the hopefulness of Arnold Wesker gave way to doubts and loss of faith. There was a premonition of the frightening development of revolutions

---

Kate Nelligan and Edward Fox in David Hare's Knuckle *(1974) at the Comedy Theatre, Eastbourne.*

past in Brenton's *Thirteenth Night* (1981), which was presented in the Royal Shakespeare Company's production at their London studio theatre the Warehouse, with Michael Pennington in the leading part. In this play there was a left wing coup in Britain, the very thing towards which Brenton had for years been moving, sometimes with angry, sometimes with majestic tread. But this coup did not bring about the millennium. The breakdown of the system led to a still worse system, with murder and violence the only solutions, leading of course to still further violence and murder, as in the oldest Greek tragedies.

A still more intense fear permeated Ken Campbell's production of Kenny Murphy's adaptation of Karel Capek's *The War of the Newts* in the same year (1981). Some of the anarchic Campbell's old insolent high spirits remained in scenes like the ducking of the Prince of Wales and his future princess in a swimming pool. But you could see the knees shivering. *The War of the Newts* was a parable, and, though there was joyous lampooning of Michael Foot and Enoch Powell, there was terror at its heart; and bewilderment, too. The newts were oppressed; and then liberated; and then exploited by a Labour Government; then they rose in rebellion and very soon they had conquered the whole earth. Is freedom to be granted only at the loss of our own freedom? Can the shackles of the deprived parts of the world be removed only if we put them on ourselves? These questions haunted Campbell's hilarious, knockabout production, as indeed they haunt nearly all modern drama. The freedom which liberal thought insisted on giving to the newts resulted in the destruction of the West. The play ended with a curiously sad and beautifully symbolic scene in which, in a small boat amidst endless desolation, Malcolm Muggeridge and Sir Robin Day unceasingly, dispiritedly aimlessly and uselessly pondered the ruin round them.

There was a despair just as real, though dramatically more elegant, at the heart of Ronald Millar's *A Coat of Varnish* (1982), in which, with masterly finesse, Millar raised the question of whether even justice may not be too passionately desired and pursued. In *A Coat of Varnish* Peter Barkworth, pathologically coughing his way both to the apprehension of the criminal and his own death, gave one of the finest, suavest, and most disquieting performances of the still young decade.

The Bread and Puppet Theatre and *The War of the Newts* belonged to one of the most flourishing developments of the drama between Suez and the 1980s. This was known as the Alternative Theatre. It was outrageous, defiant, unconventional, and believed all established things (including comfortably upholstered theatres) to be evil. It was epitomized in the Arts Laboratory which Jim Haynes, a young, diligent, free-living, and amiable American, set up in Drury Lane during the year of student rebellion, 1968. The Arts Laboratory ridiculed all conventional drama and behaviour; the audience picked its way through a long room over the prostrate bodies of drug addicts to the small curtained-off space at the back where plays were given. The Arts Laboratory was welcomed with enthusiasm by young anti-bourgeois intellectuals, but it acquired a doubtful reputation which led to its decline. But other Fringe theatres

Ken Campbell's production of The War of the Newts *(1981) at the Riverside Theatre, London.*

proliferated, and some of them achieved a lasting reputation. Dan Crawford at the King's Head, but above all Verity Bargate at the Soho Poly did work of consistently high standard. Verity Bargate, whose life was tragically cut short whilst she was still comparatively young, discovered many enterprising new dramatists, amongst whom the compassionate and indeed heroic Barry Keeffe is especially notable.

The most famous outpost of the Alternative Theatre was not in London, but in Edinburgh. In a sinister little room half way up a winding stone staircase ideally suited to medieval plotting and murder, the Traverse (for some years under the stimulating direction of Michael Rudman) gave productions which, particularly during the annual Edinburgh Festivals, became widely celebrated. Its work was often fantasticated, and always shocking to complacency. In the year in which Haynes set up the Arts Laboratory in London the Traverse presented one of its most typical productions, *The Lunatic, the Secret Sportsman, and the Women Next Door*. This play was by Stanley Eveling, a Durham University man who was lecturing in philosophy in Edinburgh.

The Lunatic, the Secret Sportsman, and the Women Next Door had four characters or maybe only three (for two of them may be one), and appeared to spring from the conjunction in Eveling's mind of Christ's 'Noli me tangere' with a celebrated phrase of Cyril Connolly's. This phrase came out on the programme as 'Inside every fat man there is a thin lunatic trying to get out', and the play did in fact open with the lunatic taking a flying leap over a table chased by the fat man. The term lunatic was, of course, ambiguous, for the wisdom of the wise is in some eyes foolishness. 'Sportsman', too, could not be taken literally, for though the fat man Teddy had at one point a cricket bat, boxing gloves, and a model horse on his walls he probably read *Penthouse* more assiduously than *The Field*.

Yet even *Penthouse* may have been too normal for him. The Alternative Theatre specialised in sexual deviation: for instance, Simone Benmussa's production of an adaptation of George Moore's *Albert Nobbs* ten or so years later, with Susannah York, was as pure and delicate a work as anyone could imagine; yet it was based on transvestism. Ever since a scrap with Carruthers minor at school, Teddy had been partial to boys, though sometimes the boys were really girls. He was fortunate in having next door a brothel run by a vast female named Elsie baroquely dressed in violently coloured silks over Turkish trousers, and Teddy changes clothes with her just before going to gaol – Holloway, of course. Elsie was rather randy, very broadminded, sincerely religious (always ready for a prayer) and extremely refined. There is one client whom she particularly admires – 'T. J. Crabtree,' she muses with relish, 'a real gentleman. Before entering one of my girls he washes his hands and says, "May I intrude?"' She provided Teddy with Doris, a north-country girl suitably dressed like a Gainsborough painting of an attractive youth. Doris sat on Teddy's knee (this was one of several scenes which would not have been accepted in mainstream theatre at that time) whilst he fumbled with her Blue Boy fly-buttons.

These things were an essential part of the spirit of the Alternative Theatre. Its attack was directed as much at conventional morals as at conventional politics. But there were other things in Eveling's play. There was, for instance, the lunatic himself. All this time the lunatic stood forlorn, with hanging head. There was blood on his clothes, and he looked like some deserted pierrot who had been playing in the open air at a third-rate seaside resort where it had been raining all summer, and there had been fights and quarrels among the members of his sorry company. His voice was gentle and he did not speak of his wounds. Darkness came upon the face of the theatre, and it was of him that Doris, even when she was in bed with Teddy and obeying his unusual requests, used to think.

Immediately after this Doris had a remarkable scene with the lunatic. It was played with arresting intensity and horrified silence by Derrick O'Connor and by Pamela Moiseiwitsch in Doris's torrent of beseeching words. In her tortured simplicity she desired to touch this man, even the edge of his garment, this real being, this fugitive and fragile personality. But he shrank from this harmless, this so tiny contact. So psychologically penetrating was the playing that one felt that if Doris were actually to touch the lunatic, even one of the beads that hung round his neck, the theatre would explode. For each man is an island, and the shore of his being is not to be violated by any invader. This delicacy, this *pudeur* was at the heart of *The Lunatic, the Secret Sportsman, and the Women Next Door*; it was its unique quality, and it was magistrally displayed to the desperate shocked unease of those who feared blasphemy and the upsetting of conventional propriety.

The same dark spirit brooded everywhere in the advanced sections of the theatre, those sections which traditionally give to it its especial glory. The RSC's production of Barrie's *Peter Pan* (1982) tried to free the play from its old accretion of dusty mediocrity, and presented it as a freshly conceived masterpiece. But the result was that the play seemed to be full of hatred, and poisonous to the minds of children: making it, in fact, only too clear that it conditioned the minds of the unfortunate children who first heard it to ready acceptance of suicide and disaster.

Sometimes, however – and chiefly in the plays of David Storey and Tom Stoppard – a feeling of poetry and of intellectual legerdemain, as in *The Contractor* (1969) and *Rosencrantz and Guildenstern Are Dead* (1967) and *The Real Thing* closed one's mind to the surrounding despair. In *Albert's Bridge* (1969) Stoppard showed ingeniously that something apparently so simple as a bridge has strange, imaginative ambiguities. To travellers a bridge is merely a way of getting from A to B; to engineers a challenge in dynamics; to Albert's parents and to Albert's wife a dangerous enemy; and to Albert himself his Dulcinea and his Holy Grail. To Albert, painting a bridge was a rewarding and indestructible passion. Albert, a man of sense as well as of determination, was also a philosopher; and this enabled Stoppard to weave from these conflicting views of something which, as an objective reality (if such a thing as objective reality exists) wreaks through human carelessness a terrifying vengeance, a play that was exceedingly funny, thought-provoking, and curiously exciting.

There was a grave beauty in the hopeless sadness of Lindsay Kemp's adaptation of *Flowers* from Genet's *Notre-Dame des fleurs* (1974), a beauty that was not perhaps sufficiently acknowledged. For to praise an entertainment that is passionately steeped in the conviction that homosexual love, preferably homosexual love between criminals and outcasts, is the only kind of love that deserves the name; that what we have known as love from the days of *Romeo and Juliet* to William Douglas Home's *The Secretary Bird* is only a game and a deception lays the reviewer open to all kinds of possible misunderstandings.

All the same, *Flowers* was a quite extraordinary creation, as extraordinary as *Notre-Dame des fleurs*, whose lyrical ecstasy it translated into mime, was extraordinary. It created with a terrifying and revolting beauty the awful world of the Place Blanche and the Place Pigalle and the milieu that obscenely fascinate Jean Genet; the perverse cafés; the horrible public lavatories (when he was poor Genet knew every public lavatory in Paris that had a seat); the readiness to spill blood and the worship of the naked male body; and invested these things with that blasphemous reverence for the Mass, and that haunted confusion between the criminal and the saint that make him unique amongst the great modern masters of French prose.

Through this foul and evil world, so glorious to Genet, moved Kemp's timid, sad Divine, tottering like a more than consumptive Lady of the Camelias, doomed to an exhausted passion and a bloody end. The exceeding slowness of Lindsay Kemp's performance, a mark that, in Genet's world of transcendental viciousness, he has passed from time into eternity, was a true rendering of Genet's shocking, unmatchable prose; the work of Lucifer rejoicing in being hurled from Paradise, but remembering its former purified splendour, a masterpiece of the damned.

In David Storey's *In Celebration* (1969) there was, as there is in all Storey's work, a more generally acceptable beauty that was still irreclaimably melancholy. During the brief intervals that separated the various scenes of *In Celebration* one heard the simple and comforting strains of a tinkling piano nostalgically playing 'Jesus Loves Me'. Bathed in the warmth of this old-time religion, we saw the Shaws in their small miners' house celebrating the fortieth anniversary of their wedding. For the occasion they were visited by their three sons, for whom they had done exceedingly well, since they had given them a university education.

Colin, the middle son, was now a prosperous executive, not very articulate, but kind and generous. The youngest, Steven, was a teacher, full of affection for his parents, who were unfashionably fond of him and of each other. The eldest son, Andrew, in this united and Christian family, was the odd man out. He had been a solicitor, but was now an artist, uninspired and unsuccessful; and in the bitterness of his mocking tongue he seemed bent on destroying the happiness around him.

But there had been a fourth child, a child less wanted than the others. Whereas they had been treated with unvarying kindness, he, in Andrew's searing memory, had been beaten black and blue; and at the age of seven he had died of pneumonia. Andrew could not, or at least did not, forget this; and alone in the contented household he was obsessed by the fact that his brother Steven also nursed an inexplicable grief.

In the light of these things it was impossible to take the hymn tune at its superficial value; and very difficult to accept any interpretation of the play that saw it as a sweet domestic idyll, a Yorkshire collier's Garden of Eden invaded by a malicious and poisonous serpent.

Lindsay Anderson's fine production of the play was too full of disturbing nuances for that. In its compelling ambiguity it perhaps even went so far as to suggest (though not to Andrew or to me) that it is better to compound cruelty to a child than to let its memory become the mainspring of vengeful action. It might have implied that the consequences of evil can never be erased, even to the third or fourth generation; or it may have meant that though the penalty for wrong-doing is always exacted, it is sometimes exacted (since Mr and Mrs Shaw are visibly happier than either Steven or Andrew) not from the wrong-doer, but

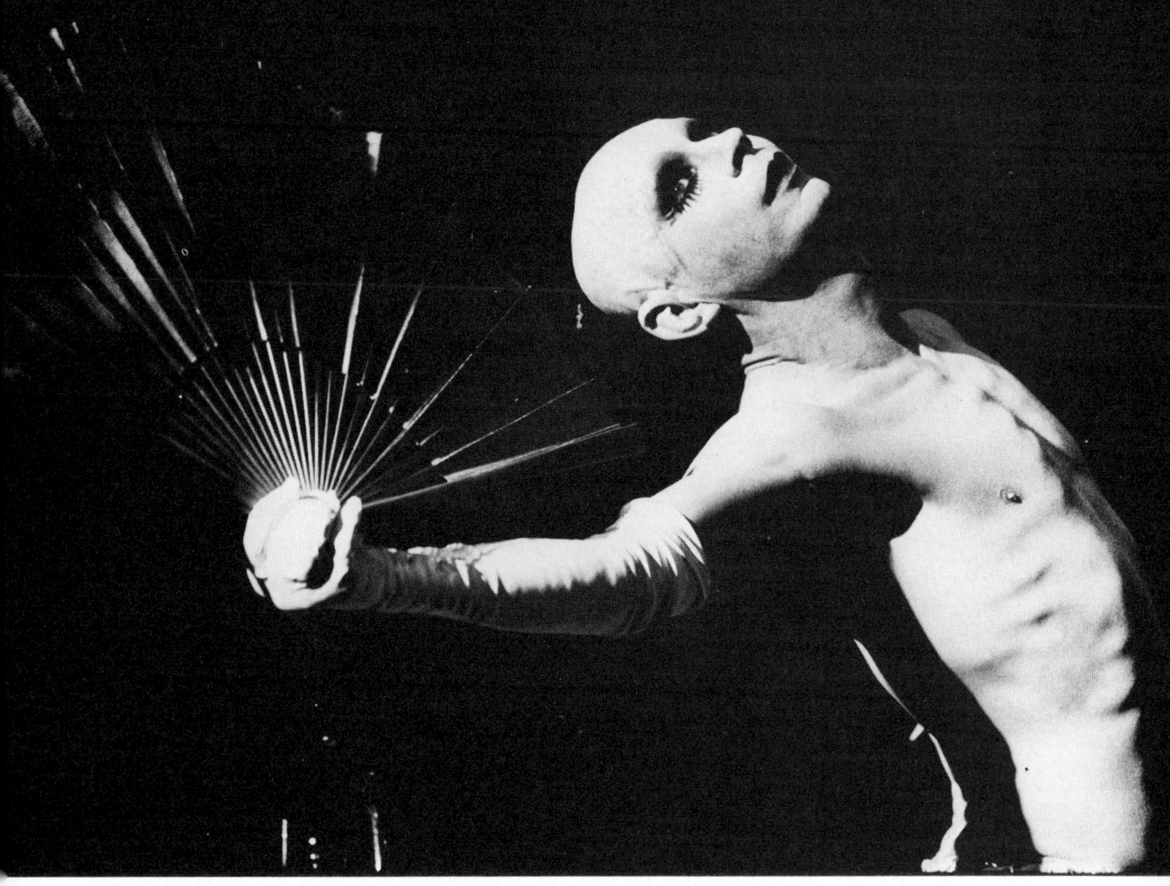

Lindsay Kemp in his Flowers *(1974) at the Regent Street Polytechnic, London.*

from the innocent. But a quiet tale of comfort and joy (as it seemed to some people) is precisely what it could not possibly be. It was better, it was more subtle than that. With Andrew I could not but remember the dead, bruised child, as I remembered, in *Now Barabbas*, the killed policeman.

This may not be what Storey intended. If so, it would not be the first time that a profound and moving play produced in a spectator deeply touched by it an impression other than had been foreseen. (This happens at every performance of *Mother Courage*, and, after the 1982 production, it seems likely that it will happen with *Peter Pan*.) But this is a sign, not of failure, but of richness, and *In Celebration* is a very rich play. It was beautifully written, and its beauty was appropriate to the circumstances and the class of its characters. And it had reverberating echoes of great men, as when Colin was said to measure out his life in motor cars.

It was perfectly acted by James Bolam as the upright and successful son, and by Brian Cox, who bore memorably Steven's uncommunicated sorrow. As for Andrew, for whom went all my sympathy, Alan Bates gave to him a bright ferocity that made the play vibrate with life. Lindsay Anderson's direction showed that characteristic yet amazing understanding of northern existence and northern passion that is so rare in well-born, intellectual, public school Socialists.

Tragic though many aspects of *In Celebration* and *Albert's Bridge* were, the final impression was not one of total despair. The same could be said of Alan Drury's one-act, one-man play, *An Honourable Man* (Cottesloe, 1982). The central, indeed the only figure in this touching monologue was a teacher who had been accused of assaulting one of his pupils. John Price, in telling his story, offered us a picture not so much of wronged innocence as of a bruised grief that the man's friends and colleagues should even be able to think him capable of such a crime. In a remarkably effective gesture he gazed in wonder at his outstretched hands, as if they were as bloodied as Lady Macbeth's.

The French theatre had, soon after the end of the war, brought new life into the British theatre. But in the 1980s it had begun to share the British theatre's gloom. Even the lighter stage, always more gallant in spirit than the serious theatre, felt the same desperate sense of something lost, something no longer believed in, yet not to be forgotten, and for which no substitute had been found.

The French, unlike the British, underpinned with a philosophy the pessimism of their theatre. As John Ardagh says in *France in the 1980s* (1982), in the late 1960s 'a new trend emerged into fashion: structuralism. To an extent it grew out of Existentialism, with which it shares an atheistic rejection of the bourgeois view of history and morality. But whereas [Existentialism] saw man as the free captain of his own conscience and destiny, the structuralists regard him as the prisoner of a determined system. [Existentialism] sprang from the humanist tradition: [structuralists] use the language and methods of anthropology, psycho-analysis and linguistic philosophy. Roughly they believe that man's thoughts and actions have been determined, throughout history, by a network of structures, social and psychological, where free will plays a minimal part; and that history is like a series of geological layers, each created by the pressure of the preceding one.' Michel Foucault, in *Les Mots et les choses* (1966), argued 'Man with a capital M is an invention; if we study thought as an archaeologist studies buried cities, we can see that Man was born yesterday, and that he may soon die.'

British dramatists had no such formidable philosophy to support them, nothing more, in fact, than an emotional reaction to temporary conditions weighed on the dissolving scales of a local perspective. But they reached more or less the same conclusions without the benefit of rational thought, and in John Antrobus's and Spike Milligan's extravaganza, *The Bedsitting Room* (revived in 1983), in which the Prime Minister has turned into a parrot and a charwoman has inherited the throne, what the critic Anthony Masters calls 'the crucial line' is 'Man is finished – and we asked for it' (*The Times*, 2 February 1983). It is the

---

John Price in Alan Drury's An Honourable Man *(1982) at the Cottesloe Theatre, London.*

same conclusion as Foucault's, with only this difference, that according to Foucault, Man would be finished whether he asked for it or not.

I might suitably end this very personal survey of the modern British stage with a play, *What If You died Tomorrow?*, by an Australian, David Williamson, which was produced at the Comedy Theatre in 1974. It is one of those plays that one occasionally encounters that take an old form, and breathe into it new life. Underneath an outer brashness it subtly and gradually transformed what at first seemed no more than a routine exercise in uninhibited sex, family quarrels, business bitchiness, and four-letter words into something thoughtful and intimidating.

The process of transformation went on, for the most part unperceived, until it was completed at the play's last moment, when the director, Robin Lovejoy, revealed to us, literally to the final brick and pulley, the important and beautiful structure which he and the author had been unobtrusively building all through the evening.

It was then, when Williamson's central character, Andrew Collins, a successful novelist, walked off the stage for the last time, with a lingering, rueful glance at the fantastic, industrial site which he had half absent-mindedly erected with a child's box of bricks, and, after a moment's pause the curtain descended on a scene of silence and emptiness, that one realized what it was that the play had so powerfully and, despite the loud, abundant laughter, been sadly saying; and that its title, which, since no one in the cast was in real danger of dying, might have seemed irrelevant, was in fact the crux of its meaning.

Andrew Collins lived, fairly sumptuously, in a Melbourne suburb with Kirsty, a married woman who had left her husband and brought her children with her, whilst Andrew's are with their mother, who has divorced him. From time to time Kirsty's children made a great noise, upstairs and offstage, and Andrew, though he had been a doctor before becoming a best-selling novelist, was patently unable to quiet them down.

The evening when the events of the play happened was tumultuous. All Collins's acquaintances came at him at once. His publisher, Harry Bustle, boisterous, cigar-smoking, foul-mouthed, not unlikeable, was trying to get him to sign the contract for his latest book. His agent, Michael O'Hearn, homosexual, unhappy, with a keen eye to the most lucrative bargain, had brought a rival publisher, the highly-sexed, more cultured Carmel Scott, who wanted both his book and his body.

As they struggled over him, and the children yelled, and Kirsty talked ruthlessly about the wife that Andrew had deserted, and the audience roared at the sexual jokes as they fell thick and fast, this scene of human carnage, in all its vigour and life was watched – need I say disapprovingly – by Collin's parents, who had unexpectedly returned from a long sea voyage, bringing with them a love-lorn Italian-speaking Swede, Gunter, whose fiancée had rejected him on the long journey.

All this might suggest a conventional comedy, rather old-fashioned, yet shocking even in 1974 to Puritanical ears. But in speaking of Collins's books, Williamson gave a hint early in the play that the superficial values of a creative work were not necessarily its real values. This judgement worked against Collins, but not, as it turned out, against Williamson. Even under the hail of jokes that scored off the conventional (the prim, acidulated matron, for example) there were undertones that implied a subtler scale of values than appeared on the surface. The matron was, after all, the only person for whom the children showed any respect. Much as personal freedom was given the edge over stuffiness, in the play's early scene of copulation, it was significant that desire, and with it accomplishment, failed; and though there was no danger of dying, both the Swede and the agent were close to the contemplation of suicide.

It was these things that gave to the play's last scene, with not a word spoken, its great force. Suppose, after all, you *were* to die tomorrow. What have you done in the world that anyone should respect you, that anyone should have for your memory the least touch of sadness? Has anyone been the better for your presence, or happier? For all the crowd of people with their modern and uneasy ethics that Williamson shows us, Collins's rueful smile as he sees the pile of bricks that he has built, supplies a sufficient answer. Only in that pile of bricks was there nothing to regret. *It* at least had done no one any harm. It might even in the morning give a little pleasure to Kirsty's children when they come down to breakfast. But Collins knows desperately that it will do nothing of the kind. For he is the man who does strange things to their mother which she seems to enjoy; he is the supplanter of their father, and they hate him with a hatred that he will never conquer.

And what if the theatre itself were to die tomorrow, or next month, or next year, or in ten years' time? Would the modern tale be the same as Collins's? Not quite, perhaps, but uncomfortable, nevertheless. In answer to the question 'What has the post-war drama achieved?' I do not see that anything more reassuring could be said than 'Not as much as could have been expected.' Since the war it has established both the National Theatre and the Royal Shakespeare Company, and given us a long programme of stimulating productions more or less based on the work of our greatest dramatist. It has driven out the lordly gentlemen and the brilliant ladies, and put in their place working men and women. It has substituted new concrete blocks and labyrinthine passages for the plush, romantic glitter of the commercial theatre it has almost completely destroyed. It has turned minority audiences into a minority of minority audiences. Under the imminence of war its intelligent predecessors withdrew from the conflict. Many of their advanced successors, faced by the contemporary world, rage and bluster, and whimper and cry defeat, which is perhaps an improvement. But it is humiliating to admit that the world of entertainment has always been and continues to be braver than the world of thought.

True, we now have freedom of speech on the stage. We are no longer gagged by the Lord Chamberlain. But many of those who most gallantly fought for his abolition as Censor might be disconcerted by what has resulted from the

The National Theatre, South Bank, London, opened in 1970.

The
Lyttelton
Theatre

The Royal Exchange Theatre, Manchester, opened in 1976: the 'space module' auditorium set up in the 19th-century Corn Exchange.

accomplishment of their desire. In the theatre today there is too much talk of sex and not enough of love. There is an excessive preoccupation with homosexuality. The unjustified contempt for entertainment plays increases. There has been a continuous degeneration of language. Freedom of speech may be allowed, but freedom of thought is not. Finally, there has been an almost complete loss of what Aristotle held to be the chief mark of a dramatist – the capacity to construct a plot. All the causes – Beckett, Osborne, Pinter – for which I fought have been won, and there have been several brilliant achievements. We still have people

The foyer of the Lyttelton Theatre, opened in 1976: part of the National Theatre complex on the South Bank, London.

like Peter Gill, Ian MacKellen, John McGrath, Barry Keeffe, Michael Gambon, John Price, Simon Gray and Alan Drury. Nevertheless, on the whole the result has been desolation. The battles will have to be fought all over again, and the other way round, until it once more becomes possible on the stage for a young man to fall in love with a girl, or speak of his country without contempt; or for an audience once again fully to understand and share such tenderness and longing, such soaring exaltation, as Robert Tear brought to the singing of Giuseppe Giordani's love song *Caro mio ben* ('without you my heart languishes') in Westminster Abbey on 17 November 1983, in a service of thanksgiving for the life and work of Sir Ralph Richardson, an actor so often mentioned with affection, admiration and gratitude in the preceding pages.

INDEX

Numbers in italic refer to illustrations.

ACKNOWLEDGEMENTS

BBC Hulton Picture Library, 34, 37, 43, 53, 61, 64, 69, 87, 115, 119, 124, 178; Photo by Cecil Beaton courtesy of Sotheby's Belgravia, 2, 33, 78; Nobby Clark, 206, 227; A. C. Cooper, 47; Donald Cooper, 96, 185, 198, 203, 207, 209, 221; Dominic Photography, 187, 192, 195; Julia Hamilton, 189; Douglas H. Jeffery, 201, 215; Keystone Press, 42, 45, 95, 116, 155; Denys Lasdun & Partners (photo: Donald Mill), 232–3; Sandra Lousada (Susan Griggs Agency), 213; Angus McBean (photo: Shakespeare Birthplace Trust), 171; Mander & Mitchenson Theatre Collection, 12, 15, 25, 31, 38, 56, 57, 73, 89, 91, 102, 113, 127, 130, 145, 177, 186; Mansell Collection, 8; Michael Mayhew, 229; National Theatre, 234; Punch Magazine, 173; Riverside Studios (photo: Chris Marris), 223; Royal Exchange Theatre, 235; Royal Shakespeare Company, 219; Roger Taylor, 65; Times Newspapers Ltd., 167, 181, 194; Victoria and Albert Theatre Museum, 11, 23, 26, 29, 36, 41, 48, 55, 62, 76, 99, 101, 106, 132, 143; John Vickers Archives, London, 135, 136, 137.